Microsoft® Access 2010:

Level 2 of 3

PAMELA R. TOLIVER
Soft-Spec, LLC

LABYRINTH
LEARNING™

El Sobrante, CA

Microsoft Access 2010: Level 2
by Pamela R. Toliver

LABYRINTH
LEARNING™

Labyrinth Learning
P.O. Box 20818
El Sobrante, California 24820
800.522.9746
On the web at lablearning.com

President:
Brian Favro

Product Development Manager:
Jason Favro

Managing Editor:
Laura A. Lionello

Production Manager:
Rad Proctor

eLearning Production Manager:
Arl S. Nadel

Editorial/Production Team:
Donna Bacidore, Pamela Beveridge, Belinda Breyer, Everett Cowan, Alec Fehl, Alona Harris, Sandy Jones, PMG Media

Indexing: Joanne Sprott

Interior Design:
Mark Ong, Side-by-Side Studios

Cover Design:
Words At Work

ITEM: 1-59136-318-7
ISBN-13: 978-1-59136-318-7

Manufactured in the United States of America.

10 9 8 7 6 5 4 3 2 1

Table of Contents

Quick Reference Tables

Preface

Microsoft® Access 2010: Level 2 provides thorough training of Access 2010 intermediate skills. This course is supported with comprehensive instructor resources and our eLab assessment and learning management tool. And, our new work-readiness exercises ensure students have the critical thinking skills necessary to succeed in today's world. After completing this course, students will be able to successfully face the challenges presented in the next book in this series, *Microsoft Access 2010: Level 3*.

Visual Conventions

This book uses many visual and typographic cues to guide students through the lessons. This page provides examples and describes the function of each cue.

`Type this text`	Anything you should type at the keyboard is printed in this typeface.
TIP	Tips, Notes, and Warnings are used throughout the text to draw attention to certain topics.
Command→ Command→ Command, etc.	This convention indicates how to give a command from the Ribbon. The commands are written: Ribbon Tab→Command Group→Command→ Subcommand.
FROM THE KEYBOARD [Ctrl]+[S] to save	These margin notes indicate shortcut keys for executing a task described in the text.

Exercise Progression

The exercises in this book build in complexity as students work through a lesson toward mastery of the skills taught.

- **Develop Your Skills** exercises are introduced immediately after concept discussions. They provide detailed, step-by-step tutorials.
- **Reinforce Your Skills** exercises provide additional hands-on practice with moderate assistance.
- **Apply Your Skills** exercises test students' skills by describing the correct results without providing specific instructions on how to achieve them.
- **Critical Thinking and Work-Readiness Skills** exercises are the most challenging. They provide generic instructions, allowing students to use their skills and creativity to achieve the results they envision.

A Note About Lesson and Page Numbering

You will notice that this book does not begin with Lesson 1 on page 1. This is not an error! The lessons in this book are part of a larger text. We have repackaged the large book into smaller books – while retaining the original lesson and page numbering – to accommodate classes of varying lengths and course hours.

All content in this book is presented in the proper, intended order.

Designing a Relational Database

LESSON OUTLINE

LEARNING OBJECTIVES

After studying this lesson, you will be able to:

- Identify and apply principles for good relational database design
- Modify field settings and create Lookup fields that return multiple values
- Create a split form
- Identify database relation-ship types and create and print a relationships report
- Identify object dependencies

By now, you should have a good understanding of the basic features of a database. As you move forward in your study of Access, it is important to get a better idea of what makes Access a relational database management system. Because of the tasks associated with building databases, it is often easy to lose track of the careful planning and design that must go into each relational database. Carefully constructed relational databases reduce the amount of redundant data that is stored in database objects and create ties between the objects that help make them more efficient to use.

In this lesson, you will study the basic concepts and properties of relational databases and examine how objects in the database relate. In addition, you will modify tables and field properties to enhance the relational aspects of the database and create forms and reports for the database. Finally, you will examine and create relationships between the tables and prepare database documentation that displays and demonstrates relationships.

Student Resources labyrinthelab.com/acc10

Relating Database Objects

Welcome to Green Clean, a janitorial product supplier and cleaning service contractor to small businesses, shopping plazas, and office buildings. Green Clean uses environmentally friendly cleaning products and incorporates sustainability practices wherever possible, including efficient energy and water use, recycling and waste reduction, and reduced petroleum use in vehicles. In addition to providing green cleaning services, the company also sells its eco-friendly products directly to customers.

Ahn Tran, office manager, and Michael Chowdery, purchasing manager, have recently undertaken the task of developing a new database for the company that is easy to use, places all data for the business in one concise file, and tracks sales and inventory for maintenance purposes. After reviewing the tables and other objects contained in the database, they have determined that several improvements will make the database more efficient and will improve data entry: modifying the properties of the database tables and creating a lookup field that enables users to quickly identify suppliers of inventory items. Examining and working with object relationships will help ensure that the relationships define the database appropriately. The activities in this lesson add the following items to the database:

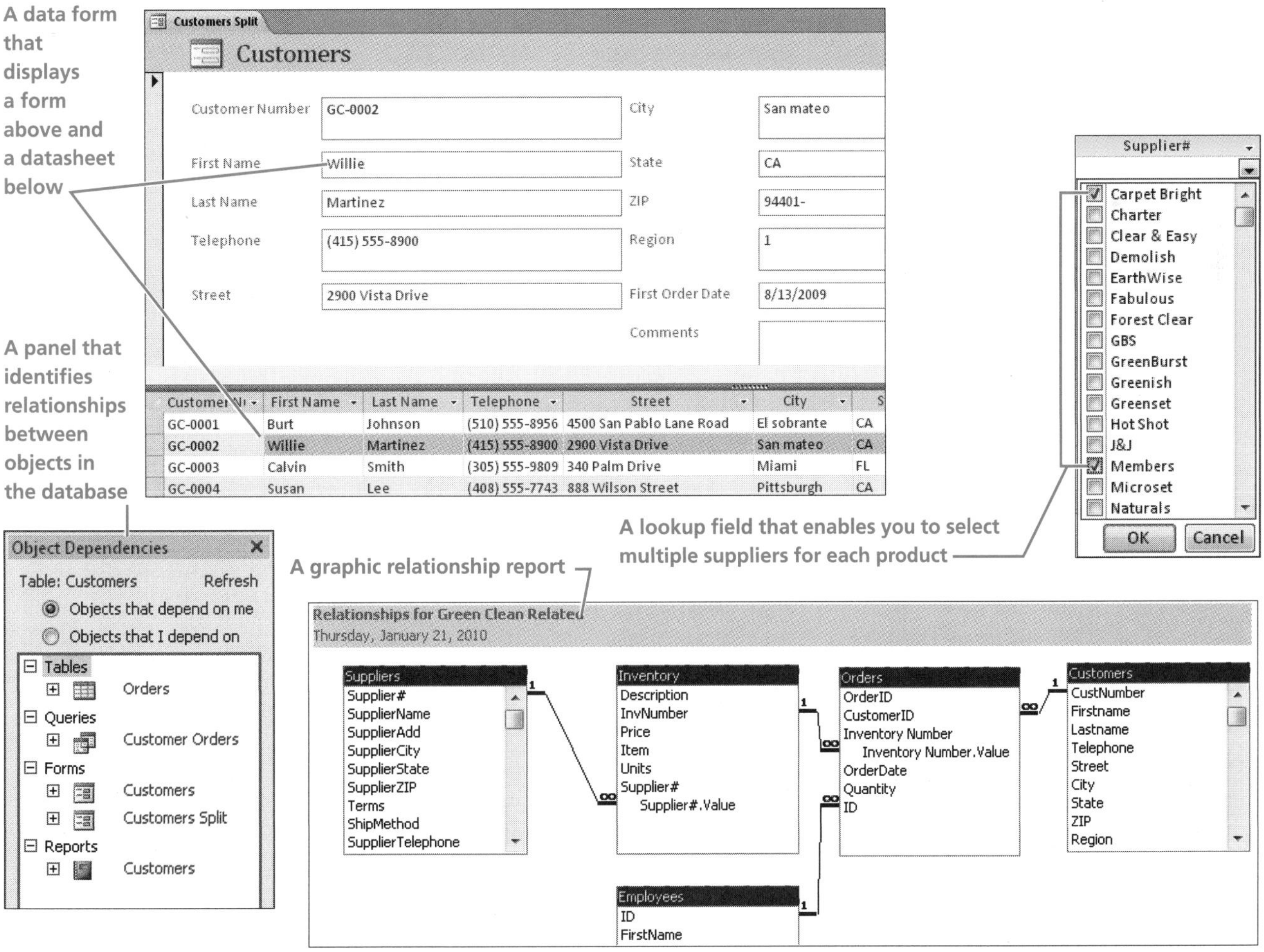

5.1 Designing a Relational Database—An Overview

Video Lesson labyrinthelab.com/videos

Early database programs stored all data in one large flat file similar to a spreadsheet. Such databases stored data over and over again for each record. Such repetitive data entry was not only time consuming but required voluminous storage space to store the ballooning data. Access 2010, on the other hand, is considered a relational database management program. Relational database programs separate repetitive data from the larger database flat file and store the data separately so that it can be accessed without being repeated.

Flat file databases repeat data for each record.

Relational databases separate data into tables to reduce data repetition.

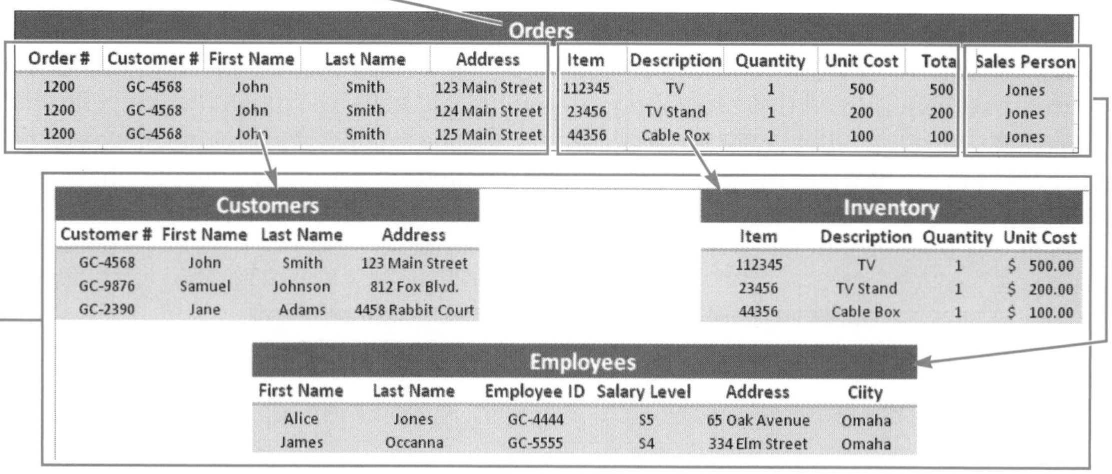

Principles for Good Database Design

As you consider designing a great database, you will discover that certain principles guide you through the process. These principles are essential to good database design.

- Divide data into subject-based tables to reduce redundant data. Data that is repeated wastes space and increases errors and inconsistencies.
- Set up the database in such a way that Access knows how to connect the data in one table to data in other tables. In other words, show Access how data in all tables relates to the scope or purpose of the database.
- Ensure that your data is complete and accurate. Although this goes without saying, incomplete and inaccurate data results in inaccurate processing and reporting and invalidates the integrity of the database—and it's more common than you might think.
- Include report formats, forms, and queries to process data and report the information that meets the needs intended for the database.

Planning a Relational Database

It is common for personnel within an organization, or for consultants who are called in to work with a business, to be asked to design a database using very little data and information. As a result, having a working plan with which to develop the design is very helpful. Many professionals who design and build relational databases work backward to develop complex databases. That is, they start with the reports the organization wants to generate, identify data required to generate the reports, and then define the fields and database objects required to store the data. A well-defined plan is essential to successful design. Several steps are involved:

QUICK REFERENCE — DESIGNING DATABASES

Step	Task
1	Identify the purpose of the database.
2	Locate and organize detailed information about what the database should contain, such as employee data, customer information, and inventory details—many of these will become fields.
3	Separate the details into related groups—these will make up your tables.
4	Identify additional breakdowns in information details, such as breaking Name into first name and last name. Also, separate information such as totals calculated using values in other fields. You won't need these in the tables.
5	Specify a primary key for each group of data.
6	Relate tables to each other by identifying how data in one table can be connected to data in other tables, and then add the necessary fields to tables or create new tables to help connect the data.
7	Create the database in Access and test the design. By creating the tables and entering sample data into each table, you can test the design to ensure that it provides the expected results. Refine as needed.
8	Apply normalization rules and make any necessary adjustments.

Applying Design Steps

If you apply these steps to designing a relational database for a utility company, you might use a utility bill as the required result of the database and build from there:

Design Step/Task	Result
Identify the purpose of the database.	To generate a utility bill
Locate and organize detailed information about what the database should contain.	Customer name, address, amount of power used, associated costs, company info
Separate the details into related groups.	Customer details, billing history, cost of power, utility company details
Identify additional breakdowns in information details.	Customer first name, last name, street, city, state, ZIP Code, telephone, etc.
Specify a primary key for each group of data.	Customer number
Relate tables to each other by identifying how data in one table can be connected to data in other tables.	Customer number added to other tables to connect the tables
Create the database in Access and test the design.	Create the tables to determine whether or not you can generate the billing statement
Apply normalization rules and make any necessary adjustments.	Review the design using the normalization levels (described elsewhere) and determine the normalization level attained

Sketching Out the Design

Graphically, you could use the following plan to accomplish the database design:

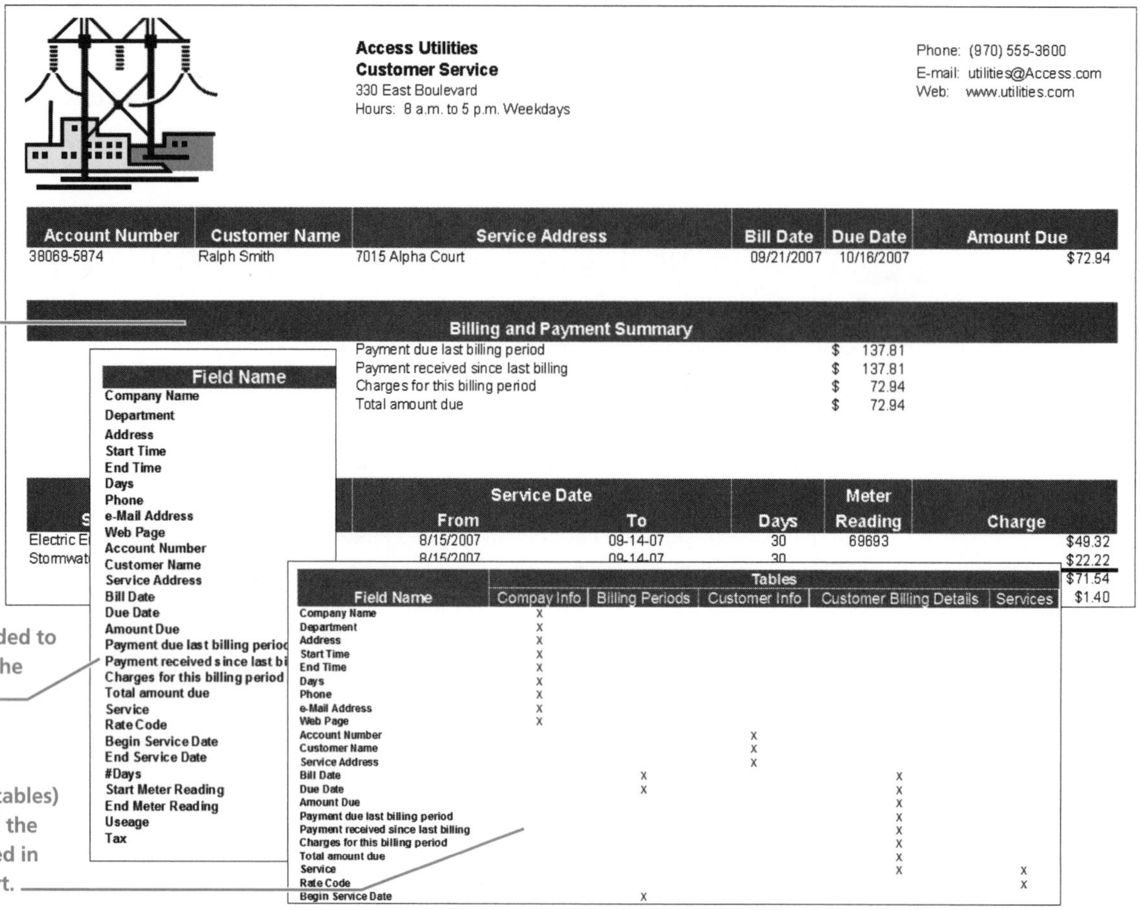

A common report showing a billing statement for an electric company.

Fields needed to generate the report.

Objects (tables) that hold the fields used in the report.

Normalizing Data

The goal of every database is to allow data retrieval as rapidly and efficiently as possible. As a result, the database designer tries to structure the data in a way that eliminates unnecessary duplication of data entry and streamlines the search path to all necessary information. The process of refining tables, keys, fields, and relationships to create an efficient database is called *normalization*. Normalizing forms the basis for laying out the design elements required for a relational database.

Normalization Defined

Normalization is the process of discarding repeating groups, minimizing redundancy, eliminating composite keys for partial dependency, and separating non-key attributes. Normalization is a complex process with many specific rules and different levels of intensity. Each table should describe only one type of entity (such as a person, place, customer order, product item, etc.).

Identifying Stages of Normalization

You can normalize most simple databases by following a simple rule of thumb: Tables that contain repeated information for multiple records should be divided into separate tables to eliminate duplication. To accomplish normalization, you can separate the tasks into numerous stages, sometimes referred to as *normal forms*. Each normal form is a rule that leads to normalization, and the first three normal form rules are considered essential to good relational database design. As you review the stages toward normalization, you'll notice many of the design elements you considered as you planned the databases you've created.

NORMALIZATION RULES	
Normal Form	**Rules**
First normal form	■ Eliminate repeating groups in individual tables. ■ Create a separate table for each set of related data. ■ Identify each set of related data with a primary key.
Second normal form	■ Create separate tables for sets of values that apply to multiple records. ■ Relate the tables using foreign keys.
Third normal form	■ Eliminate fields that do not depend on the primary key.

As you work through the activities in this lesson, you will begin to shape the relationships among database objects toward normalization.

5.2 Examining and Editing Database Objects

Video Lesson labyrinthelab.com/videos

As you examine database tables, one of the most important features to look for is the presence of repeating groups. After you modify and format tables in a database, you will examine the relationships between database tables and ensure that the database tables contain no repeating groups. In addition, setting field properties and creating lookup fields where appropriate will improve the accuracy of the data and ensure consistent formatting for all records.

Modifying Table Field Settings

Maintaining the integrity of a database, the validity of data, and data format are important considerations to building a database that works the way you want it to work and presents data on a report in a consistent format. Setting a field as a primary key field ensures that data entered in the field is unique or different for each record. It does not, however, ensure that each person entering data in the field capitalizes the data, or that the data contains the required number of characters, or that the values entered fall within valid data ranges.

Setting Common Field Properties

Setting field properties—characteristics, format, and values allowed for each table field—helps control many of the characteristics and values entered in database tables to ensure data validity. Frequently-used field properties often set for table fields include Field Size, Captions, Input Masks, Validation Rules and Text, Default Values, and Required.

COMMONLY SET FIELD PROPERTIES	
Property	**Description**
Field Size	Controls the number of characters Access allows in the field
Input Mask	Sets the appearance of field data entered, adds standard characters such as parentheses, slashes, and hyphens to the data, formats data in all caps or lowercase, and so forth
Caption	Displays alternate text in place of the field name in datasheets, on forms, and in repots. Caption text is usually more descriptive, especially when field names are cryptic
Default Value	Sets a data value that Access enters for a field when no other data is entered
Validation Rule	Sets rules for data entered in a field so that Access can check the data entered to ensure that it meets value limitations
Validation Text	Provides instructional information to help data entry personnel correctly enter data for a field containing a validation rule; Access displays validation text in a message box when invalid data is entered for a field
Required	Sets the field as a required field so that data must be entered into the field

Setting Text and Memo Format

Table fields are unique in the types of field properties available for formatting data. Text and Memo data type fields are no exception. Because they often contain many more characters than number, date, and other field types, Access provides a Format field that enables you to force all characters in the field to a specific format by simply typing a single symbol such as @, >, and <. Using the Format property eliminates the need to spend valuable time entering multiple characters in the Input Mask property.

QUICK REFERENCE	FORMATTING SYMBOLS FOR TEXT AND MEMO FIELDS
Format Symbol	**Description**
@	Requires data entry of a character or space
>	Forces all characters in the field to uppercase
<	Forces all characters in the field to lowercase
&	Text is not required

Creating Custom Text and Memo Field Formats

Access field formats cannot, of course, meet the needs of every text or memo field contained in every database. Access provides tools for creating custom formats to meet special needs. Custom formats for Text and Memo fields can contain two sections:

- Section 1: Contains a symbol and is followed by a semicolon when a second section is entered.
- Section 2: Contains the value of the alternate value when no value is entered. This alternate value is enclosed in quotation marks with no space between: "".

An example of a two-section format for a text field would be: @; "N/A". In this example, the @ symbol tells Access to display text from the field to be displayed if it is entered; the second section tells Access to display N/A when no value is entered.

Setting Text and Memo Field Unique Properties

Text and Memo fields are formatted to hold text characters, symbols, etc., and numbers on which no mathematical calculations will be performed—ZIP Codes and phone numbers, for example. Because of the broad scope of data that these two data type fields can contain, Access provides several field properties for controlling and formatting data entry in the field.

TEXT AND MEMO FIELD UNIQUE PROPERTIES

Property	Description
Allow Zero Length	Allows data entry of zero length in a field. Zero length data is entered as open and close parentheses with no character or space between, as (). The purpose of this entry is to show that there is no value to enter. For example, if you have a field in a Customers table that requires a phone number and the customer you are entering has no phone, you would enter () in the field. If, however, the phone number is simply unknown, you would leave the field blank and type the data when it is available.
Text Format	In fields set using the Memo data type, this property sets the text as Plain Text or Rich Text. You can format rich text by applying text enhancements, different fonts, font size, and other attributes to format the values.
Text Align	Positions the text on the left, center, or right side of the field box or column. The default setting is General, which aligns the text within the column. You can also select the Distribute setting and Access will spread the text out to fill the column or text box size.
Append Only	In fields set using the Memo data type, this property adds a series of date-stamped comments to a single memo field, making it easy to create a history log of comments and when they were added to memo fields. The multiple entries are stored in a separate table and accessed through the Append Only memo field.

Identifying Field Size for Number Fields

Number fields are identified by special formats in the Properties panel. In general, number fields should be set to define the largest value anticipated for the field. Setting the proper field size controls, to some extent, the speed with which Access processes the data and optimizes database performance. The following table identifies each Number field format and describes the type of data each stores.

Field Size Property	Description
Byte	Stores whole numbers between 0 and 255 using one byte and allows no fractions or decimal points
Integer	Stores whole numbers between –32,768 and 32,767 using 2 bytes rather than the standard 7 bytes normally used for high values
Long Integer	Stores whole numbers between –2,147,483,648 and 2,147,483,647 using 4 bytes rather than the standard 14 bytes normally used for high values
Single	Stores positive and negative numbers to exactly seven decimal places using 4 bytes
Double	Stores positive and negative numbers to exactly 15 decimal places using 8 bytes
Replication ID	Identifies replication of tables, records, and other objects in Access 2003 or earlier databases using 16 bytes
Decimal	Stores positive and negative numbers to exactly 28 decimal places using 12 bytes

Entering Field Properties

Access provides three basic techniques for setting field properties:

- Type the value into the property box.
- Choose the value from the property list. (For example, click the list button to change a property setting from No to Yes or to select a valid entry.)
- Click the Build [...] button that appears at the right side of a field property to open the wizard associated with that property. Then, choose the settings you want to apply from the screens presented. For example, click the Build button to open the Input Mask Wizard to format the display of text and field dates.

You will use each of these techniques as you complete the tasks in the following exercises.

DEVELOP YOUR SKILLS 5.2.1

Modify Field Settings

In this exercise, you will modify fields contained in the Customers table of the Green Clean database by setting field properties and editing data types.

NOTE

Setting data types that are consistent with the data they hold helps ensure that the data will report and display properly when included in related database objects.

1. **Open** the Green Clean database in the Lesson 05 folder and **save** the file as a new database named **Green Clean Related**.
2. Open the **Customers** table in your Green Clean Related database.
3. Choose **Home→Views→View** to display the table in Design View.
4. Follow these steps to change the data type for the FirstOrder field:

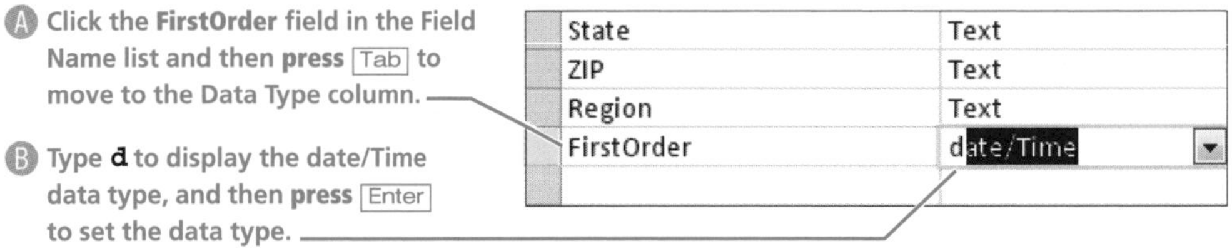

A Click the FirstOrder field in the Field Name list and then press Tab to move to the Data Type column.
B Type d to display the date/Time data type, and then press Enter to set the data type.
State
Text
ZIP
Text
Region
Text
FirstOrder
date/Time

Add a New Memo Field

Now you will add a new field to the table to hold comments.

5. Add the following new field to the **bottom** of the field list:

Field Name	Data Type
Comments	Memo

6. Select each field identified in the following table and set the **field size** and **caption properties** to the values shown:

Field	Field Size	Caption
CustNumber		Customer Number
FirstName	20	First Name
LastName	20	Last Name
Street	30	
City	30	
State	2	
ZIP	10	
Telephone	14	
FirstOrder		First Order Date

Set Input Masks and Validation Rules

Input masks and validation rules help ensure the integrity of data entered into this table.

7. **Save** changes to the table, click **Yes** when advised that some data may be lost, and then set the following **Input Mask** for the associated fields:

Field	Input Mask
CustNumber	“GC-”0000
FirstName	>L<???????????????????
LastName	>L<???????????????????
City	>L<?????????????????????????? ???
State	>LL

8. Follow these steps to create an input mask using the Input Mask Builder:

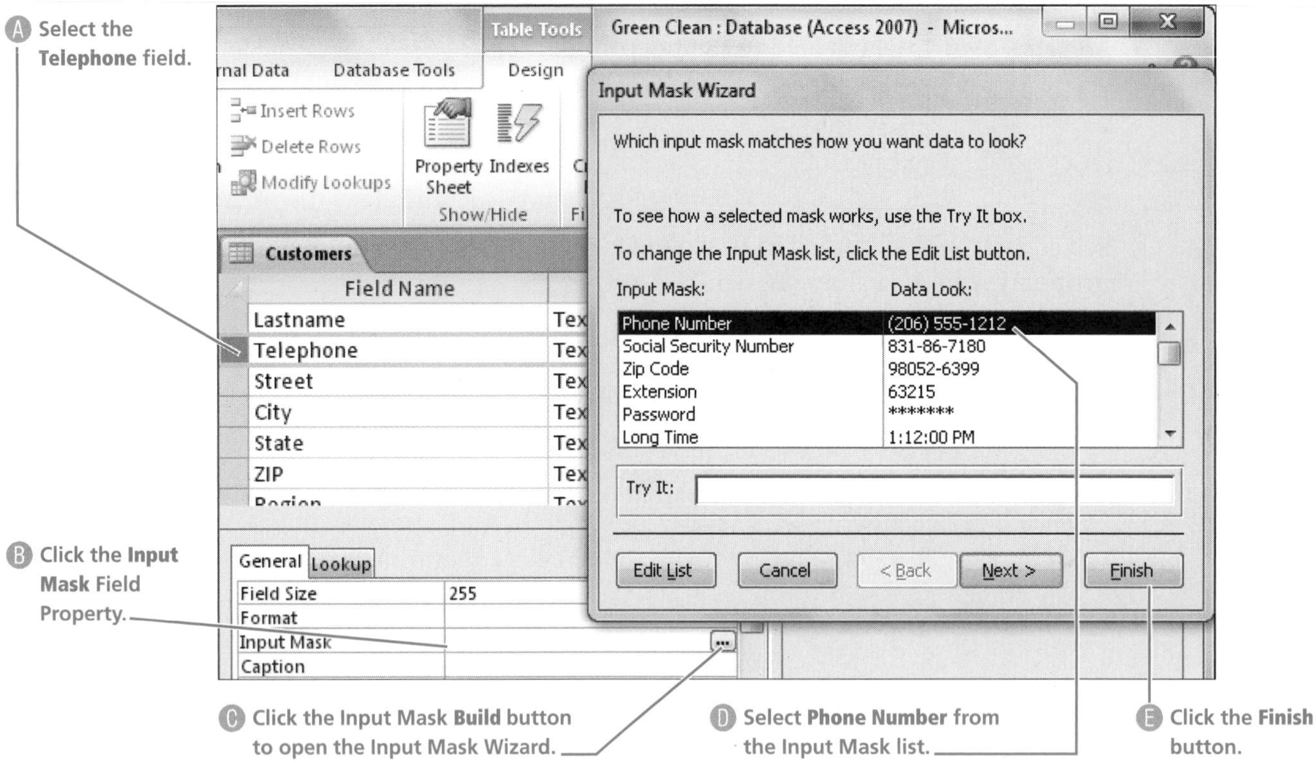

9. Repeat the procedures shown in **step 8** to create a ZIP code format Input Mask for the ZIP field.

10. Select the **FirstOrder** field and set the following **Validation Rule** and **Validation Text** properties:

Field	Validation Rule	Validation Text
FirstOrder	<=Now()	The first order date must occur today or prior to today. Please enter today's date or a previous date.

Identify Required Fields and Set Additional Properties

Now you will set required fields and additional properties to control data entry.

11. Select the following fields in the **Field Name** list and change the Required property to **Yes**: **LastName**, **ZIP**, **FirstOrder**.

12. Select the following text and memo fields and set the properties identified to the values shown:

Field	Property	Value
Telephone	Allow Zero Length	Yes
Comments	Append Only	Yes
FirstName	Format	@
LastName	Format	@

13. **Save** changes to the table, click **Yes** when advised that data integrity rules have changed, and then **close** the table.

Testing Control Settings

Video Lesson labyrinthelab.com/videos

Now that you have formatted controls to format data appropriately, you can test the format by entering sample records.

DEVELOP YOUR SKILLS 5.2.2

Enter Data into a Table

In this exercise, you will enter a record into the Customers table to test the data.

1. Open the **Customers** table in the Green Clean Related database.
2. Choose **Home→Records→New** to create a new record.
3. **Type** the following data into the columns indicated exactly as shown:

Column	Value to Type
Customer Number	1001
First Name	geraldo
Last Name	BAKER
Telephone	5025553390
Street	Main Street
City	Louisville
State	Ky
ZIP	40216
Region	3
First Order Date	*Current Date*

4. Review the format of the data to ensure that Input Masks and other formatting properties work properly.
5. **Save** changes to the table and then **close** it.

Creating Lookup Fields

Video Lesson labyrinthelab.com/videos

By now, you have most likely already created a lookup field that enabled you to select an item from a list as you entered records into a table. Access 2010 enables you to set up a list of valid data values in such a way that you can select multiple values to enter for each lookup field. For example, it is conceivable that an inventory item is available from more than one supplier. As a result, you may wish to set up the field to allow you to select all suppliers for an item. To create a selection list, you simply check the Multiple Items option as you move through the Lookup Wizard screens.

DEVELOP YOUR SKILLS 5.2.3

Create Lookup Fields for Selecting Multiple Values

In this exercise, you will create a lookup field in the Inventory table that allows you to select multiple suppliers for an item.

NOTE: Creating lookup fields automatically creates a relationship between fields in both tables.

1. Display the **Inventory** table in your Green Clean Related database in Design View.
2. Follow these steps to launch the Lookup Wizard:

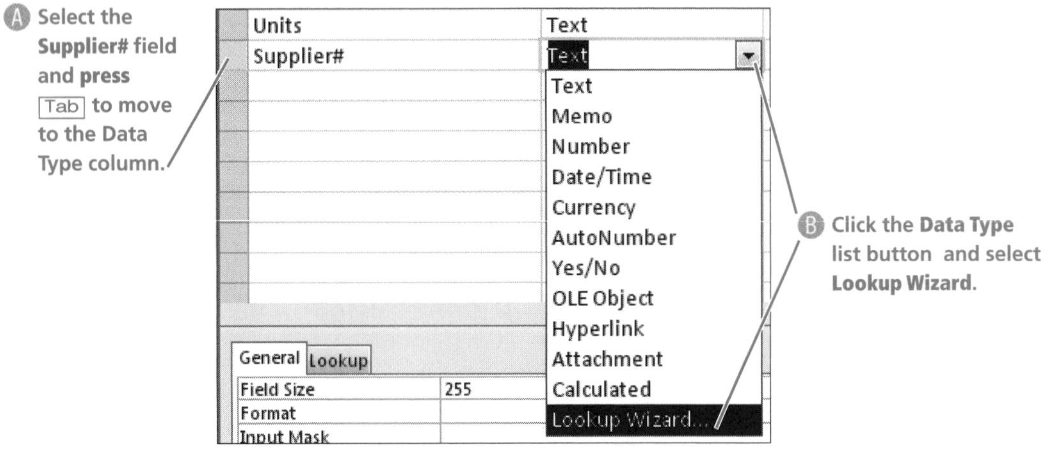

3. Select the **I Want the Lookup Field to Get the Values from Another Table or Query** option and then click **Next**.
4. Select **Table: Suppliers** and then click **Next**.

5. Follow these steps to identify the fields to include in the lookup:

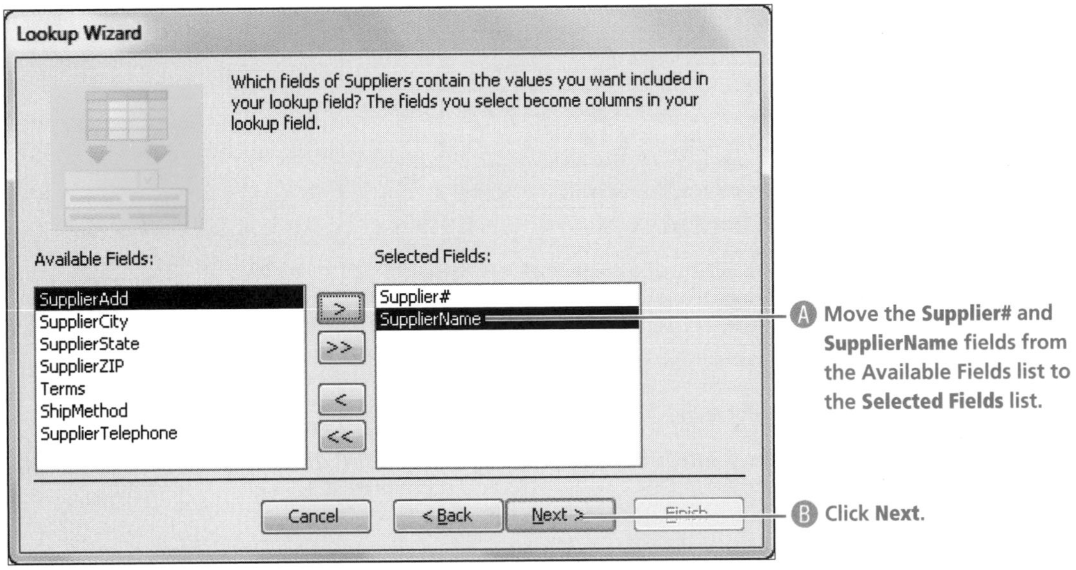

6. Select **SupplierName** from the sort order 1 drop-down list, leave the sort order as **Ascending**, and click **Next**.

7. Click **Next** to accept the default settings for the appearance of the columns.

8. Follow these steps to finalize the lookup field:

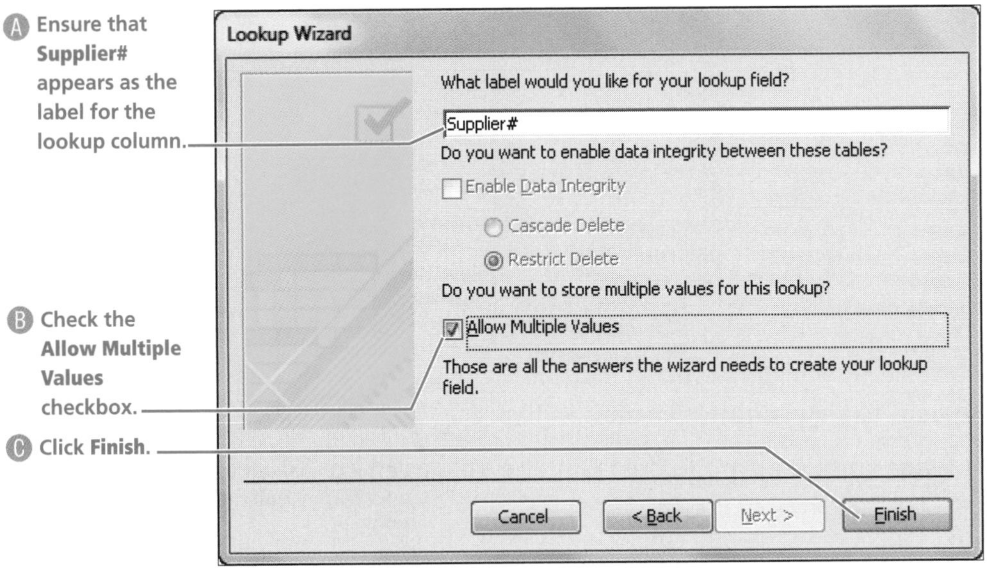

9. Choose **Yes** when prompted to confirm that you want to store multiple values. *Access displays a warning message that data may be lost.*

10. Choose **Yes** to save the changes to the table.

11. Click the **Lookup** tab in the Field Properties pane to view the settings for the lookup field.

General	Lookup
Display Control	Combo Box
Row Source Type	Table/Query
Row Source	SELECT [Suppliers].[Supplier#], [Suppliers]
Bound Column	1
Column Count	2
Column Heads	No
Column Widths	0";1"
List Rows	16
List Width	1"
Limit To List	Yes
Allow Multiple Values	Yes
Allow Value List Edits	No

Test the Multiple Values Lookup Field

Now that you have created the lookup field you will test it and see how it can help maintain the integrity of the database.

12. Choose **Design→Views→View** to display the Datasheet View.

13. Follow these steps to select multiple suppliers for an item:

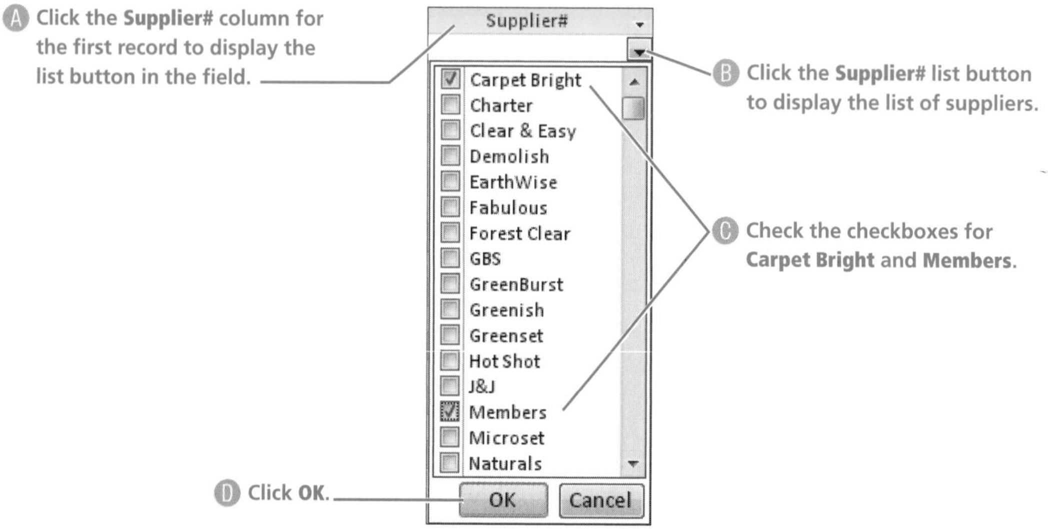

C Check the checkboxes for Carpet Bright and Members.

14. Follow these steps to view multiple entries:

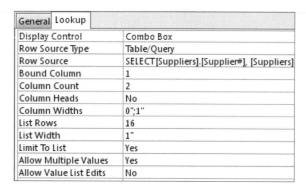

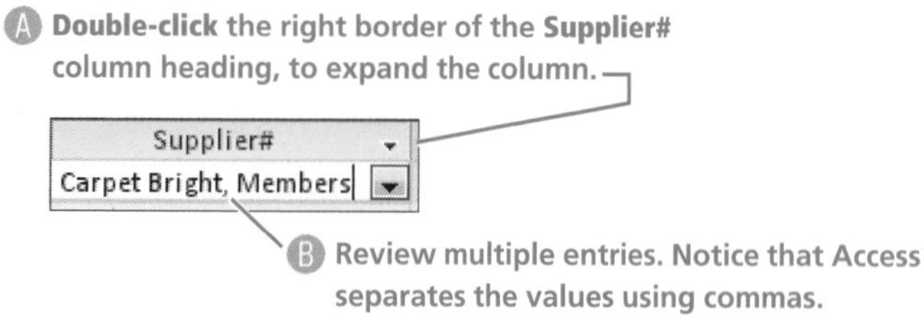

A Double-click the right border of the Supplier# column heading, to expand the column.
Supplier#
Carpet Bright, Members
B Review multiple entries. Notice that Access separates the values using commas.

Database users can quickly see all suppliers that provide each item.

15. **Close** the table, **saving** changes if prompted.

5.3 Creating a Split Form

Video Lesson labyrinthelab.com/videos

Forms in Access databases provide an efficient way to enter new data into database tables and also to edit data contained in tables. Many times, those who are responsible for entering and editing data work both in table datasheets to view multiple records in a table-like display as well as in forms, which display records onscreen one record at a time. Switching between the table datasheet and the form can become cumbersome. As a result, you may want to create a split form that displays data from a table in two formats: a datasheet in one pane and a form layout in a second pane. You can adjust the size and layout of each pane to change the display of data and to make the form more efficient to use. Displaying the datasheet in the upper pane enables you to select the record you want to view without navigating through many records. Access then displays data from the selected record in the form in the lower pane.

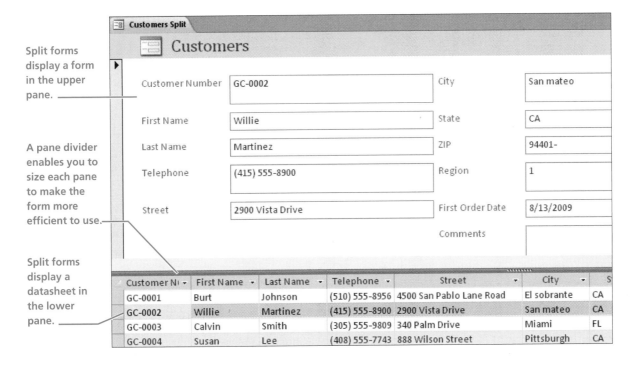

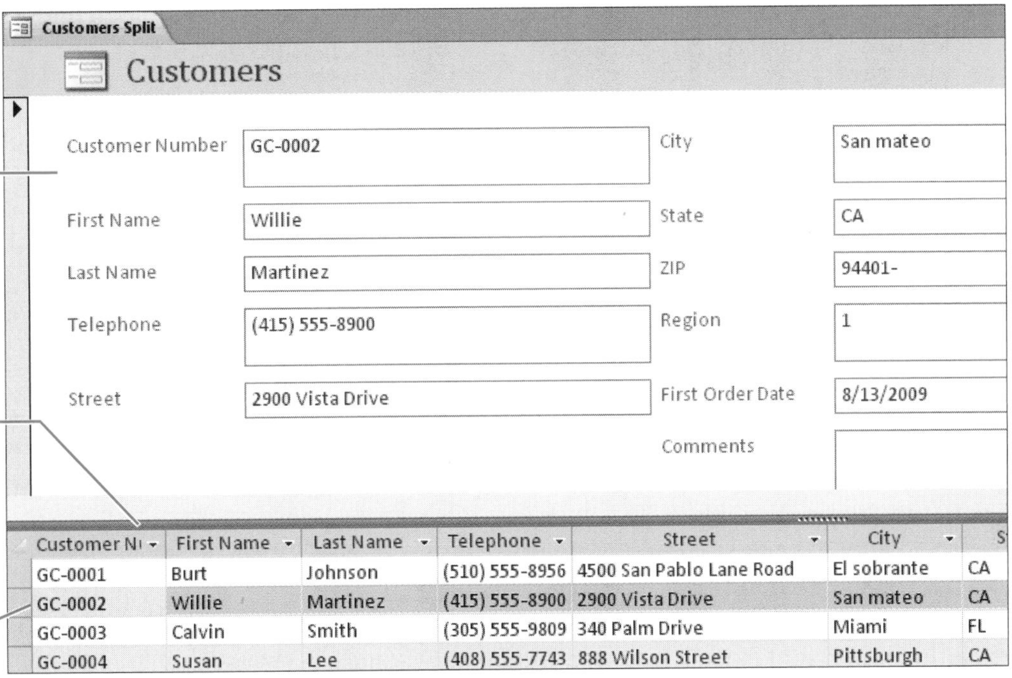

Split forms display a form in the upper pane.

A pane divider enables you to size each pane to make the form more efficient to use.

Split forms display a datasheet in the lower pane.

DEVELOP YOUR SKILLS 5.3.1

Create a Split Form

In this exercise, you will create a split form for the Customers table.

1. Select the **Customers** table in your Green Clean Related database.
2. Choose **Create→Forms→** More Forms **menu** and select **Split Form**.
   Access creates the split form automatically and formats the lower pane of the form using all table fields.
3. **Save** the form using the form name **`Customers Split`** and then **close** it.

5.4 Working with Relationships

Video Lesson labyrinthelab.com/videos

Relationships are ties that bind objects to each other within a relational database, and are what give a relational database management system (RDBMS) program, such as Microsoft Access, its power. Relationships enable you to share information among tables and specify rules about how records relate. As you work with databases and perform tasks such as creating lookup fields, Access identifies the ties between tables and creates the relationship automatically. Sometimes, however, it is necessary to create the relationship manually.

Identifying Relationship Types

Individuals and teams within organizations establish relationships to effectively interact and cooperate with other teams. The same is true of tables within an Access database—*relationships* must exist. Relationships in Access databases connect data in one table to data stored in other tables. Access supports three different types of relationships:

- One-to-one
- One-to-many
- Many-to-many

One-to-One Relationships

A one-to-one relationship between database tables is the least frequently used relationship. Using two tables, A and B, a one-to-one relationship means that each record in Table A can have only one matching record in Table B and each record in Table B can have only one matching record in Table A. This type of relationship is the least common because most of the data related in this type of relationship would be stored in the same table. Such a relationship might exist if two separate tables, a personnel table and payroll table, store data related to employees.

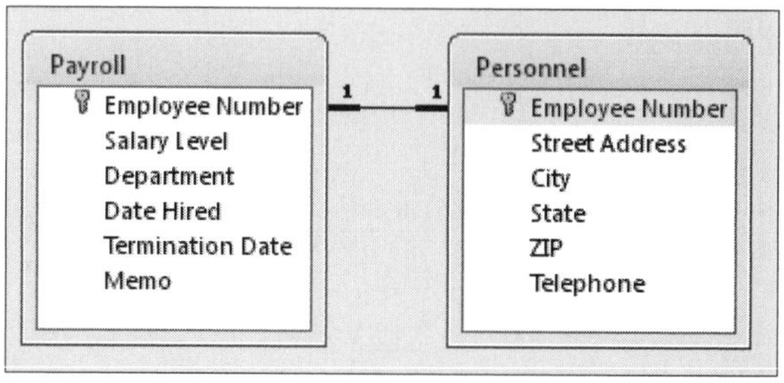

In this one-to-one relationship, each employee's address information is stored in one table while payroll data is stored in a separate table. Each employee has only one record in each table. Notice that the 1 on each end of the join line identifies the relationship type.

One-to-Many Relationships

A one-to-many relationship is the most common type of relationship between Access database tables. Using the same analogy of two tables, A and B, in a one-to-many relationship, each record in Table A can have multiple matching records in Table B, but a record in Table B can have only one matching record in Table A.

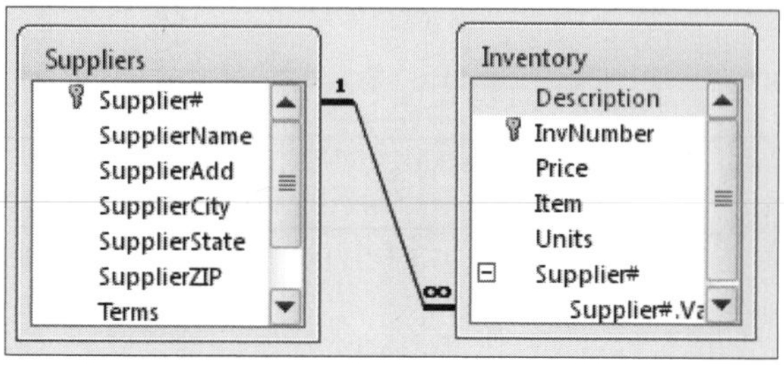

In this one-to-many relationship, each supplier listed in the Suppliers table could have multiple records in the Inventory table. Notice that the 1 on the Suppliers field list end of the join line and the infinity sign at the Inventory field list end of the join line identify the one and many sides of the relationship.

Many-to-Many Relationships

Many-to-many relationships often employ a third table to tie other tables to each other to complete the relationship. Using the analogy of two tables, A and B, each record in Table A can have multiple matching records in Table B, and each record in Table B can have multiple matching records in Table A. To create a many-to-many relationship you create a third table, C, called a *junction table*, using the primary keys of both Tables A and B as foreign keys in Table C. The junction table generally has a one-to-many relationship to each table.

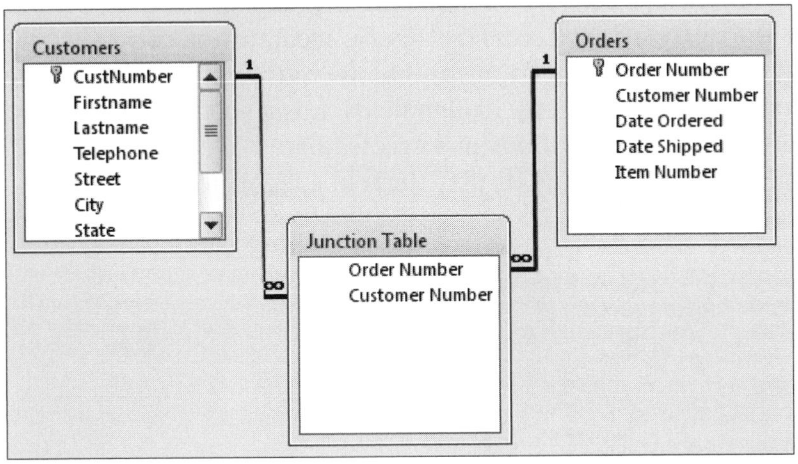

In this many-to-many relationship, items in the Orders table have a one-to-many relationship with the Junction Table (which contains the keys from tables that need to be related); and customers in the Customers table also have a one-to-many relationship with the Junction Table. As a result, customers could have many different orders for many items and each item could be ordered by many different customers.

TYPES OF ACCESS DATABASE RELATIONSHIPS

Relationship Type	Description	Example
One-to-one	Each record in Table A can have only one matching record in Table B, and each record in Table B can have only one matching record in Table A. This type of relationship is the least common because most of the data related in this type of relationship would be stored in the same table.	Each item in an Inventory table can be related to only one manufacturer in a Manufacturer table.
One-to-many	Each record in Table A can have multiple matching records in Table B, but a record in Table B can have only one matching record in Table A. This is the most common type of relationship.	Each franchise in the Franchises table could be related to many records of employees in a Franchise Employees table.
Many-to-many	Each record in Table A can have multiple matching records in Table B, and each record in Table B can have multiple matching records in Table A. To create a many-to-many relationship you create a third table, C, called a junction table, using the primary keys of both Table A and B as foreign keys in Table C. The junction table generally has a one-to-many relationship to each table.	Each student in the Students table can be listed on the class list for many classes (Class Schedule table), and each class can be listed on the registration form for many students. The Registration table would contain the foreign keys for ClassID from the Class Schedule table and StudentID from the Students table to relate many students to many classes.

Using Redundant Fields

As you work with databases, you will realize the need for *redundant fields*—fields that appear in multiple tables in the database. Redundant fields are required to establish relationships between database tables—they hold the connection that relates tables and other objects to each other. At the same time, extensive use of redundant fields makes maintaining data in the database more difficult—each time you update data in one table, you must remember to update the data in other tables. By establishing relationships between database tables, you can remove all redundant fields except those that establish the relationships between fields.

Creating and Modifying Relationships

As you build tables and other objects in a relational database, Access examines each table and often creates the relationships between tables using the data and structure of fields in each table. Most often, the relationships Access creates are accurate and correctly relate fields in the tables. For example, Access creates relationships between tables that you include in a query as well as between tables you use to set up lookup fields. It is a good idea to examine the relationships to determine what relationships Access might have set, and edit or establish additional relationships manually and display them in a report to add to the database documentation.

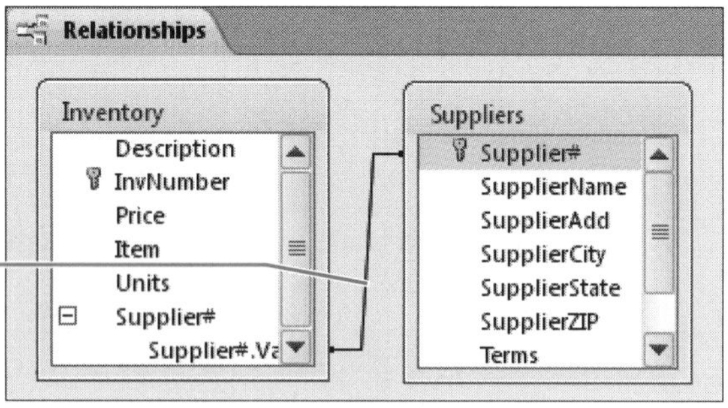

In this example, the relationship was established when you created the lookup field.

Defining Referential Integrity

Referential integrity is a system of rules that Access uses to ensure that relationships between tables are valid. As a result, when you manually create a relationship between database tables, the Edit Relationships dialog box opens so that you can identify the rules you want Access to check:

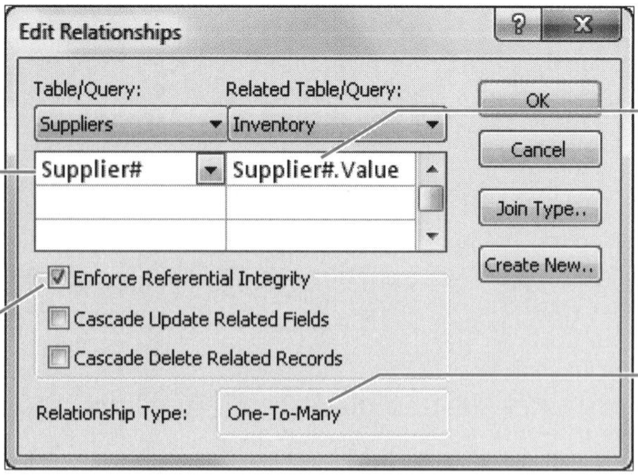

When you enforce referential integrity in a one-to-many relationship, Access displays characters at each end of the join line to identify the type of relationship created.

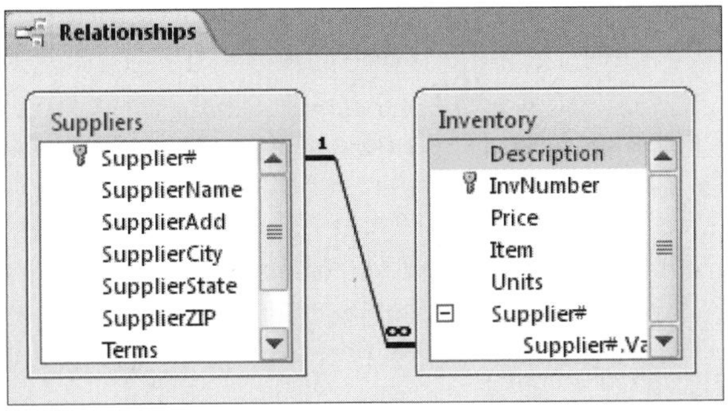

This join line shows how Access adds characters to the join line—the end close to the Suppliers table displays a 1 and the end close to the Inventory table displays an infinity sign. This shows that each supplier might have many items in inventory.

Identifying Referential Integrity Requirements

Access uses referential integrity to do more than just validate data. It also uses referential integrity to ensure that you don't delete or change a record in one table that is related to data contained in another table. The following conditions must be met to set referential integrity between table fields:

- The matching field from the primary table must be a primary key or contain unique data.
- The data types of the related fields must be the same or compatible.
- Both tables must belong to the same database.

After you establish referential integrity between tables, Access enforces the following rules:

- Only values in the related table that exist in the table containing the primary key are allowed. Therefore, you cannot enter an inventory item for a supplier into the Inventory table until you create the supplier record in the Suppliers table.
- No record from the table containing the primary key can be deleted if a corresponding record appears in the related table. For example, after you enter data for a new item into the Inventory table, you cannot delete the record for the supplier from the Suppliers table.
- The primary key value in the table containing the primary key cannot be changed if a corresponding record exists in the related table. For example, after you enter data for a new supplier into the Suppliers table, you cannot edit the data in the primary key field (the Supplier# field) in the Inventory table.

QUICK REFERENCE	VIEWING RELATIONSHIPS
Task	**Procedure**
View a relationship	Choose Database Tools→Relationships→Relationships.

Setting Relationship Cascade Options

Two additional options are available in the Edit Relationships window that you can set to control updates to related tables. Each of these options has a unique function for maintaining database relationships, and it is important to know what these options control before you activate them.

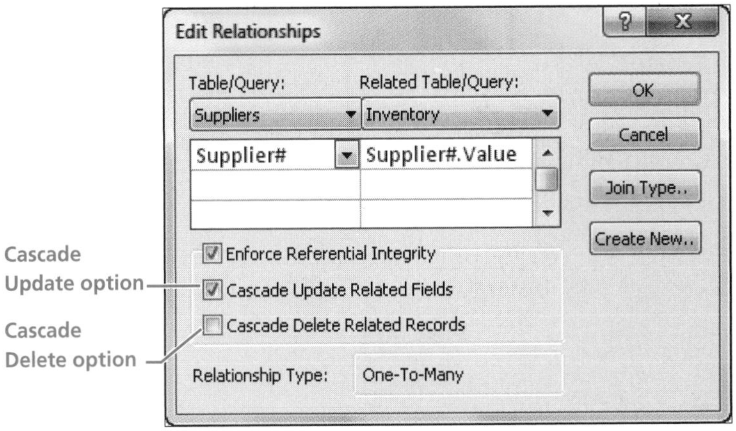

CASCADE OPTIONS	
Cascade Option	**Description**
Cascade Update	Updates the value in the key field of a related table if you change the primary key value in the primary table. For example, if you change a customer number in the Customers table, the customer number field value in the Orders table updates for each order.
Cascade Delete	Deletes records in a related table any time you delete related records in the primary table. For example, if you delete a customer from the Customers table, Access deletes all orders for that customer. Access notifies you before deleting related records when the Cascade Delete option is active.

DEVELOP YOUR SKILLS 5.4.1

Create and Modify Relationships

In this exercise, you will display the Relationships window, add a table to the window, and create a relationship between tables. In addition, you will set referential integrity for the relationship.

1. **Close** all database objects in your Green Clean Related database.
2. Choose **Database Tools→Relationships→Relationships** on the Ribbon to open the Relationships window.
3. Follow these steps to add tables to the Relationships window:

Ⓐ Choose **Design→Relationships→Show Table** on the Ribbon to display the Show Table dialog box.

Ⓑ **Double-click** each table name that does not already appear in the Relationships window to add it to the window.

Ⓒ Click **Close** on the Show Table dialog box to close it.

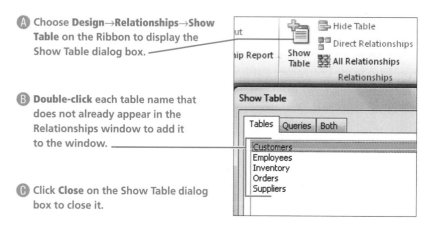

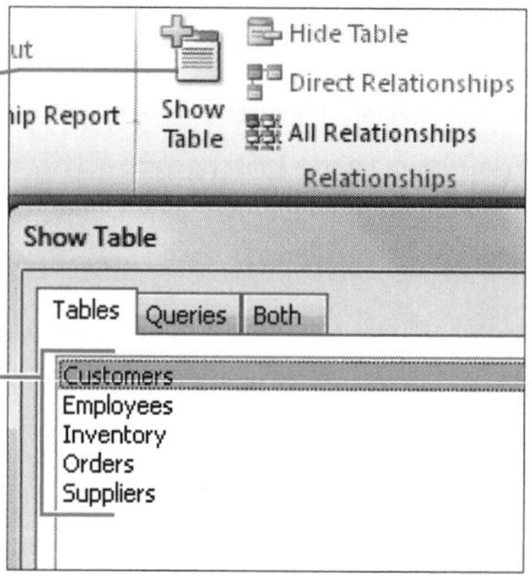

The Inventory and Suppliers tables should already appear on the Relationships window. If they do, add the Customers, Employees, and Orders tables.

4. Follow these steps to arrange the table field lists in the Relationships window:

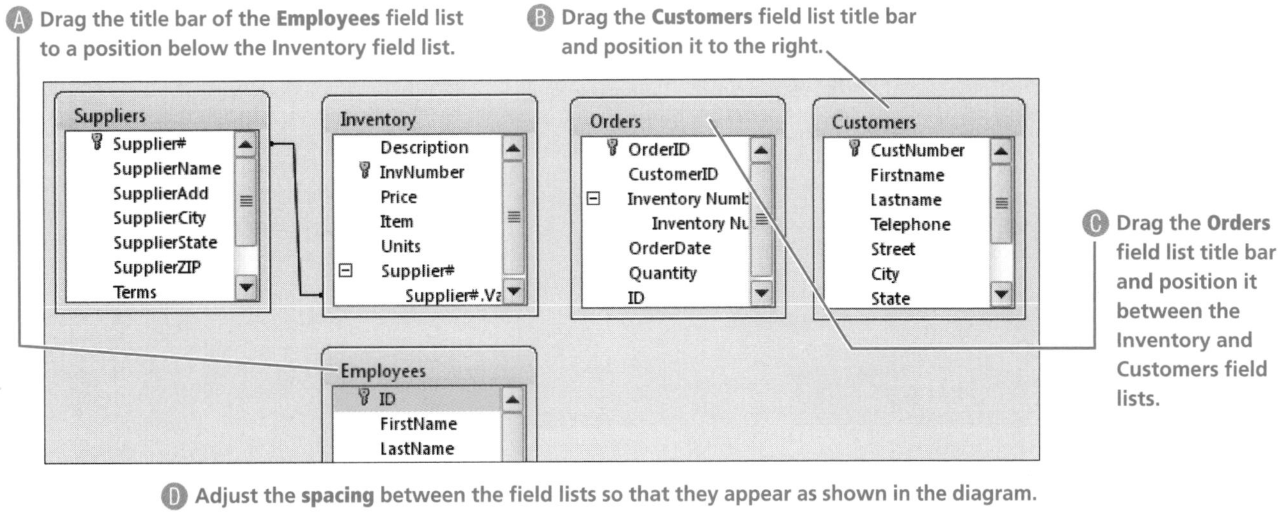

Now you will set up relationships between the Orders table and the Employees table.

Manually Set Relationships

5. Follow these steps to create a relationship between the Orders table and the Employees table:

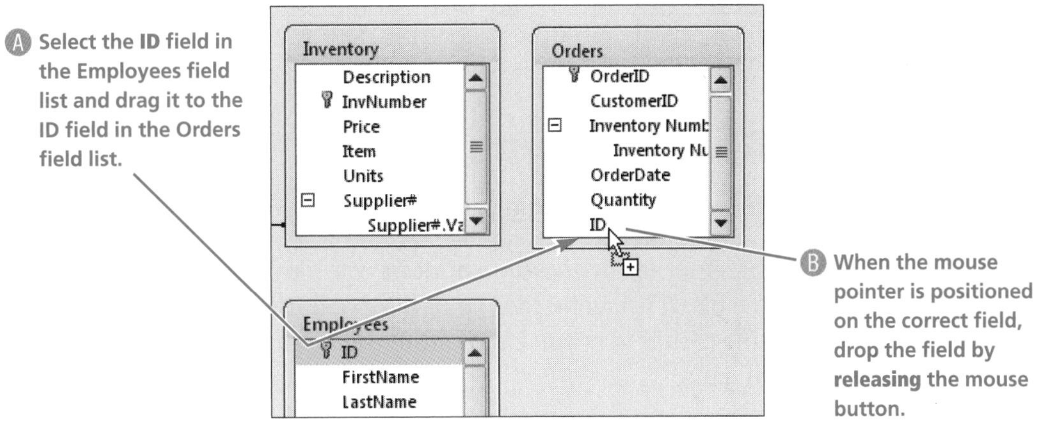

The Edit Relationships dialog box opens.

6. Follow these steps to set referential integrity between the tables:

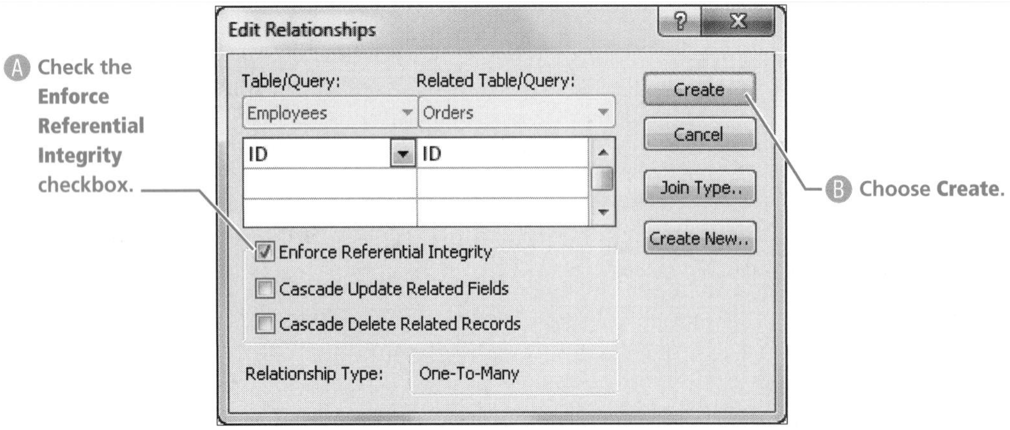

Access adds characters to the join line—the end close to the Employees table displays a 1 and the end close to the Orders table displays an infinity sign.

7. Repeat the procedures outlined in **step 5** to create relationships between the following fields in the corresponding tables without enforcing referential integrity in either of the additional relationships:
   - **Inventory Table:** Inventory Number field→Orders Table: Inventory Number field
   - **Orders Table:** CustomerID field→Customers Table: Customer Number field
8. **Save** changes to the Relationships window and leave it **open**.

Editing Relationships

Video Lesson labyrinthelab.com/videos

As you might imagine, setting cascade options can have a ripple effect on records and data in a database. As a result, it is a good idea to back up a database before setting options and then testing the settings. That way you can restore the database from the backup if the setting results in loss of data.

When to Review Relationships

Anytime the structure of a table changes—whether it's through adding or removing fields or simply changing data types or creating lookup fields—you need to review and update the relationships among database tables. In this lesson you have modified the Customers table in the Green Clean Related database and created lookup fields between the Inventory and Suppliers tables. You now need to update and save changes to the relationships.

DEVELOP YOUR SKILLS 5.4.2

Edit Relationships and Set Options

In this exercise, you will review the relationships in the database, edit the relationships, and set relationship options.

Before You Begin: The Green Clean Related database should be open with the Relationships window displayed.

1. **Right-click** the join line between the Orders table field list and the Customers table field list and choose **Edit Relationships**.
2. Follow these steps to edit relationship options:

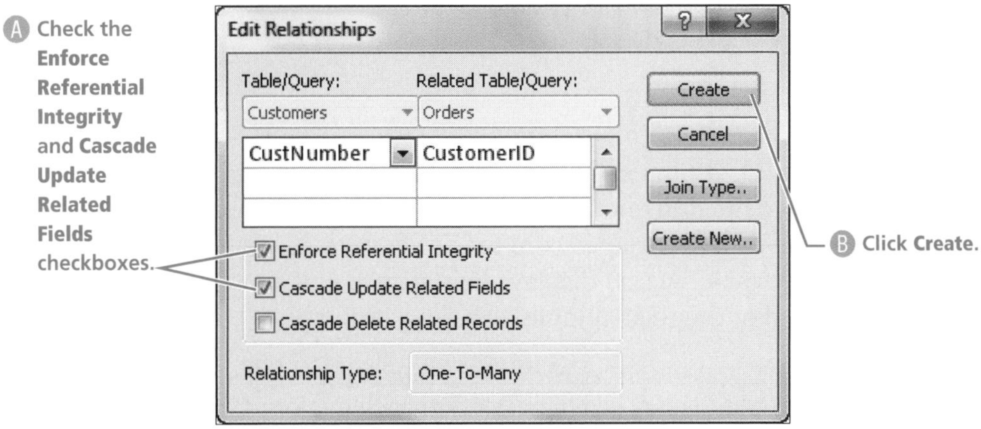

3. Follow these steps to set Referential Integrity and Cascade options for another join:

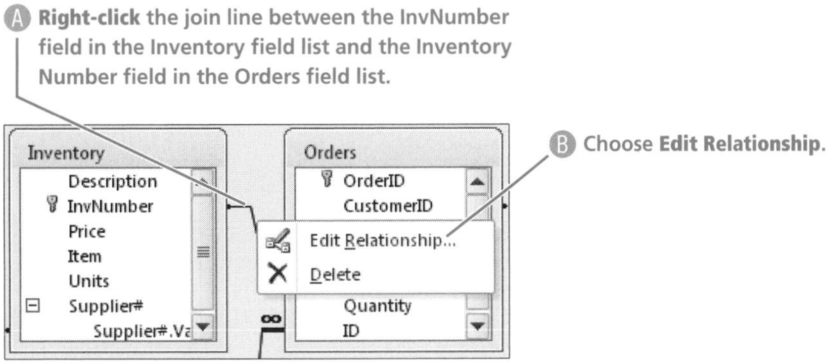

4. Check the **Enforce Referential Integrity** and **Cascade Update Related Fields** checkboxes.
5. **Save** changes to the relationships.

Reviewing Effects of Relationships on Datasheets

Video Lesson labyrinthelab.com/videos

After relationships are created between two database tables, Access recognizes those relationships and displays related data in the table datasheet. You may already have noticed the plus (+) symbol in a column at the left end of each record in the datasheet. The appearance of the plus symbol is another indicator that relationships exist between the active table and another table in the database.

The plus (+) symbol appears at the left end of a record in one table when relationships are established.

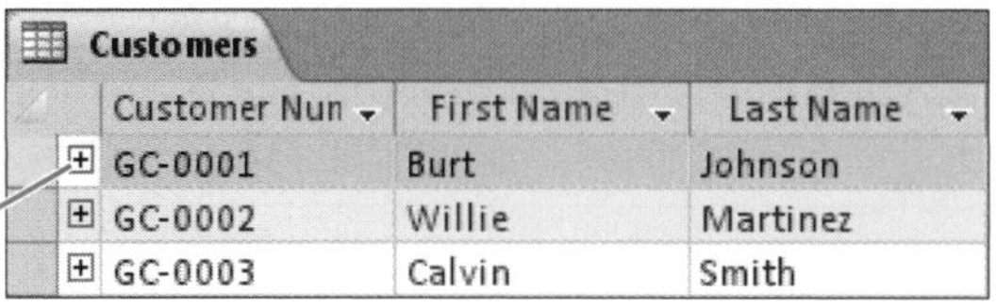

Viewing Subdatasheets

The plus symbol in a datasheet acts as an expansion tool to display a *subdatasheet*—a mini-datasheet that displays data contained in another table that is related to the active record. The subdatasheet appears immediately below each record in the active table. If there are no related records for a record in the active table, Access displays field names and a new row so that you can enter data into a new record of the related table.

For example, if a Customers table in a database is related to the Orders table in the database, opening the Customers table would display orders related to each customer in the subdatasheet. If a customer calls and wants to place a new order, you can enter the order details into the fields of the subdatasheet and Access stores the record in the Orders table.

The customer name is found in the Customers table of the database.

The subdatasheet appears immediately below the customer record and displays an existing order from the Orders table.

The expand (+) button changes to a collapse (–) button when the subdatasheet is shown.

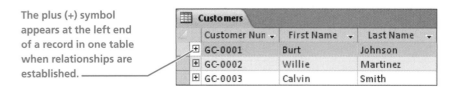

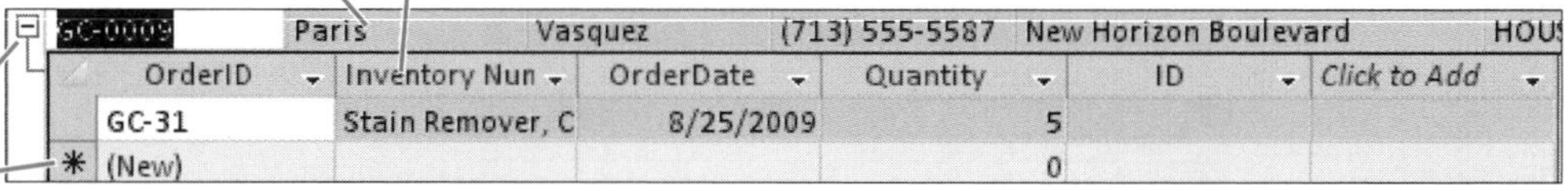

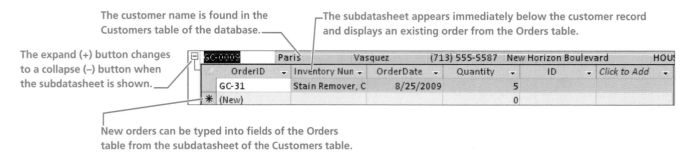

New orders can be typed into fields of the Orders table from the subdatasheet of the Customers table.

Printing Relationships

After you save the database relationships, you can save the document as a report and then print it just as you can print other database reports. Access displays the relationships in Print Preview and places the data and title of the document on the page for reference. You can then update the report to show new relationships as the database develops.

DEVELOP YOUR SKILLS 5.4.3

Print Relationships

In this exercise, you will create a Relationships report and print the relationships.

Before You Begin: The Relationships window for the Green Clean Related database should be open.

1. Follow these steps to create a Relationships report:

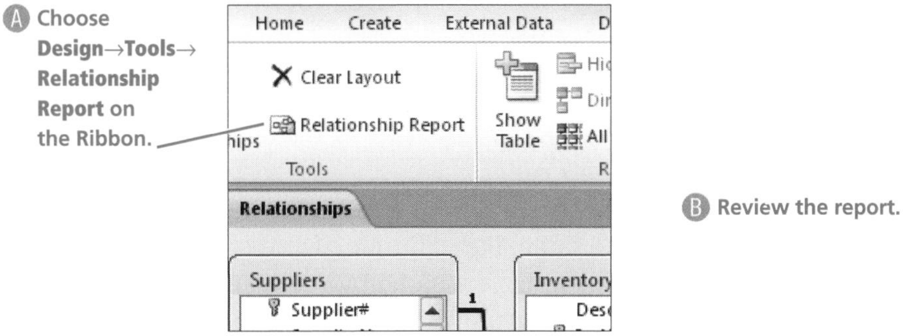

2. **Save** the report using the default name Access assigns.

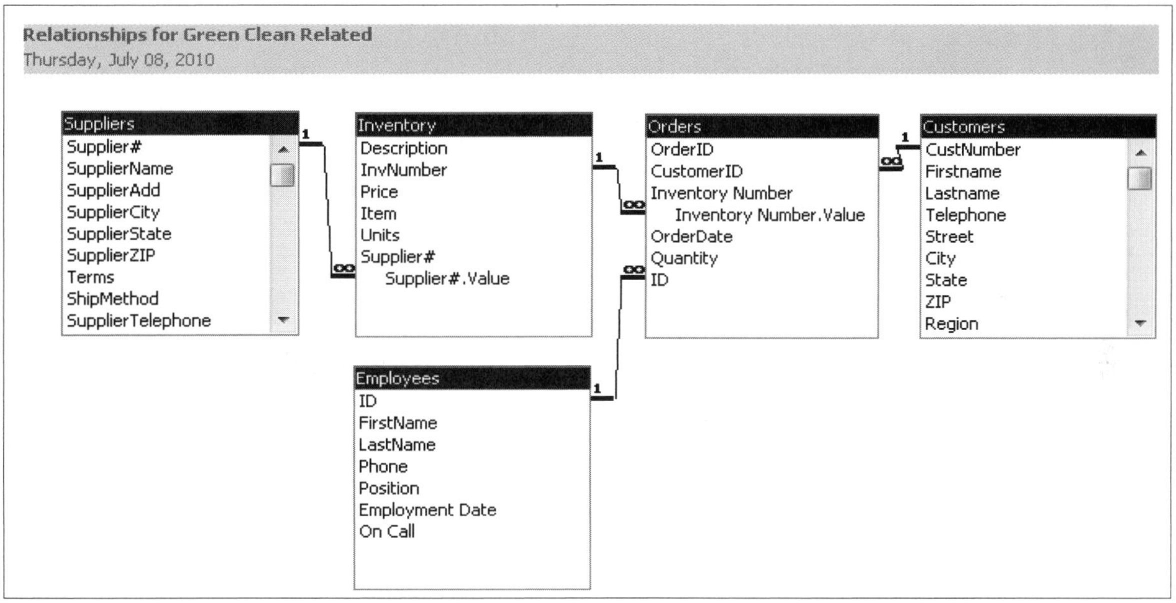

3. **Print** the report and retrieve the printout.

4. **Close** the report and the Relationships window.

5.5 Reviewing Relationship Join Properties

Video Lesson labyrinthelab.com/videos

Depending on the type of query you create and the data you want Access to display when you run the query, it is sometimes necessary to change the join properties between tables in the query. Join properties control the circumstances under which a record from related tables appears when you run the query.

Setting Join Properties

Normally, when you create a query, Access displays only those records from related tables when the values of data in related fields are the same. For example, if you create a query that displays data for all employees in an Employees table for which an order is recorded in the Orders table, Access displays only those records for employees with orders—i.e., the employee IDs in both tables match. Suppose, however, that you want to display all employees from the Employees table and include data from the Orders table for employees with sales. You can select the join properties option that instructs Access to display all records from one table and only data from the other table with matching data in related fields.

Standard Query

First Name	Last Name	Employee ID	Order Number
Alice	Jones	GC-68	GC-1234
Alice	Jones	GC-68	GC-2345
Alice	Jones	GC-68	GC-3456
Alice	Jones	GC-68	GC-4567
Alice	Jones	GC-68	GC-5678
James	Occana	GC-64	GC-1345
James	Occana	GC-64	GC-2456
James	Occana	GC-64	GC-3567
James	Occana	GC-64	GC-4678

Results display only those records for employees with orders.

By setting join properties, you can create a query that displays results for all employees and still identify the orders placed for some records.

Edited Join Property Results

First Name	Last Name	Employee ID	Order Number
Julie	Adams	GC-72	
Jessica	Allen	GC-34	
Destiny	Baker	GC-71	
Morgan	Gonzalez	GC-70	
Jose	Green	GC-73	
Hailey	Hall	GC-01	
Jasmine	Hernandez	GC-87	
Gabriel	Hill	GC-75	
Alice	Jones	GC-68	GC-1234
Alice	Jones	GC-68	GC-2345
Alice	Jones	GC-68	GC-3456
Alice	Jones	GC-68	GC-4567
Alice	Jones	GC-68	GC-5678
Benjamin	King	GC-67	
Brandon	Lopez	GC-32	
Kaitlyn	Nelson	GC-69	
James	Occana	GC-64	GC-1345
James	Occana	GC-64	GC-2456
James	Occana	GC-64	GC-3567
James	Occana	GC-64	GC-4678
Zachary	Scott	GC-74	
Kayla	Walker	GC-98	
Logan	Wright	GC-43	
Victoria	Young	GC-65	

Identifying Join Types

Three join types are available in Access. It is important to note that only the description of the join appears in the Join Properties dialog box.

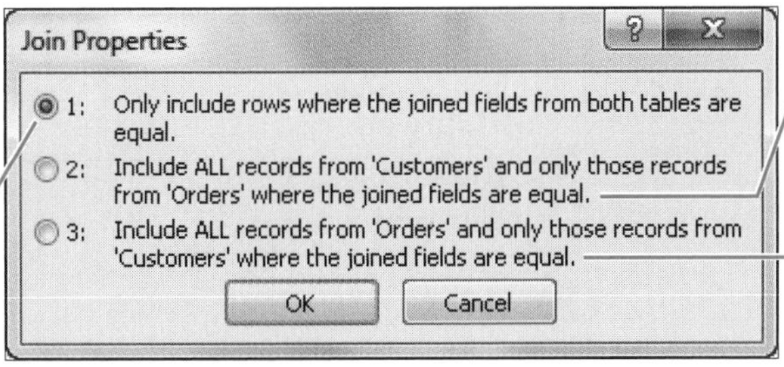

Inner Join: Default option displays only those records where data in both tables matches.

Left Outer Join: Includes ALL records from 'Customers' and only those records from 'Orders' where the joined fields are equal.

Right Outer Join: Include ALL records from 'Orders' and only those records from 'Customers' where the joined fields are equal.

QUICK REFERENCE — IDENTIFYING RELATIONSHIP JOIN TYPES

Join Type	Description
Inner join	Checks for records with matching values in the join field and displays only those records for which the values match.
Left outer join	Displays all records from the table on the left or one side of a one-to-many relationship even if there are no matching records in the other table(s).
Right outer join	Displays all records from the table on the right or many side of a one-to-many relationship even if there are no matching records in the other table(s).

Defining Left and Right Joins

The Inner Join is the most common join type used in Access databases and is the default join property. You can modify join properties using the Relationships window so that the settings affect all queries, or set the join properties in the query Design window so that the settings affect only the active query. Knowing how to change the join properties to display all records in one of the tables is also important when you need it.

Many people think that the *left* and *right* referred to in the join definitions refer to the arrangement of the tables in the Relationships window. That is not necessarily the case. The Edit Relationships dialog box displays related tables and the fields in each table that relate the tables. The table on the one side of a one-to-many relationship is always listed in the left column of the Edit Relationships dialog box. The table on the many side of a one-to-many relationship is always listed in the right column of the Edit Relationships dialog box. As a result, the left and right referred to in the Join Properties dialog box refer to the tables listed in the Edit Relationships dialog box rather than the physical arrangement of tables in the Relationships window.

The table on the left shows the table on the one side of a one-to-many relationship.

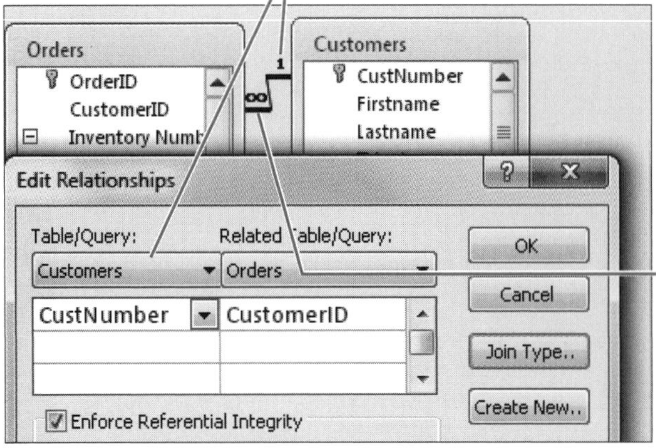

The table on the right shows the table on the many side of a one-to-many relationship.

DEVELOP YOUR SKILLS 5.5.1

Review Join Properties

In this exercise, you will display the join properties for a database in both the Relationships window and a query window.

Before You Begin: Your Green Clean Related database should be open.

1. Choose **Database Tools→Relationships→Relationships** on the Ribbon to open the relationships window.
2. Follow these steps to display the Join Properties dialog box:

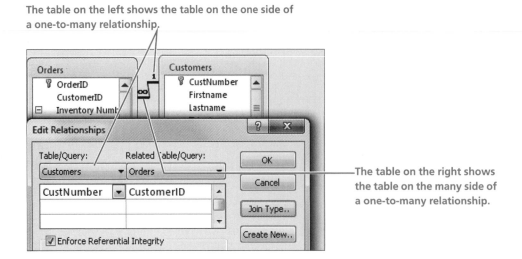

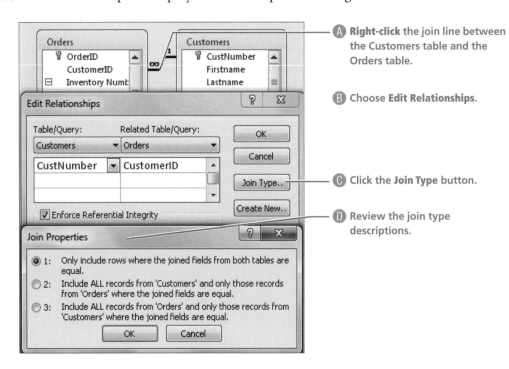

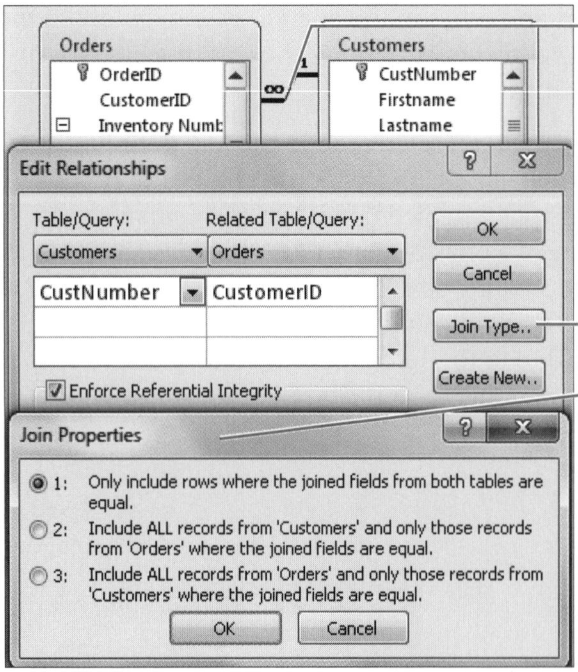

A. **Right-click** the join line between the Customers table and the Orders table.

B. Choose **Edit Relationships**.

C. Click the **Join Type** button.

D. Review the join type descriptions.

3. Click **OK** twice and then **close** the Relationships window, **saving** changes, if prompted.

View Join Properties in Query Design View

4. **Right-click** the Customer Orders query in the Navigation Pane and choose **Design View**.
5. Drag the **Inventory Number** field in the Orders field list to the **InvNumber** field in the Inventory field list, **right-click** the join line connecting the Orders field list to the Inventory field list, and choose **Join Properties**.
   Access opens the Join Properties dialog box. Notice that the dialog box displays the table names and field names differently from those displayed in the Relationships window.

TIP: If Join Properties is missing from the shortcut menu, try pointing closer to the center of the join line and then right-click again.

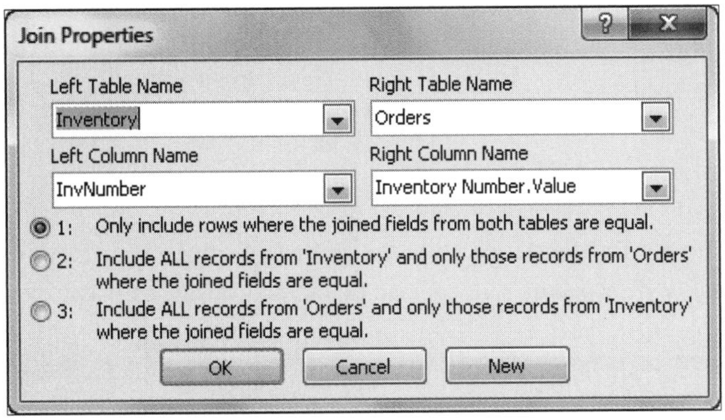

6. Click **Cancel** to close the Join Properties dialog box, and then **close** [×] the query without saving changes.

5.6 Identifying Object Dependencies

Video Lesson labyrinthelab.com/videos

Each object in a database is, in some way, connected to other objects. In many cases, one object may totally rely on another object for its data. For example, a form may be created for a table and if you delete the table, the form has no object from which to obtain its data. Access contains a tool that enables you to display a list of objects that depend on another object in the database so that you can identify how modifications you make to the database affect other objects. Object dependencies display in a panel within the database window when you call for them.

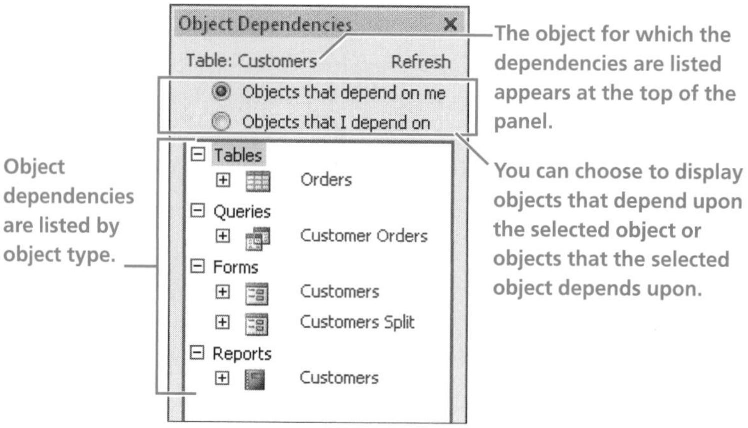

QUICK REFERENCE	VIEWING OBJECT DEPENDENCIES
Task	**Procedure**
View object dependencies	■ Select the object for which you want to view dependencies. ■ Choose Database Tools →Relationships→Object Dependencies.

DEVELOP YOUR SKILLS 5.6.1

Display Object Dependencies

In this exercise, you will display object dependencies for the Customers table.

1. **Close** all open database objects and then **select** (but do not open) the **Customers** table in the Navigation Pane of the Green Clean Related database.
2. Choose **Database Tools→Relationships→Object Dependencies** and click **OK** if a message appears advising you that the object dependencies need to be updated.
3. Choose the **Objects That I Depend On** option to display objects on which the Customers table depends.

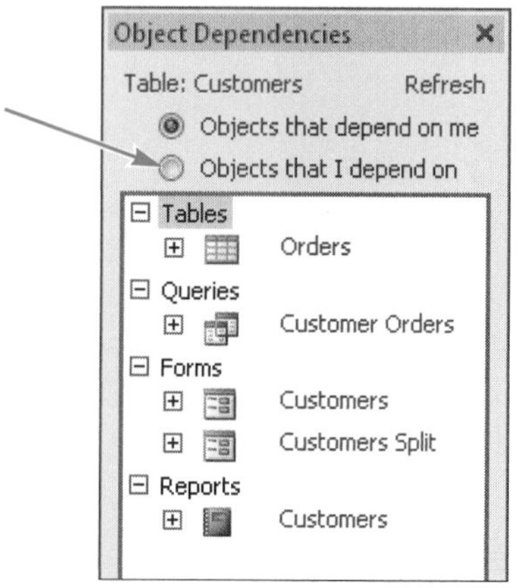

4. Follow these steps to display objects on which the Customers Split report depends:

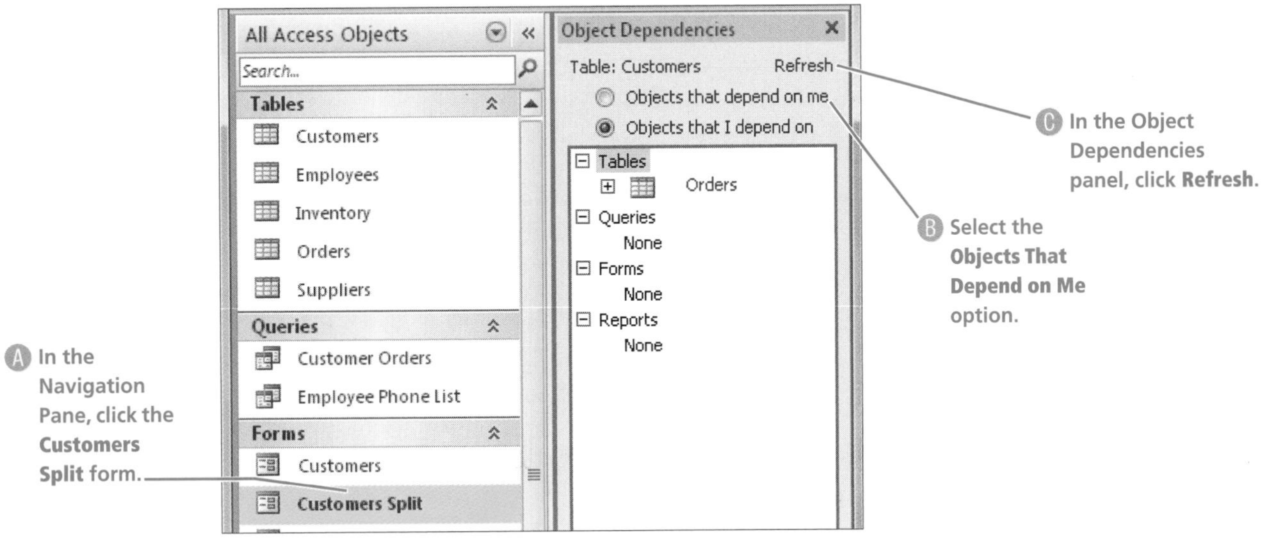

5. **Close** [X] the Object Dependencies panel, **close** the Navigation Pane, and then **exit** Access.

5.7 Concepts Review

Concepts Review labyrinthelab.com/acc10

To check your knowledge of the key concepts introduced in this lesson, complete the Concepts Review quiz by going to the URL listed above. If your classroom is using Labyrinth eLab, you may complete the Concepts Review quiz from within your eLab course.

Reinforce Your Skills

REINFORCE YOUR SKILLS 5.1

Create a Field Lookup

Raritan Clinic East is now developing a database that contains staff scheduling data. They have built a number of related tables and have also entered numerous records. They would like to create lookup fields that enable data entry personnel to select valid entries from a list. In this exercise, you will create a lookup field in the Schedule table that enables you to add multiple values from the Resources table.

1. **Open** the rs-Raritan Clinic East Schedule database from the Lesson 05 folder and **save** the file using the filename `rs-Raritan Schedule Rev`.
2. Open the **Resources** table, review the data, and then **close** the table.

Create Lookup Fields

3. **Right-click** the Schedule table in the Navigation Pane and select **Design View** to open the table design.
4. Display the **Data Type** list for the ResourceID field and select **Lookup Wizard** to launch the wizard.
5. Select the following settings for each Lookup Wizard screen, clicking Next to advance to the next screen:
   - Screen 1: Select the **I Want the Lookup Field to Get the Values from Another Table or Query** option.
   - Screen 2: Select **Table: Resources**.
   - Screen 3: Move the ResourceLastName and ResourceID fields to the **Selected Fields** list.
   - Screen 4: Select **ResourceLastName** from the sort box 1 list.
   - Screen 5: Leave default settings **active**.
   - Screen 6: Select the **ResourceLastName** field.
   - Screen 7: Check the **Allow Multiple Values** checkbox, and then click **Finish**.
6. Choose **Yes**, if prompted, to create a lookup for multiple values.
7. Choose **Yes** when prompted to save the table.
8. Display **Datasheet view** and select the following resources from the Resource ID field for the first record (1NW): Arnold, Carpenter, Carrol, and Dunn.
9. **Double-click** the right border for the Resource ID column heading to widen the column and then **close** the table, **saving** changes when prompted.
10. **Close** all open objects and **close** the database.

REINFORCE YOUR SKILLS 5.2

Create a Split Form

Additional forms are required for the Raritan Clinic East Nurse Schedule. In this exercise, you will create a split form for the Schedule table.

1. **Open** your rs-Raritan Schedule Rev database from the Lesson 05 folder and select the Schedule table in the Navigation Pane.
2. Choose **Create→Forms→More Forms→Split Form** to create a new form based on the Schedule table.
3. Review the data shown for the first table record.
4. **Save** the form using the form name **`Schedule Split`**, and then **close** it.

REINFORCE YOUR SKILLS 5.3

Work with Relationships

After creating the lookup field and a new form for the database, the relationships in the database have changed. As a result, you need to review the relationships and update them to reflect the relationships. As personnel leave the clinic for other positions, it is important to maintain an up-to-date list of valid resources. As such, when a Resource is removed, you want to be sure to remove it from the list of available resources. In this exercise, you will edit and create relationships and set relationship options.

1. **Open** your rs-Raritan Schedule Rev database, if it is closed.
2. Choose **Database Tools→Relationships→Relationships** to open the Relationships window.
   Notice that Access created a relationship between the Resources table and the Schedule table.

Edit Relationships

3. **Right-click** the join line for the relationship Access created and choose **Edit Relationship**.
4. Ensure that **Resources** appears as the table on the left side of the Edit Relationships dialog box, and then choose **ResourceID** from the field drop-down list for that table.
5. Click **OK**.

Create Relationships

6. Drag the ResourceTypeID field from the **Resources** table and drop it on the ResoureTypeID field in the **Resource Types** table.
7. Check the **Enforce Referential Integrity** checkbox and the **Cascade Update Related Fields** option in the Edit Relationships dialog box, and then click **Create**.
8. Choose **Design→Relationships→Show Table** to display the Show Table dialog box that contains a list of tables in the database.
9. **Double-click** the Assignment Location table, and then click **Close** to close the Show Table dialog box.

10. **Drag** the following fields contained in the tables identified to create relationships without enforcing referential integrity:

Field	From Table	To Table
StationID	Schedule	Schedule Details
StationID	Schedule	Assignment Location
StationID	Schedule Details	Assignment Location

11. **Save** changes to the Relationships window.

REINFORCE YOUR SKILLS 5.4

Create a Relationship Report and View Dependencies

Now that the relationships are set, you can create the relationships report and add it to the database documentation. In this exercise, you will create a relationship report and display object dependencies for the new form.

1. **Drag** the field list title bars to arrange them in the relationships window so that no lines overlap.
2. Choose **Design→Tools→**Relationship Report to create a new report.
3. **Save** the report using the default report name and **print** a copy of the report.

Display Object Dependencies

4. **Close** all open objects, and then **select** (but do not open) the **Schedule** table in the Navigation Pane.
5. Choose **Database Tools→Relationships→Object Dependencies** and click **OK** when prompted to turn on Track name AutoCorrect.
6. Select the **Objects that I Depend On** option in the Object Dependencies panel.
   - How many tables depend on the Schedule table? _____
   - How many Queries depend on the Schedule table? _____
   - How many Forms and Reports depend on the Schedule table? _____
7. **Close** all open database objects, **close** the database, and **exit** Access.

Apply Your Skills

APPLY YOUR SKILLS 5.1

Create a Database and Import Data

The Flower Pot is a small flower store in Denver that has seen a rapid growth in sales in the last few months. They have been storing their customer data in an Excel worksheet and now plan to move the data into a database to make managing the data more efficient. In this exercise, you will create a new database to hold the data and then import data from both Excel files and text files to create three tables in the database.

1. Create a **new** blank database named **`as-The Flower Pot`**.
2. Choose **External Data→Import→Text File** on the Ribbon to launch the Get External Data wizard and **import** the file for the first table using the following information and clicking **Next** to move to the next screen:
   - Choose **Import** the source data into a new table in the current database.
   - Click **Browse** and locate and **open** the file named as-Flower Pot Customers.txt in your Lesson 05 folder.
   - Select options to tell Access that as-The Flower Pot Customers file is a delimited file, separated by tabs, that contains field names in the first row.
   - All fields should be imported and the CustNo field should be the **primary key**.
3. Create a second **new** table named **`Employees Mailing Labels`**, by importing data from a worksheet named Employees Mailing Labels contained in an Excel file named **`as-Flower Pot`**. As you import the file, select appropriate options to accommodate the data, as shown here:
   - The first row contains column headings and all fields **except** the DOB field should be imported.
   - The table contains **no** primary key.
4. Create the final **new** table, name it **`Departments`**, by importing the Excel data stored on the Departments worksheet in the as-Flower Pot workbook. Note the following as you select options during import:
   - The first row contains column headings.
   - The Department ID field is the **primary key field**.
5. **Open** all tables and review the data.

APPLY YOUR SKILLS 5.2

Create a Lookup Field and Set Field Properties

Now that you have created the database for The Flower Pot and added tables to the database, you can begin formatting the data and making data entry more efficient. In this exercise, you will create a lookup field that enables you to select a valid department when entering data into the Employees Mailing Labels table. In addition, you will modify tables by changing the data type and setting field properties.

1. **Open** your as-The Flower Pot database and display the Departments table in Design View.
2. Change the **Data Type** for the DepartmentID field to **Number**, if necessary, and then add an **input mask** that formats the DepartmentID as FP- followed by two digits.
3. **Save** changes to the table and **close** it.
4. Display the **Employees Mailing Labels** table in Design View and make the following changes to the fields and data types:
   - Change the ZIP and Telephone fields to **Text**.
   - Change the Dept field name to **DepartmentID**.
   - Change the DepartmentID data type to **Number**.
5. Use the **Input Mask Builder** to create standard input masks for the ZIP and Telephone fields, **saving** the table changes when prompted.
6. Set the following field properties for the corresponding fields:

Field	Field Size	Caption	Default Value
FirstName	15	First Name	
LastName	15	Last Name	
City	15		Denver
State	2		CO

7. Set the following field input masks for the corresponding fields:

Field	Input Mask
FirstName	>L<??????????????
LastName	>L<??????????????
State	>LL
DepartmentID	"FP-"00

8. **Save** changes, **close** the table, and then **open** the Flower Pot Customers table in Design View.

9. Change the **data type** for the ZIP field to **Text** and then make the following changes to associated fields in the table:

Field	Field Size	Caption	Input Mask
CustNo		Customer Number	"FPC-"000
FirstName	15	First Name	>L<??????????????
LastName	15	Last Name	>L<??????????????
City	15		>L<??????????????
State	2		>LL
ZIP	11		Build
Telephone	14		Build

Create a Lookup Field

10. Display the **Employees Mailing Labels** table in Design View and launch the Lookup Wizard for the **DepartmentID** field.

11. Make appropriate selections from Lookup Wizard screens to create a lookup field that:
    - Looks up data from the Departments table.
    - Uses both fields from the Departments table and sorts them by department name.
    - Hides the key column and displays the department name.
    - Allows multiple values to be selected.
    - Uses the default value Access assigns as a label.

12. **Display** the table datasheet and enter the following department values for the employees:

Last Name	Departments
Silva	Annuals, Seasonal
Pearson	Accessories, Garden Tools
Holland	Landscaping, Ponds & Pool
Douglas	Administration
Fleming	House Plants, Seasonal
Jenson	Trees & Shrubs, Ponds & Pools
Vargas	Stocking, Annuals
Byrd	Stocking, Annuals
Davidson	Garden Tools, Accessories
Hopkins	House Plants, Seasonal

13. **Save** changes to all objects and **print** copies of each table.

14. **Close** the database.

APPLY YOUR SKILLS 5.3

Create Special Forms

Input forms make data easier to enter. In this exercise, you will create a form for each database table.

1. **Open** your as-The Flower Pot database and **select** (but do not open) the **Departments** table in the Navigation Pane.
2. Create a **simple form** for the table.
3. **Save** the form using the default name Access assigns.
4. Select the **Flower Pot Customers** table and create a **split form** for the table.
5. **Save** the form using the default form name Access assigns.
6. Select the **Employees Mailing Labels** table in the Navigation Pane.
7. Create a **simple form** for the table.
8. **Save** the form using the default name Access assigns.
9. **Print** a copy of each form, and then **close** the forms and **close** the database.

APPLY YOUR SKILLS 5.4

Review, Edit, and Print Relationships

Activities you have performed on The Flower Pot database have established relationships. In this exercise, you will review the relationships, edit them, and print a copy of the relationships report.

1. **Open** your as-The Flower Pot database and display the Relationships window.
2. Display the **Show Tables** dialog box, add the **third** table to the window, and then **close** the Show Tables dialog box.
3. Display the **Edit Relationships** dialog box for the join that exists and **enforce referential integrity**.
4. Create a **Relationship Report**, **save** it using the default report name Access assigns, and **print** a copy of the report.
5. Display **object dependencies** for each object in the database.
6. **Close** all open database objects, **close** the database, and **exit** Access.

Critical Thinking & Work-Readiness Skills

In the course of working through the following Microsoft Office-based Critical Thinking exercises, you will also be utilizing various work-readiness skills, some of which are listed next to each exercise. Go to labyrinthelab.com/workreadiness *to learn more about the work-readiness skills.*

5.1 Share Data with Lookups

Green Clean is exploring new ways to encourage people to recycle their unused treasures. Ahn Tran has located the ct-VonHamburg Tomb database (Lesson 05 folder), which contains plain, unformatted data. She would like to use it as an example of the types of items lying around the house that can be recycled by selling them to others. In essence, they can become someone else's treasure. Before distributing the database to customers who have expressed a need to get rid of their clutter, she wants you to edit the table format and create a lookup field to tie the Format or Selling Format field in each table to the Selling Format table. Modify table structures by changing data types and adding field properties, create lookup fields to establish the relationships among the tables, and create and print a relationship report to show Ahn. Then, create a split form for each table to display the table data, saving each split form with the word *Split* in the object name.

WORK-READINESS SKILLS APPLIED

- Reasoning
- Seeing things in the mind's eye
- Acquiring and evaluating information

5.2 Build a Relational Database

The utility bill for Green Clean has just arrived and D'Andre Adams, Facilities Services Manager, passes it to you as a good example of a statement that might be used by Green Clean's accounting department. Review ct-Utility Bill.pdf (Lesson 05 folder) and use it to develop a data dictionary for a database that could generate the statement. Then, start a new database named **`ct-GC Sample Statement`** and create two of the tables you have designed. Include lookup fields, field properties, referential integrity, forms, and reports. Print a relationships report and a copy of each object in the database.

WORK-READINESS SKILLS APPLIED

- Seeing things in the mind's eye
- Acquiring and evaluating information
- Reasoning

5.3 Field of Study Usage

Green Clean is preparing to expand its consulting group to include environmental engineers who can provide solutions to companies struggling to meet environmental quality controls. Each field of study has a particular set of courses that each student must complete to fulfill graduation requirements. Use your school's website to locate a list of courses required for majors in environmental engineering. Then, using Word, compile a list of fields that should be added to the Employees table in the database to identify employee educational background and qualifications for their positions. Save your work in the Lesson 05 folder as **`ct-New Fields`**.

WORK-READINESS SKILLS APPLIED

- Seeing things in the mind's eye
- Acquiring and evaluating information
- Reasoning

Creating Complex Queries

LESSON OUTLINE

6.1 Identifying Advanced Query Features—An Overview

6.2 Creating Select Queries

6.3 Creating and Running Parameter Queries

6.4 Creating a Calculated Field in a Query

6.5 Creating and Running Action Queries

6.6 Protecting and Repairing a Database

6.7 Concepts Review

Reinforce Your Skills

Apply Your Skills

Critical Thinking & Work-Readiness Skills

LEARNING OBJECTIVES

After studying this lesson, you will be able to:

- Create a select query involving multiple tables
- Create a report based on multiple tables in a query
- Create and run parameter queries
- Create a calculated field in a query
- Create and run action queries
- Analyze, compact, repair, backup, and restore a database

As the volume of data stored in database tables grows, so does the number of edits required to keep data in thousands of records up to date. Although relational databases reduce redundant data, which reduces the number of places and times that you must edit data, it does little to improve the accuracy and validity of data. Consequently, it becomes a challenge to maintain a database in a timely fashion.

In this lesson, you will explore five types of queries designed to improve the timeliness and accuracy of large relational databases. You will discover queries that automate data updates, delete out-of-date records, and summarize data. In addition, you will use special query features to display a subset of data to make updating or selecting records from the data more efficient. Finally, you will learn techniques for repairing databases that become corrupt and for backing up databases to prevent unwanted loss of data.

Student Resources labyrinthelab.com/acc10

Handling Growing Databases

Green Clean has just turned database management tasks over to Allen Sedgwick, manager of computer information systems for the company. He is responsible for implementing data retrieval from the growing number of records stored in the database. He plans to develop queries that will make updating records in the database more efficient. With one query, he wants to limit the query results to display information for whichever customer the customer service representative is helping. He also wants to create additional queries designed to perform cleanup and automation tasks in the Green Clean database.

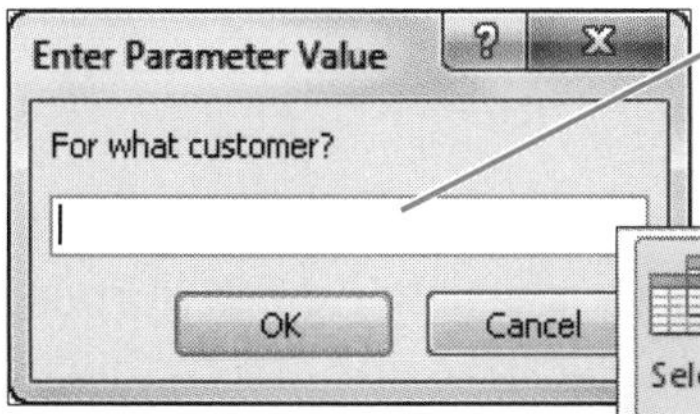

A Parameter Query prompts the user for a value in one or more table fields.

The Query Type section of the Design tab of the Ribbon provides easy access to creating queries that automate database tasks.

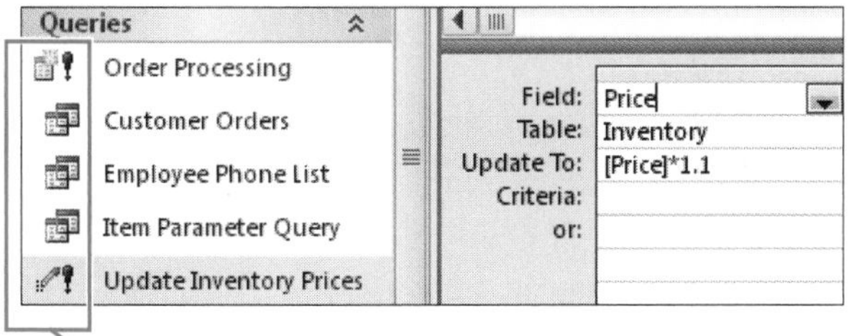

Query types are identified by icons in the Navigation Pane.

6.1 Identifying Advanced Query Features—An Overview

Video Lesson labyrinthelab.com/videos

One goal of relational databases is to store data in such a way that you can retrieve it from multiple tables quickly and efficiently. Telephone order clerks and department of motor vehicle personnel retrieve data and information daily—and often at a moment's notice. They can locate a customer's address by entering a telephone number or customer ID or the owner of a car based on the license plate number. When data is stored in tables in a relational database, you can retrieve data from one or more database tables and extract records that meet specific criteria using a *query*—a database object used to locate and list records based on conditions you set. You may have already used several types of queries: the select query, the crosstab query, the unmatched query, and the duplicates query. Each of those queries was designed to locate records that met special circumstances or specific criteria.

Access contains additional query types that are designed to perform specific actions or meet specific needs. Now that you have advanced in your study of Access, identifying the purposes of each query type and how they are set up to meet specific needs is important. Each query type, from the select query through each advanced query type, is identified in the following table.

QUICK REFERENCE **IDENTIFYING ACCESS QUERY TYPES**

Query Type	Description
Select Query	Contains fields from one or more database tables, criteria to select data from corresponding tables, conditions for matching data in multiple fields, settings to group or summarize record data, and/or calculated fields. When you run a select query, Access retrieves records containing data that meets the criteria.
Parameter Query	Prompts data entry personnel for a data value so that Access filters records in a large database and displays a subset of records that match the value entered. For example, if you want to display products from a specific category of items, you could set a parameter query to request a category name so that Access displays only those products in the category.
Crosstab Query	Summarizes values—such as sums, counts, and averages—from a table field and groups records based on summary fields. Access places one set of data on the left side of the datasheet and summarizes the data based on another field across the top of the datasheet. For example, if you wanted to display a total inventory of items available by category, you could create a crosstab query that calculated the total of each category and displayed only the total value of inventory.
Action Query	Performs one of four different types of actions on a group of records: delete records, update records, append records, or create a new table.
SQL Query	Uses a structured query language (SQL) statement to create a query. Common SQL queries include the union query, data-definition query, and subquery.
Unmatched Query	Locates records in one table that have no related records in another table. For example, you could create an Unmatched Query to ensure that each record in the *Orders* table has a corresponding record in the *Customers* table.
Duplicates Query	Locates records containing duplicate field values in a single table or query. For example, you could create a Duplicates Query to locate records in the *Orders* table that were entered twice or inquiries submitted more than once.

Querying Tables Containing No Relationships

Relationships between database objects play an important role in creating successful queries. When tables in a database have no established relationships, running queries on the tables can produce some very unexpected results.

Cartesian Product Lists

Cartesian product lists are simple lists that display all combinations of results from querying a database using fields from two unrelated tables. Without established relationships, Access has no idea how to relate the data contained in each table, so it presents every possible combination of records between the two tables. If, for example, one table contains 15 records, the other table contains 100 records, and you add fields from both tables to a query, Access displays 1,500 records (15 x 100) in the query results datasheet—*the Cartesian product,* which is sometimes called a *cross product*—because the list represents the product of every possible combination of each record in both database tables. The Cartesian product lists the same record many times. When the number of records in each table is large, these queries take a long time to run and ultimately provide quite meaningless results.

Customer Orders

First Name	Last Name	OrderID
Calvin	Alaverz	GC-13
Calvin	Alaverz	GC-13
Calvin	Alaverz	GC-13
Calvin	Alaverz	GC-13
Calvin	Alaverz	GC-13
Calvin	Alaverz	GC-13
Calvin	Alaverz	GC-13
Calvin	Alaverz	GC-13
Calvin	Alaverz	GC-13
Calvin	Alaverz	GC-13
Calvin	Alaverz	GC-13

Example of Cartesian product query results where the same record is listed many times, compounding the number of records.

Avoiding Cartesian Products

To prevent Cartesian product lists when you run a query, you should establish relationships before creating a query or by connecting fields between tables in the query grid. By ensuring that a join line connects fields in different tables and also that referential integrity is established, you can control, to some degree, the results of the query.

6.2 Creating Select Queries

Video Lesson labyrinthelab.com/videos

Select queries are the most common type of query. They are designed to display data from specific fields contained in one or more database tables in a single datasheet. You can design a select query to select records based on criteria, sort records in the query results datasheet, and summarize data by grouping data and using *aggregate functions*—sum, max, min, count and so forth—to display field totals. In addition, you can create calculated fields using values contained in other fields to summarize data. Select queries process no data—they simply display the data. One great advantage to running queries is that they are dynamic, meaning they display up-to-date data together in a single datasheet each time you run the query. You can then edit the data or use the data to create reports and other database objects based on the query when necessary, but the data remains stored in the database tables—*not* in the query results datasheet.

DEVELOP YOUR SKILLS 6.2.1

Create a Select Query

In this exercise, you will create a select query that displays data from three different database tables for Green Clean.

1. **Open** the Green Clean Queries database from the Lesson 6 folder and **save** it as a new file using the filename **Green Clean Advanced Queries**.
2. Open the **Navigation Pane** and review the table objects contained in the database.
3. Choose **Create→Queries→Query Design** on the Ribbon to create a new query.
4. **Double-click** each of the following table names to add their field lists to the query grid: **Customers**, **Inventory**, and **Orders**.
5. **Close** the Show Table dialog box and **drag** the field list title bars to position them as shown.

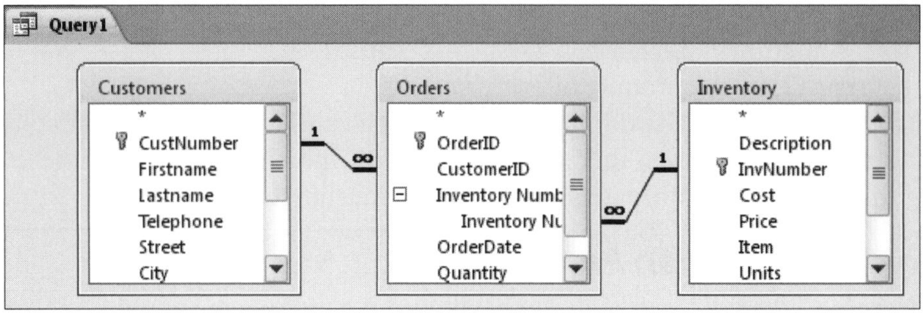

6. **Double-click** the OrderID field in the Orders table to add the field to the query grid.
7. Repeat the procedures outlined in **step 6** to add the following fields from the corresponding tables to the query grid:

Table	Fields
Orders	CustomerID, Inventory Number, Quantity
Customers	LastName, FirstName
Inventory	Description, Price

8. Choose **Design→Results→Run** on the Ribbon to run the query and review the results.

Access displays 75 records in the query results datasheet.

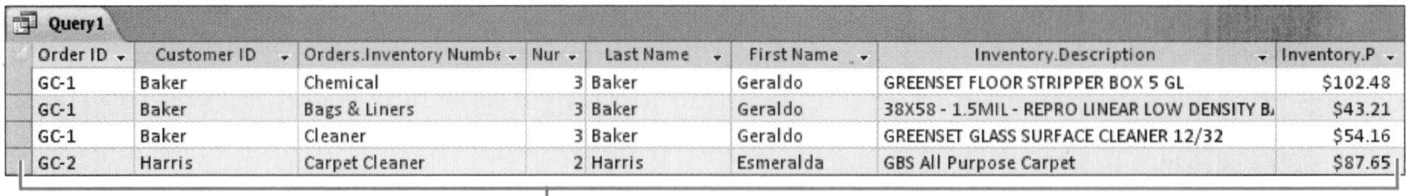

Query1

Order ID	Customer ID	Orders.Inventory Numbe	Nur	Last Name	First Name	Inventory.Description	Inventory.P
GC-1	Baker	Chemical	3	Baker	Geraldo	GREENSET FLOOR STRIPPER BOX 5 GL	$102.48
GC-1	Baker	Bags & Liners	3	Baker	Geraldo	38X58 - 1.5MIL - REPRO LINEAR LOW DENSITY B.	$43.21
GC-1	Baker	Cleaner	3	Baker	Geraldo	GREENSET GLASS SURFACE CLEANER 12/32	$54.16
GC-2	Harris	Carpet Cleaner	2	Harris	Esmeralda	GBS All Purpose Carpet	$87.65

Field values from selected fields from all three tables display.

9. **Double-click** the right border of each column heading to size the columns to display data more appropriately.

10. **Save** the query using the query name **`Order Processing`** and then **close** it.

Creating a Multi-Table Report Based on a Query

Video Lesson labyrinthelab.com/videos

After you create a query that contains fields from multiple tables, you are able to use that query as the basis for creating a multi-table report. As you know, relationships play an important part of building multi-table objects in Access databases. To effectively build a multi-table report, the tables must be related to each other, and the fields being used in the report must be displayed in the query datasheet. If the tables are joined in a relationship, creating a multi-table report is as easy as building a simple report.

DEVELOP YOUR SKILLS 6.2.2

Create a Report Using a Query

In this exercise, you will create a new multi-table report using the Order Processing query as the source for the report.

1. Select the **Order Processing** query in the Navigation Pane to make it active, but do not open it.

2. Follow these steps to create a report using the Report Wizard:

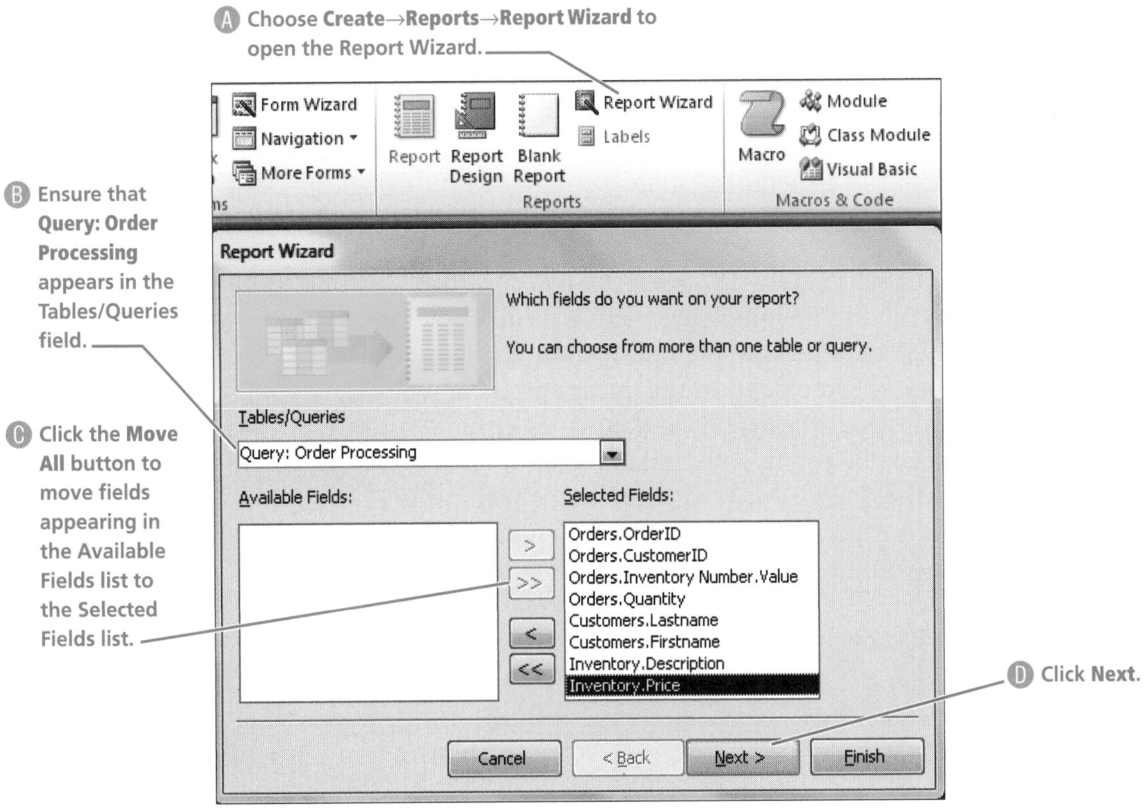

3. Click **Next** to accept the defaults for how to view the data.

4. **Double-click** the Orders.CustomerID field on the next Wizard screen to set it as the grouping level and then click **Next**.
5. Click **Next** on the next Wizard screen to leave the list unsorted.
   Access displays the Wizard screen that enables you to select a layout for the report.
6. Select *Stepped* for the layout, and *Landscape* for the Orientation, and then click **Next**.
7. Type **`Orders by Customer`** as the report title and click **Finish**.
   Your report should look something like the one pictured in the following figure.

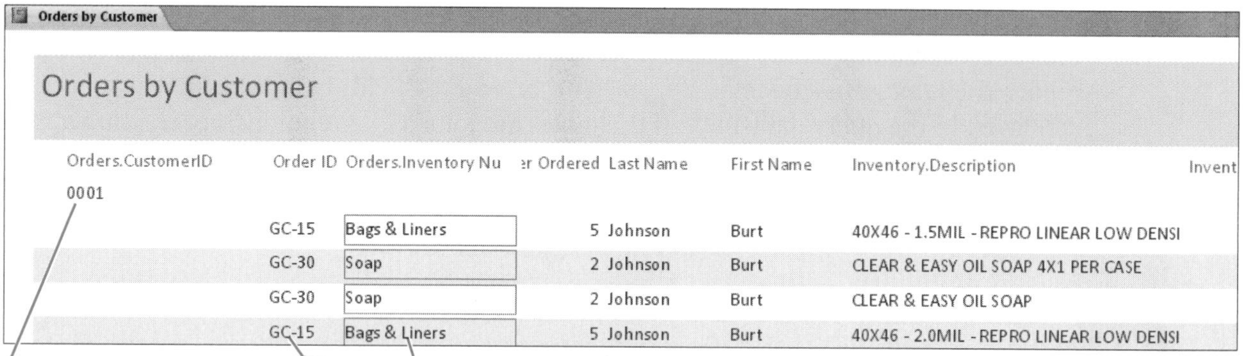

Notice the grouping level on the Customer Number field.

Each order is identified, and the items ordered for each order are shown.

8. **Close** the report, **saving** changes to the report if prompted.

6.3 Creating and Running Parameter Queries

Video Lesson labyrinthelab.com/videos

A *parameter query* is a select query to which you add controls that enable those who use the query to set criteria each time they run the query. A parameter query prompts the user to enter a value for one or more fields in the query and then delivers on-the-spot results based on the value they enter. Parameter queries enable you to enter criteria to limit results without accessing the query Design view each time you want to run the query. It is especially useful when you create a query that others who are unfamiliar with query design will use.

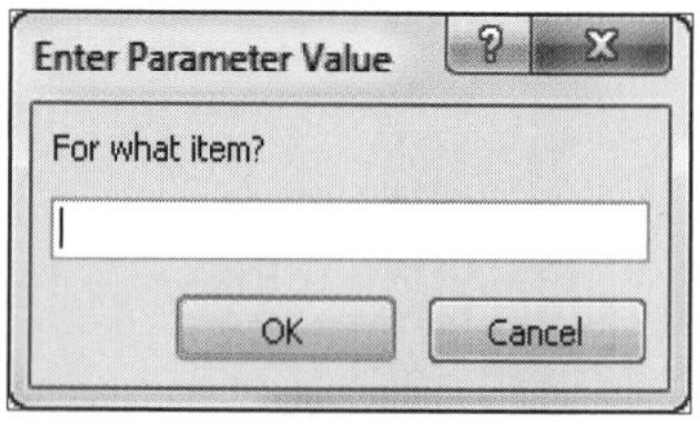

Sample of a prompt message that enables users to enter criteria when running a parameter query

Setting Up a Parameter Query

Parameter queries use the Criteria row of the query grid to create a *criteria expression*. The criteria expression contains the text that you want to appear in the prompt. When you run the parameter query, you can enter a value in the prompt box and the query results datasheet displays only records containing the value entered.

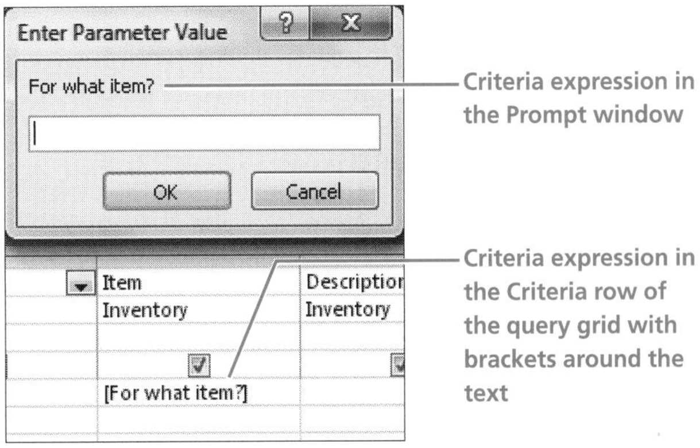

Sample query grid with criteria expression and prompt box

In many cases, the parameter field appears in the query results datasheet. However, you can also use the field to limit query results without displaying the field in the results datasheet.

Formatting the Criteria Expression

For Access to recognize text in the Criteria row as a prompt that you want to display onscreen, the criteria expression must be enclosed in square brackets ([ ]). If you omit the brackets, Access places quotation marks around the text and adds the word *Like* to the criteria. When you run a query that contains the Like comparison, Access would search the field in the table for a value that matches the text rather than placing the text as a prompt so that others can enter criteria.

Creating Complex Parameter Prompts

Normally, the text you enter for a parameter query requests that the user input specific data in the prompt message box to display records from the table. You can also combine message prompt text to create more sophisticated parameter prompts. For example, suppose you want the user to enter a product category each time you run the query. Because many products in each category are available for different suppliers, you also want the user to enter the supplier. To create multiple prompts, you add a prompt message to the Criteria row for the fields containing the values you want to search. Access displays the first prompt, allows the user to enter a value, and then presents the second prompt for a value. You can also set prompts for multiple values in the same query column or include logical criteria such as greater than and less than with the prompt message.

Examples of Parameter Criteria for a Single Field

The following table shows common examples of parameter queries and the results they would create.

Parameter Criteria	Result
Between [What is the start date?] And [What is the end date?]	Displays the first prompt to allow the user to enter the first (or starting) date. After the user enters the start date, Access displays the second prompt so the user can enter the end date. After the user completes the second prompt value, Access displays records for dates that fall between the two dates entered.
<[What is the highest price you can pay?]	Displays the prompt and when the user enters the value, Access displays all records for values less than the one entered.

QUICK REFERENCE	CREATING A PARAMETER QUERY
Task	**Procedure**
Create a parameter query	■ Choose Create→Queries→Query Design to create a new query. ■ Add tables to the query and add fields from the table field list(s) to the query grid. ■ Click the criteria row for the column for which you want to allow users to enter a value and type prompt text in a format similar to `[Parameter Expression]` in square brackets.

DEVELOP YOUR SKILLS 6.3.1

Create and Run a Parameter Query

In this exercise, you will create and run a parameter query that prompts the user for a product category and run the query.

Before You Begin: Your Green Clean Advanced Queries database should be open.

1. Choose **Create→Queries→Query Design** on the Ribbon to create a new query.
2. **Double-click** the Inventory table to add the field list to the query window and **close** the Show Table dialog box.
3. Add the following **fields** to the query grid: Inventory Number, Item, Description, Price, and Quantity In Stock.
4. **Save** the query using the query name **`Item Parameter Query`**.
5. Click the **criteria row** for the Item column and type **`[For what item?]`**.

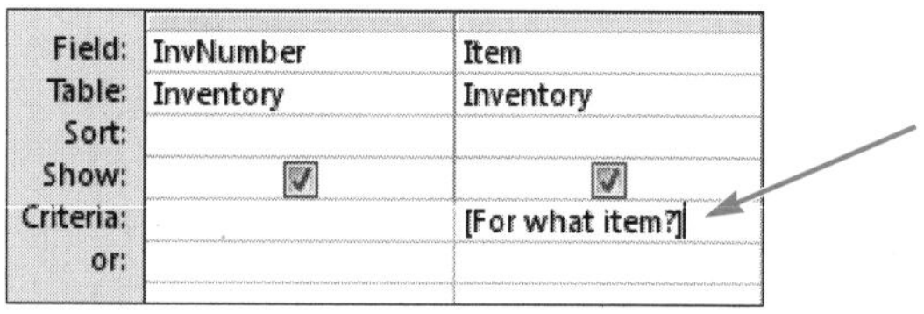

Run and Test the Query

6. Choose **Design→Results→Run** on the Ribbon to run the query, type **`Cleaner`** in the parameter box, and press Enter.
   Access runs the query and lists 17 records containing the value Cleaner in the Item field.
7. **Close** the query, **saving** changes to the datasheet if prompted.

6.4 Creating a Calculated Field in a Query

Video Lesson labyrinthelab.com/videos

Most queries, whether they are simple queries or other types of queries, display fields contained in database tables. When you want to display new data that changes depending on the values stored in table fields, you can use the query grid to create a *calculated field*. A calculated field creates a new field in the query grid, assigns a name to the field, and identifies the fields Access should use in the operation along with the mathematical or logical operations to perform. You can set properties for the field and use the field in a form or report. Using calculated fields, you can perform such operations as combining first and last names, calculating inventory value, and setting sales goals. For example:

Last Name	First Name	Name: [First Name]+[Last Name]
Brown	Samuel	Samuel Brown

By using calculated fields, you can generate up-to-date calculations each time you run the query and alleviate the need to search for and update each new calculation each time a price or other data changes.

Identifying Features of a Calculated Field

The structure of a calculated field includes a field name and expression elements that tell Access which fields, operators, and punctuation marks to use to create the field. If you have not yet created a calculated field, and as a review for those who have used these features, you need to know some of the terminology associated with building calculated fields.

Calculated Field Terms

Calculated fields perform mathematical calculations using the same order used in all mathematical equations by starting with calculations contained in parentheses and working their way through addition and subtraction. In Access, calculated fields are constructed and named, and each consists of the features and parts described in the following table:

Term	Description
Calculated Field Name	The unique name you assign to a calculated field. The field name is followed by a colon to separate the field name from the rest of the expression.
Arithmetic Operators	Add (+), subtract (-), divide (/), multiply (*), exponential (^); used to perform mathematical operations.
Logical Operators	Equals (=), greater than (>), less than (<), greater than or equal to (>=), and so on, used to compare values.
Expression	A combination of object identifiers such as field names containing values to use in the calculated field, arithmetic and logical operators, and values required to perform the calculation.
Field Names	Fields from database tables used in calculated fields enclosed within square brackets ([]).

QUICK REFERENCE	CREATING A CALCULATED FIELD
Task	**Procedure**
Create a calculated field in a query	■ Display the query in Design View and add table field lists containing the values you want to use in the expression. ■ Click the Field row for the first available column in the query grid. ■ Type the calculated field expression in the cell using the following structure: New Calculated Field Name: [Field]Operand[Field].

DEVELOP YOUR SKILLS 6.4.1

Create a Calculated Field

In this exercise, you will create a calculated field that calculates the value of inventory for in-stock items.

Before You Begin: Your Green Clean Advanced Queries database should be open.

1. **Right-click** the **Item Parameter Query** in the Navigation Pane and choose **Design View** to open the query design.
2. Follow these steps to create a calculated field:

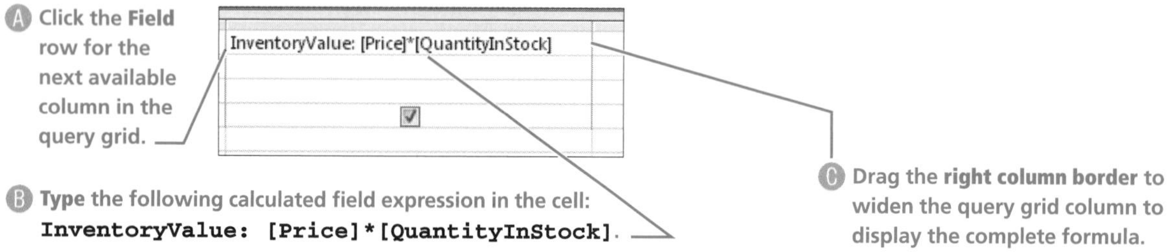
InventoryValue: [Price]*[QuantityInStock]
A Click the Field row for the next available column in the query grid.
B Type the following calculated field expression in the cell: InventoryValue: [Price]*[QuantityInStock].
C Drag the right column border to widen the query grid column to display the complete formula.

3. Choose **Design→Results→Run** on the Ribbon, type **Cleaner** in the parameter prompt, and **press** Enter to run the query.
4. Review the query results datasheet and compare your results to those shown here:

Item Parameter Query

Inventory N	Item	Description	Price	Quantity Avai	InventoryValu
fab04307	Cleaner	FABULOUS CLEANER 4/1GALLON (LAVENDER)	$61.98	95	$5,888.10
fab04373	Cleaner	FABULOUS ALL PURPOSE CLEANER OCEAN COOL 4/12	$62.00	155	$9,610.00
fcv22713	Cleaner	GLASS & SURFACE CLEANER 8/32OZ - FREE & CLEAR	$58.33	89	$5,191.37
fcv22719	Cleaner	ALL PURPOSE CLEANER 8/32 OZ FREE AND CLEAR	$58.33	664	$38,731.12
gso00451	Cleaner	GREENSET TOILET BOWL CLEANER	$47.60	95	$4,522.00
gso00452	Cleaner	GREENSET BATHROOM CLEANER SPRAY	$47.60	155	$7,378.00
gso00456	Cleaner	GREENSET ALL - PURPOSE SPRAY	$54.16	75	$4,062.00

The total value of the inventory for each Cleaner appears in the calculated field column.

5. **Close** the query, **saving** changes when prompted.

Adding Totals to Datasheets

Video Lesson labyrinthelab.com/videos

Creating calculated fields that total or perform calculations on values contained in table fields can be useful when you want to determine the total value of all items in a datasheet. For example, now that you have calculated the value of items in the Inventory list, it is possible to obtain a total value for each type of item in inventory. The Totals button appears on the Ribbon in the Records group of the Home tab.

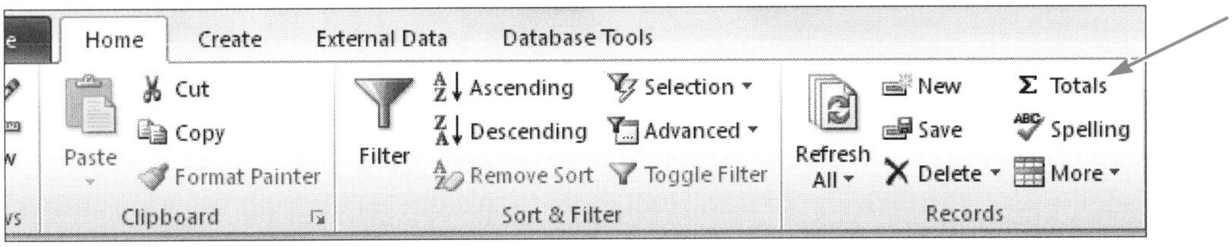

DEVELOP YOUR SKILLS 6.4.2

Add Total Row to the Datasheet

In this exercise, you will add a Total row to the Item Parameter Query results datasheet. This row will display a total value for all listings for a type of item in the database.

1. Run the **Item Parameter Query** and type **`Cleaner`** in the parameter prompt.
2. Follow these steps to add a total to the query results datasheet:

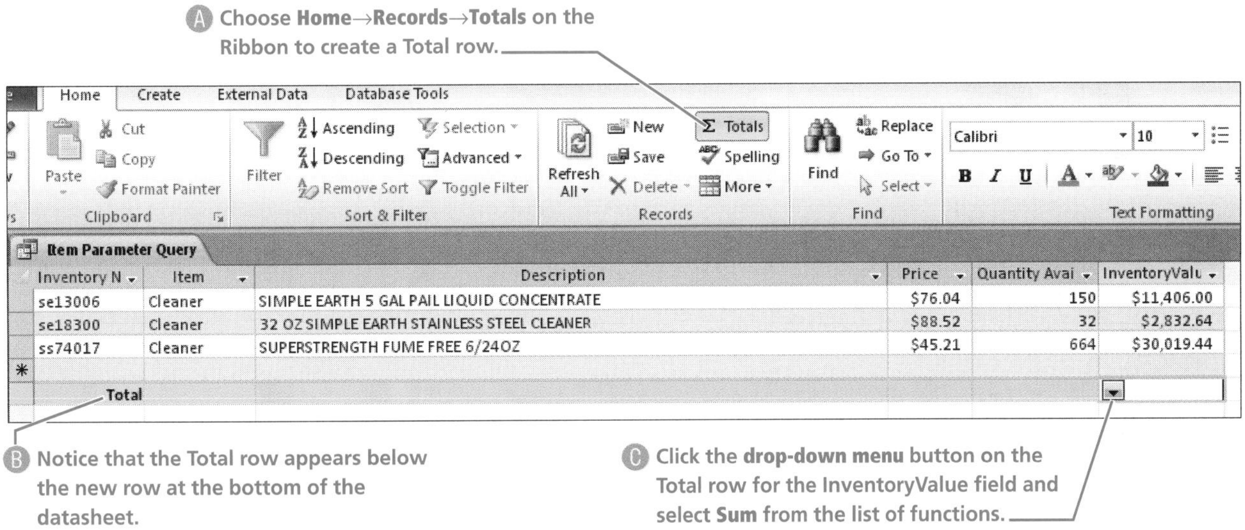

Access calculates the total value of all Cleaner items and displays $155,949.73 as the total.

3. **Save** changes to the query and **run** the query again to display **`Chemical`**.
   Access displays the total value of all four chemicals in inventory.
4. **Close** the query, **saving** changes if prompted.

NOTE To remove totals from displaying each time you run the query, choose Home→Records→Totals again to turn off the feature.

6.5 Creating and Running Action Queries

Video Lesson labyrinthelab.com/videos

Parameter queries build on the format and data displayed in select queries. *Action queries,* on the other hand, perform an action that modifies a database table or a group of records in a table. In most cases, action queries modify, move, update, or delete groups of records with a single action. You can even use an action query to create a new table using data from a query that contains fields from multiple other tables.

WARNING It is important to realize that action queries are saved as query objects in a database along with select and parameter queries. Each time you open an action query, Access runs the query. As a result, if you create a query that is designed to increase prices by 10 percent on all items in a table, Access will increase those prices every time you run the query. You may want to delete action queries after you use them to maintain validity of the data in the database.

Identifying Action Query Types

There are four basic types of action queries available in Access. They are described in the following table.

IDENTIFYING ACTION QUERY TYPES

Action Query Type	Description
Delete Query	A query that deletes a group of records from one or more tables. For example, you could create a delete query to remove records for a discontinued line of products from a table.
Update Query	A query that makes global changes to a group of records in one or more tables. For example, you can use an update query to increase the prices for all products in a specific category or update the area code for phone numbers that change when the phone company adds a new area code.
Append Query	A query that adds a group of records from one or more tables to the end of one or more tables. For example, you could use an append query to add a new customer to a database the first time the customer places an order.
Make-Table Query	A query that creates a new table from all or selected data in one or more tables. For example, you could use a make-table query to create a new table based on data from multiple tables in a database.

Identifying Queries by Their Icons

Action queries appear in the Queries list of the Navigation Pane along with select, parameter, and other types of queries. Access identifies each type of action query as well as select queries and crosstab queries using a different icon. The following table displays the various icons and their meanings.

Icon	Query Type	Icon	Query Type
	Select query		Update query
	Make-Table query		Delete query
	Append query		Crosstab query

QUICK REFERENCE	CREATING AND RUNNING ACTION QUERIES
Task	**Procedure**
Create an append query	■ Create a new query in the source database. ■ Add all table fields to the query grid. ■ Choose Design→Query Type→Append . ■ Save the query and then run the query.
Create an update query	■ Create a new query in the source database. ■ Add all table fields to the query grid. ■ Set criteria if required. ■ Choose Design→Query Type→Update . ■ Save the query and then run the query.
Create a make-table query	■ Create a new query in the source database. ■ Add all table fields to the query grid. ■ Set criteria if required. ■ Choose Design→Query Type→Make Table . ■ Save the query and then run the query.
Create a delete query	■ Create a new query in the source database. ■ Add all table fields to the query grid. ■ Set criteria if required. ■ Choose Design→Query Type→Delete . ■ Save the query and then run the query.

Enabling Content

Action queries require that content within a database be enabled. As a result, if you have not clicked the Enable Content button when you open the database before creating or running action queries, Access will present an error message advising you to enable it.

Creating an Append Action Query

An append action query is a type of action query that adds a group of records from one or more tables to the end of one or more tables in the same or in another database. For example, suppose you collect data for new customers and store the data in a new database, a new database table in the current database, or in an Excel worksheet. You could use an append query to move or add the data to a different table either in the same database or in a different database. You could also use an append action query to automatically add a new customer to a database the first time the customer places an order or add new items to a table in the main database after gathering the records in a separate database or table.

Formatting the Source and Destination Tables

When you create an append action query, Access calls the table containing the records you want to add to another table the *source table*. The table receiving the records is the *destination table*. To successfully run an append action query, the structures of both tables should be the same, and field names and data types for both tables should also be the same.

Identifying the Source and Destination Tables

Append queries appear in the database containing the source table. From the query you create, Access prompts you to identify the destination database and table using the Append dialog box:

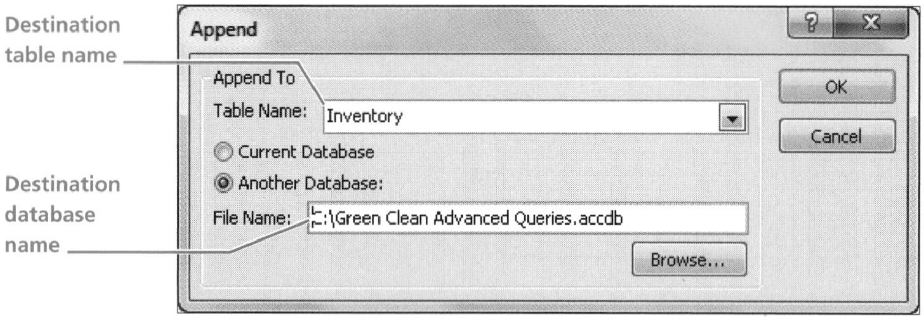

After you set the source and destination tables, Access identifies the destination table in the Append To row of the query grid:

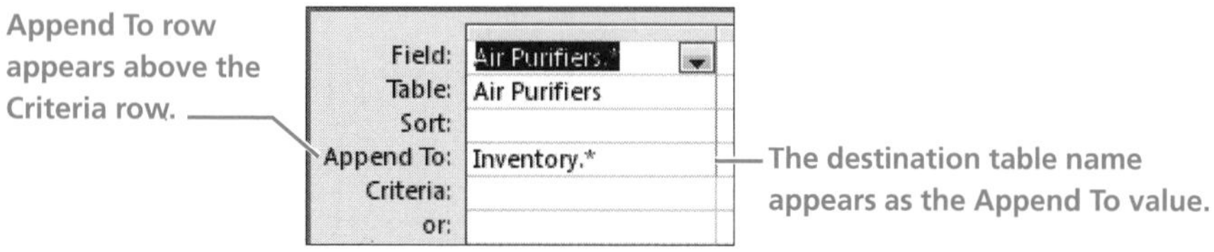

DEVELOP YOUR SKILLS 6.5.1

Create an Append Action Query

In this exercise, you will create an action query to append records for new products to the Inventory table.

1. **Open** the New Green Clean Items database and save it as a new database using the filename **`Green Clean Append Action`**.
2. Click **Enable Content** to ensure that the action queries work properly.
3. Choose **Create→Queries→Query Design** on the Ribbon to create a new query.
4. Add the **Air Purifiers** table to the query window and **close** the Show Table dialog box.

5. Follow these steps to add all fields to the query grid and run the query:

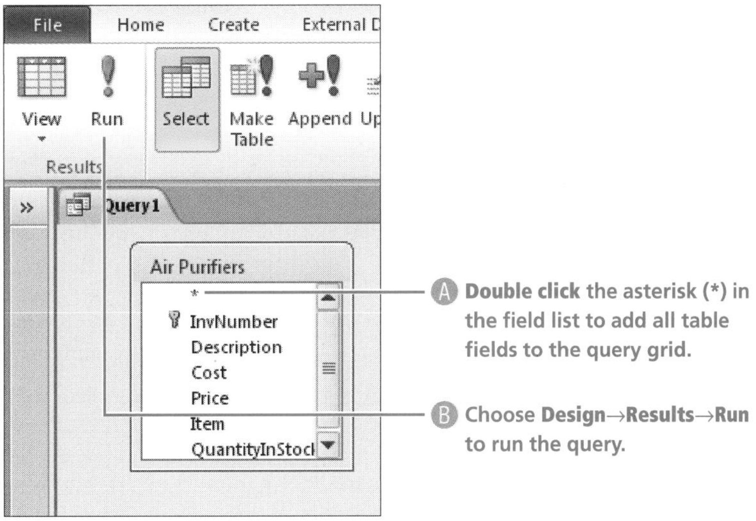

6. Switch back to Design View and follow these steps to change the query to an append query:

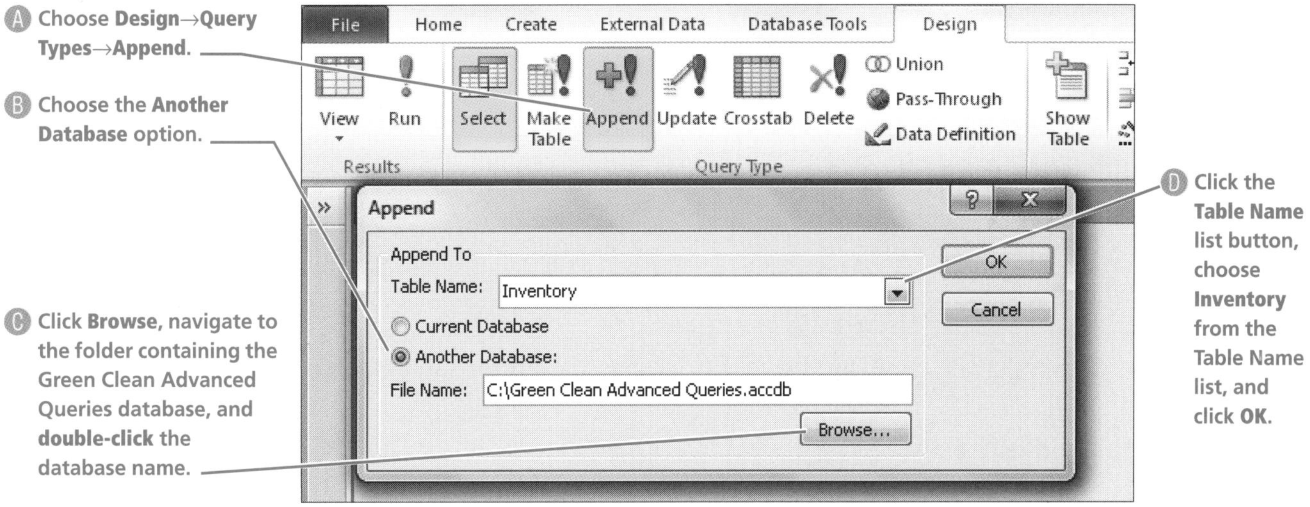

Access adds the Append To row to the query grid and places the table name that running the query will append in the row.

7. **Save** the query using the query name **`Append Inventory`**.

Run the Query and Append Records

8. Choose **Design→Results→Run** on the Ribbon to run the query.
   Access advises you that you are about to append 27 records to another table and asks you to confirm the action.
9. Choose **Yes** to proceed.

WARNING

Nothing appears to happen in the database you have open. You will only see the changes after you open the destination table to which the records were appended. DO NOT RUN THE QUERY AGAIN!

Access adds the records from this database table to the Inventory table in the Green Clean Advanced Queries database. If you run the query again, Access will again advise you that you are about to add 27 records to the destination table. Each time you run the action query, Access will add the same records to the destination table again.

10. **Close** the query, **saving** changes if prompted, and then **close** the Green Clean Append Action database.

Verify the Append Action

11. **Open** the Green Clean Advanced Queries database and then open and review the records in the Inventory table.

New inventory numbers start with number 525 and are all three-digit numbers. Products 525-551 are new to the table.

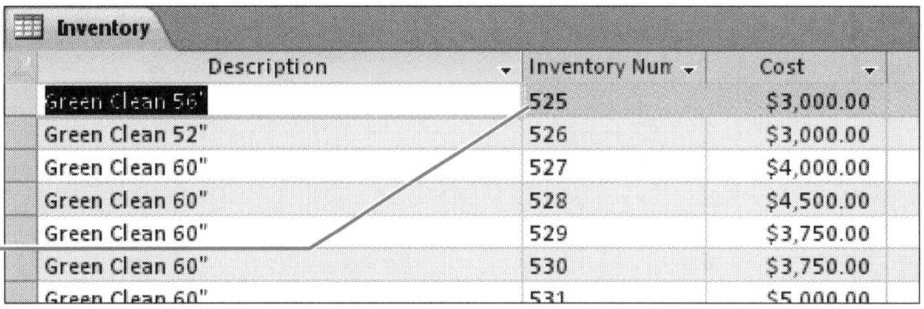
Inventory

Description	Inventory Num	Cost
Green Clean 56"	525	$3,000.00
Green Clean 52"	526	$3,000.00
Green Clean 60"	527	$4,000.00
Green Clean 60"	528	$4,500.00
Green Clean 60"	529	$3,750.00
Green Clean 60"	530	$3,750.00
Green Clean 60"	531	$5,000.00

12. **Close** the table, but leave the database **open** for the next exercise.

Creating an Update Query

Video Lesson labyrinthelab.com/videos

An update action query is a query that performs an action that makes global changes to a group of records in one or more tables. For example, you can use an update query to increase the prices for all products in a specific category or update the area code for phone numbers that change when the phone company adds a new area code.

Identifying Query Grid Update Row

As you discovered when you created the append action query, Access adds a new row to the query grid. The same is true when you create an update action query. Access places an Update row in the query grid so that you can identify the procedure to follow to update the field you want to update. In most cases, this will be changing one value to another by substitution, mathematical operation, formula, or comparison.

DEVELOP YOUR SKILLS 6.5.2

Create an Update Query

In this exercise, you will create an update action query that increases the prices of all items in the Inventory table by 10 percent.

Before You Begin: *Your Green Clean Advanced Queries database should be open with content enabled.*

1. Choose **Create→Queries→Query Design** on the Ribbon, add the Inventory table to the query, and close the Show Table dialog box.
2. **Double-click** the Price field in the field list to add it to the query grid.
3. Follow these steps to create the update action query:

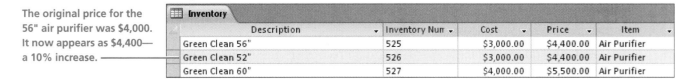

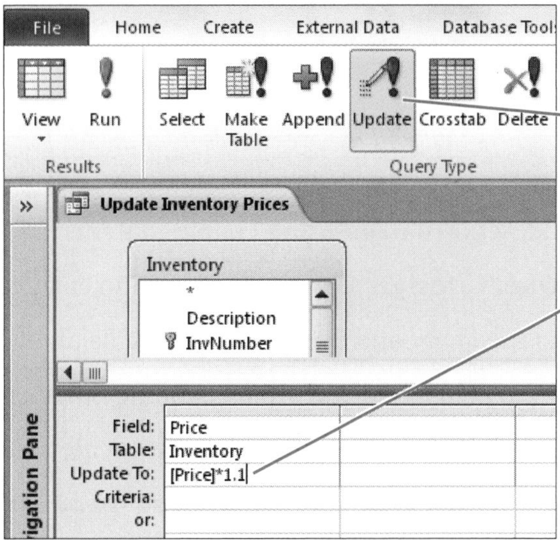

Ⓐ Choose **Design→Query Type→Update** on the Ribbon to change the query to an update action query.

Ⓑ Click the **Update To** row of the Sales Price column and type **`[Price]*1.1`**.

4. **Save** the query using the query name **`Update Inventory Prices`**.
5. **Run** the query to update the values in the Inventory table.
   Access displays a warning message that you are about to update 87 row(s) and tells you that you cannot reverse the action using Undo.
6. Choose **Yes** to run the query and then **close** the query.
   Although nothing appears to have occurred, Access ran the query and updated prices in the table.

Verify the Data Update

7. Open the **Inventory** table and review values in the Price column.

The original price for the 56" air purifier was $4,000. It now appears as $4,400—a 10% increase.

Inventory

Description	Inventory Num	Cost	Price	Item
Green Clean 56"	525	$3,000.00	$4,400.00	Air Purifier
Green Clean 52"	526	$3,000.00	$4,400.00	Air Purifier
Green Clean 60"	527	$4,000.00	$5,500.00	Air Purifier

8. **Close** the table and then **close** the database.

Creating a Delete Query

Video Lesson labyrinthelab.com/videos

A delete action query deletes a group of records from one or more tables. For example, you could create a delete query to remove records for a discontinued line of products from a table or to delete records you have appended to another table to prevent you from inadvertently running an append query multiple times.

When you create a delete action query, Access replaces the Sort row of the query grid with the Delete row. You can set criteria for specific fields in a table to identify the conditions for which Access should delete records or add all fields to the query grid to remove all records from a table.

DEVELOP YOUR SKILLS 6.5.3

Create a Delete Query

In this exercise, you will create a delete query that will remove records from the Air Purifiers table in the Green Clean Append Action database.

1. **Open** the Green Clean Append Action database and enable content.
2. Choose **Create→Queries→Query Design** on the Ribbon to create a new query.
3. Add the **Air Purifiers** table to the query and close the Show Table dialog box.
4. **Double-click** the Asterisk in the field list to add all fields to the query grid.
5. Choose **Design→Query Type→Delete** on the Ribbon to create a delete action query.
6. **Save** the query using the query name **`Delete Appended Products`** and **run** the query.
   Access presents a warning message advising you that you are about to delete 27 records.
7. Choose **Yes** to remove all records from the Air Purifiers table.
8. **Open** the Air Purifiers table and review the results.
9. **Close** all open database objects and then **close** the database.

Creating a Make Table Query

Video Lesson labyrinthelab.com/videos

A make table action query is a query that creates a new table from all or selected data in one or more tables. For example, you could use a make table query to create a new table based on data from multiple tables in a database. It's also a great way to get data from a calculated field in a query into a table. If you run a make table query multiple times, Access warns you that the existing table will be overwritten and all records in the original table will be deleted. You can then take the appropriate action to decide how to proceed.

Moving Data to Tables and Databases

When you create a new table using a make table query, Access prompts you for a table name and also allows you to save the data into another database, when necessary. As a result, you can move data from one database to another fluidly each time you want to remove it from an existing database. One such example of moving records to another database would be when they become obsolete or are no longer valid in their current table, such as when a product is no longer available.

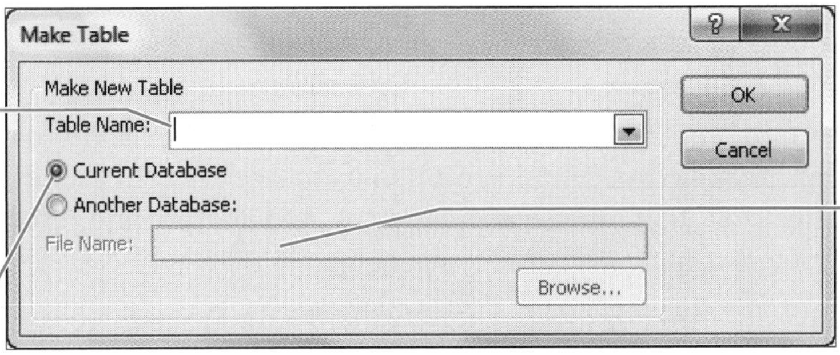

DEVELOP YOUR SKILLS 6.5.4

Create a Make Table Query

In this exercise, you will create a make table action query to save a query results datasheet as a new table.

1. **Open** the Green Clean Advanced Queries database and open the Navigation Pane.
2. **Double-click** the Order Processing query to run it.
3. Display the query in **Design View** and follow these steps to create the make table query:

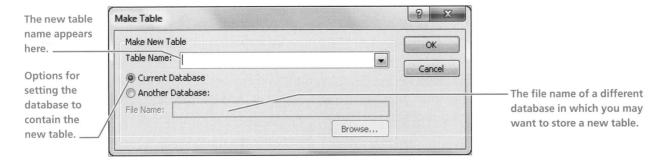

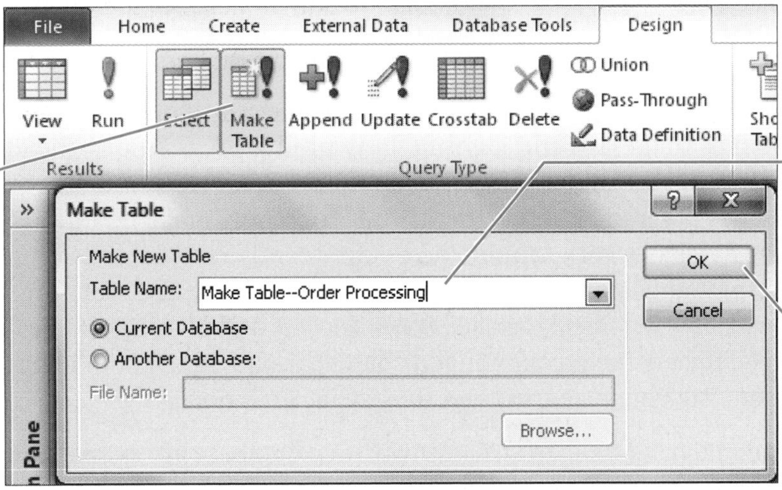

4. **Save** changes to the query and then **run** the query.
   Access displays a message advising you that you are about to paste 75 records into a new table.
5. Choose **Yes** to continue.
   Access creates the table and places it alphabetically in the list of tables in the Navigation Pane.

Verify the Table

6. **Double-click** the Make Table—Order Processing table to open it and review the data.
7. **Close** all open database objects.

6.6 Protecting and Repairing a Database

Video Lesson labyrinthelab.com/videos

Each time you make a change to the design of a database by adding new objects, editing a database table, or performing routine maintenance on a database, the chance that the database will become corrupt rises. Access contains numerous tools that help you protect your databases, document them for others to use as references, and analyze and repair those that perform poorly. These tools include:

- **Performance Analyzer—**Analyzes the performance of a database to locate and identify potential trouble spots that affect the smooth functioning of the database
- **Database Documenter—**Documents objects in the database so that you can track changes to the database design and relationships between database objects; builds an Object Definition document that provides a detailed description of each database object
- **Back Up Utility—**Creates a backup of the database and all database objects that can be used to restore the database to the state of development and completeness apparent at the time the backup was created
- **Compactor—**Compresses databases with all their objects and data into an electronic file that requires less storage room than the original file

In this section, you will use each of these tools to protect the Green Clean database you have been building.

Reviewing Performance Results

When you run the Performance Analyzer, Access reviews each object in the database, looks at all the relationships that exist, and identifies any trouble areas among the database objects that might affect database performance. Many times, Access recommends changes or provides ideas that it sees as potential improvements that you know make no difference to the smooth operation of the database. For example, Access frequently recommends that telephone numbers be formatted using the Number data type. This is unnecessary. In other cases, as you will see when you analyze this database, Access locates and identifies tables where no Primary Key is set. As you review the recommended changes, you will begin to identify those recommendations requiring your attention and those you can ignore.

Two options for analyzing the performance within a database are available. The Analyze Performance tool enables you to choose those objects that you want to analyze. The Analyze Table tool analyzes a table using the Table Analyzer Wizard.

Documenting a Database

Documentation is important to the success of every database you create. Documentation provides insight into the structure of the entire database as well as the structure of each object within the database. As you have already discovered, maintaining a database can be very time-consuming. Without proper documentation to identify potential impacts of changing field properties, object structures, and so forth, you can potentially corrupt one database object that wreaks havoc with the entire database, making it virtually worthless. Each time you change the structure of any database object, remove an object, or add an object to the database, it is important to run the documenter to provide up-to-date documentation about the database. Such documentation will prove invaluable to the next database manager when you complete your work. After running the documenter the first time to document the complete database, you can update documentation for individual items or types of objects as they change.

QUICK REFERENCE — **USING DATABASE ANALYZER AND DOCUMENTER TOOLS**

Task	Procedure
Run Database Analyzer	Choose Database Tools→Analyze→Analyze Performance on the Ribbon.
Run Database Documenter	Choose Database Tools→Analyze→Database Documenter on the Ribbon.

DEVELOP YOUR SKILLS 6.6.1

Analyze and Document the Database

In this exercise, you will analyze the performance of the Green Clean Advanced Queries database, and then document the database.

1. **Close** all open objects in the database.

Run the Performance Analyzer

2. Follow these steps to analyze database performance:

A Choose **Database Tools→Analyze→Analyze Performance** on the Ribbon.

B Click the **All Object Types** tab in the Performance Analyzer window.

C Click the **Select All** button.

D Click **OK**.

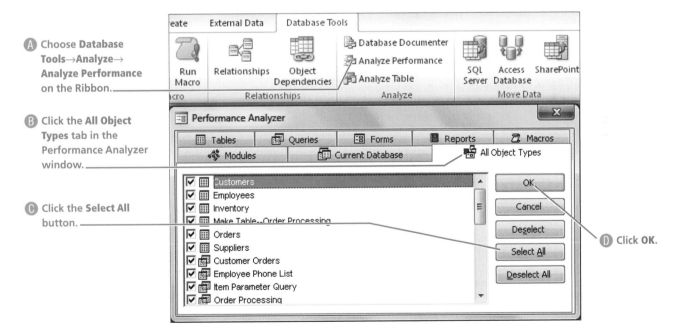

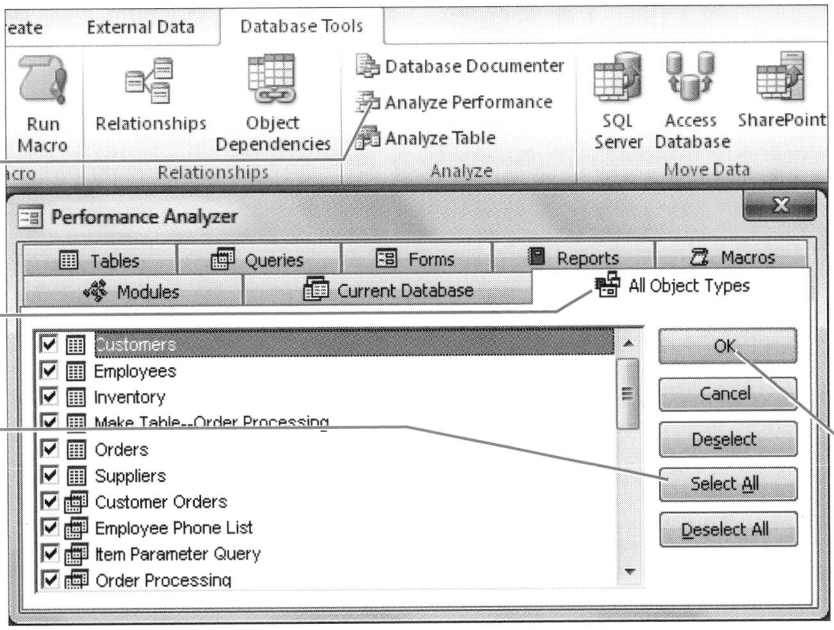

Access runs the analyzer and reports the results.

3. Follow these steps to review the Analysis Results window:

Ⓐ Select the **Idea** items identified by the light bulbs.

Ⓑ Review the **Key** to determine what type of result Access located.

Ⓒ Select the **Recommendation** items identified by the green question mark.

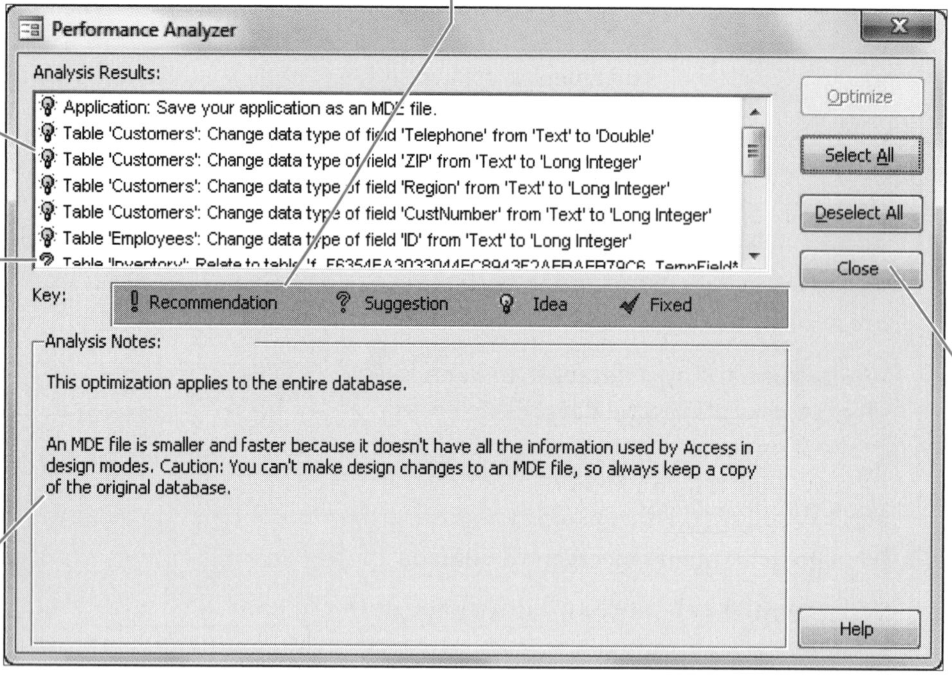

Ⓓ Review the analyzer's reasons for the recommendation.

Ⓔ Click **Close** to close the analyzer.

Run the Database Documenter

4. Choose **Database Tools→Analyze→Database Documenter** on the Ribbon to launch the Documenter, and then follow these steps:

Ⓐ Click the **All Object Types** tab in the Documenter dialog box.

Ⓑ Choose **Select All.**

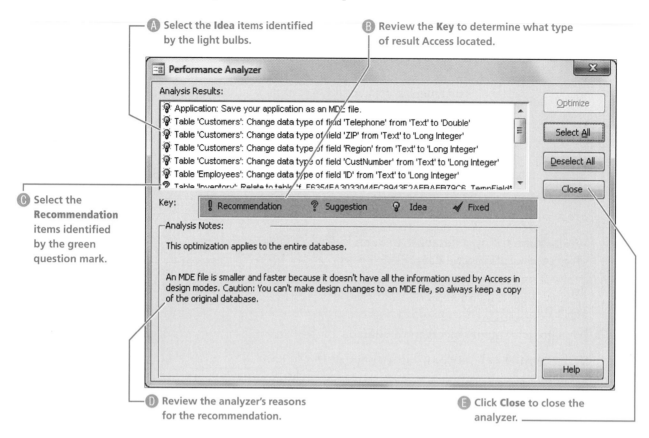

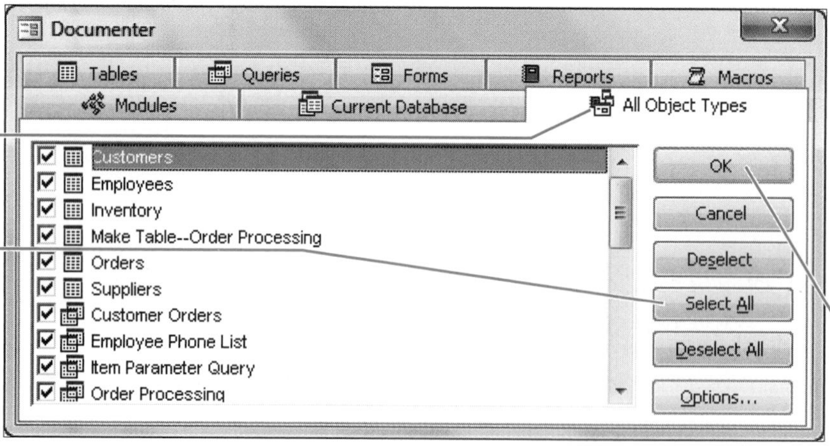

Ⓒ Choose **OK.**

Access generates a document that is roughly 268 pages long and displays the document in Print Preview.

5. Click the **page** displayed in print preview to zoom in on it and then use the navigation button to browse through the document.

6. **Close** the Print Preview window.

7. **Close** [×] all open database objects.

Backing Up a Database

Video Lesson labyrinthelab.com/videos

Databases maintained by large corporations often have hundreds of thousands of records stored within. As a result, it is important to protect that data. Most companies have a backup procedure that they use to back up a network system including all files—not just databases—on a schedule. In addition to these safety procedures for protecting data, Access contains a backup feature you can use to back up your databases. It only takes a few minutes to keep hours of work safe!

When you back up a database using Access tools, Access places the date of the backup in the filename so that you can easily identify each backup file. You choose the drive and folder in which you want to save the backup.

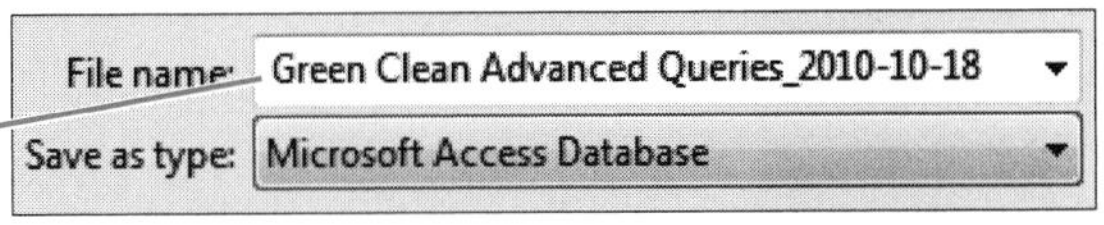

Access places the date at the end of the Filename when you create a backup.

The good news about restoring data from the backup you create using Access is that to restore the database, all you have to do is open the backup!

QUICK REFERENCE — BACKING UP, COMPACTING, AND REPAIRING DATABASES

Task	Procedure
Back up a database	■ Close all open database objects. ■ Choose File→Save & Publish→Save Database As→Back up Database. ■ Navigate to the folder in which you want to save the backup. ■ Choose Save.
Compact and repair a database	■ Close all open database objects. ■ Choose File→Info→Compact & Repair Database.

DEVELOP YOUR SKILLS 6.6.2

Back Up a Database

In this exercise, you will back up your Green Clean Advanced Queries database.

Before You Begin: The Green Clean Advanced Queries database should be open.

1. **Close** all open objects in the Green Clean Advanced Queries database.

2. Choose **File→Save & Publish→Save Database As→Back up Database**, and then click the **Save As** button.
   Access displays the Save As dialog box and places the date at the end of the database filename.

3. Navigate to the Lesson 06 folder and then click **Save** to save the backup using the default filename Access assigned.
   Access saves the new backup file to the desired location; however, the database file "in use" is still the original Green Clean Advanced Queries database. This is different from, say, using Save As with a Word Document, in which the renamed file becomes the one in use.

Compacting and Repairing a Database

Video Lesson labyrinthelab.com/videos

As you work with databases, they can become sluggish and the data stored in the databases can become fragmented—that is, separated by incidental data on the disk storage you are using. To ensure optimal performance, Access contains tools that enable you to *compact* and *repair* databases as often as you believe it is appropriate. Sometimes Access recognizes a problem with a database when you open it and attempts to repair the file before you start working with it. Even if there is no file corruption, the normal maintenance tasks of adding, deleting, and editing records, creating and running queries, and so forth, may reduce database performance. As a result, you may want to compact and repair the database manually. Compacting and repairing a database also may reduce the database file size. It's a relatively simple and quick task that can save hours of time by reducing the chance of a corrupt file. No new file is created when you compact and repair a database.

DEVELOP YOUR SKILLS 6.6.3

Compact and Repair a Database

In this exercise, you will compact and repair your Green Clean Advanced Queries database.

1. **Close** all open database objects.
2. Choose **File→Info→Compact and Repair Database**.
   The database window may disappear for a few seconds. When it reappears, Access has compacted and repaired the file. Because the database you are using is relatively small, the compact and repair process should take only a moment.
3. **Close** the database and **exit** Access.

6.7 Concepts Review

Concepts Review labyrinthelab.com/acc10

To check your knowledge of the key concepts introduced in this lesson, complete the Concepts Review quiz by going to the URL listed above. If your classroom is using Labyrinth eLab, you may complete the Concepts Review quiz from within your eLab course.

Reinforce Your Skills

REINFORCE YOUR SKILLS 6.1

Create a Select Query

State licensing departments throughout the country use databases regularly. One state is testing development of a database that they believe will revolutionize market standards for all states so that each state can maintain accurate records for licensed drivers. Database designers have entered sample data into a prototype of the database to test some of the new features that they believe states will like.

In this exercise, you will use the prototype database to create a select query that displays drivers and accidents or other violations on record.

1. **Launch** Access, open the rs-Illinois Drivers database from the Lesson 6 folder, and **save** the database as a new file named `rs-Test Queries`.
2. Open the **Navigation Pane** and then open each **table** to study the data each table contains.
3. **Close** all tables and choose **Create→Queries→Query Design** on the Ribbon to create a new query.
4. **Double-click** the Test Drivers and Test Driving Records tables to add them to the query window and then **close** the Show Table dialog box.
5. Follow these steps to set join line properties:

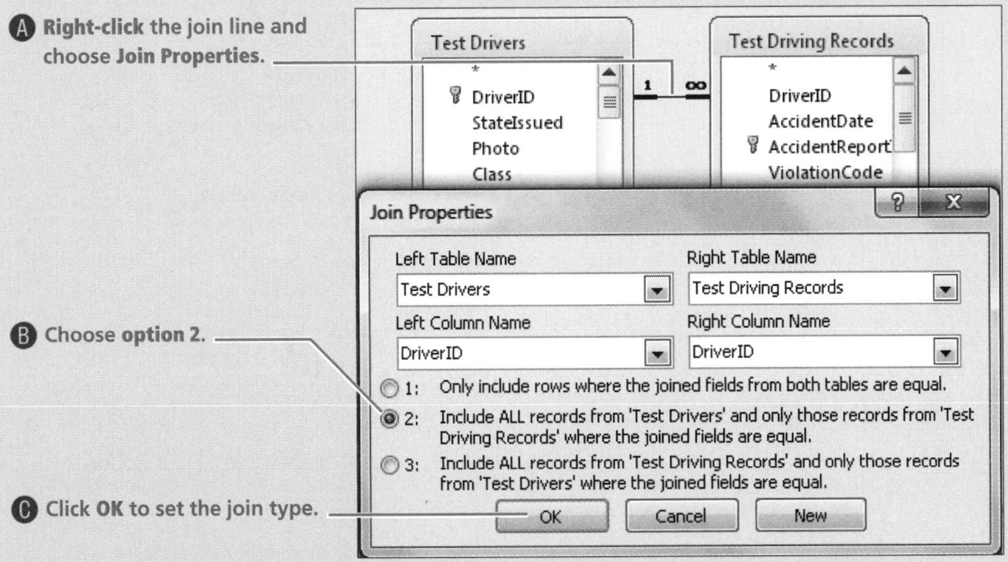

Access reformats the join line so that it now appears as an arrow from the Test Drivers field list to the Test Driving Records field list.

6. **Save** the query using the query name `Drivers with Records`.
7. **Double-click** each of the following fields from the Test Drivers table to add the fields to the query grid: DriverID, FirstName, and LastName.

8. **Double-click** each of the following fields from the Test Driving Records table to add the fields to the query grid: AccidentDate, AccidentReportID, ViolationDate, and ViolationCode.

9. Choose **Design→Results→Run** on the Ribbon to run the query.
Twelve records appear in the query results datasheet, one for each record in the Test Drivers table. Two records appear for Samuels—one for an accident and another for a violation. Other than Samuels, only Clinton and White show data from the Test Driving Records table.

10. **Save** changes to the query, **print** a copy of the query results datasheet, and **close** the query.

REINFORCE YOUR SKILLS 6.2

Set Up a Parameter Query

The rs-Test Queries database contains one select query that displays a list of all drivers and related accidents and violations. This query works well when you have only a few test records in each database table. When a state implements the database, however, the volume of records is expected to be large. Setting the select query as a parameter query so that users can enter the last name of the driver makes the database more useable. However, many states want to be able to generate a printed list of all drivers and associated driver records.

In this exercise, you will create a copy of the original query and edit the copy to create a parameter query.

Before You Begin: Your rs-Test Queries database should be open.

1. Click the **Drivers with Records** query, choose **File→Save Object As** command (not the menu ▸), and **save** the query using the query name **`Driver Parameter Query`**.

2. Display the **Driver Parameter Query** in Design View and follow these steps to create the parameter expression:

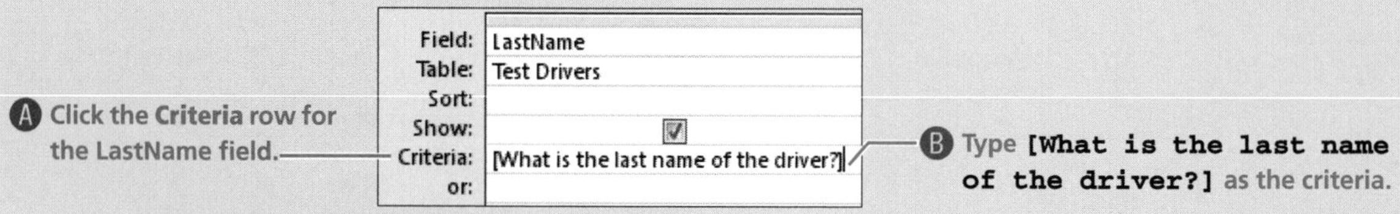

Field: LastName
Table: Test Drivers
Sort:
Show:
Criteria: [What is the last name of the driver?]
or:
A Click the Criteria row for the LastName field.
B Type [What is the last name of the driver?] as the criteria.

3. **Save** changes to the query, and **run** it.

4. Type **`Samuels`** in the Enter Parameter Value dialog box and click **OK**.
Access displays two records for Brian Samuels.

5. **Press** Shift+F9, type **`White`** in the Enter Parameter Value dialog box, and click **OK**.
Access displays one record.

6. **Close** the query and the database.

REINFORCE YOUR SKILLS 6.3

Create an Append Query

As each new driver passes the necessary tests, many states add them to a separate database and update their main database each night. Each state needs an automated procedure for adding new drivers to their main database. An append query accomplishes this task. Sample data for new drivers is located in a database named rs-New Illinois Drivers.

In this exercise, you will create an append query and test it using the prototype database.

1. **Open** the rs-New Illinois Drivers database from the Lesson 06 folder and save the database as a new file named **`rs-Append Drivers`**.
2. Choose **Create→Queries→Query Design** on the Ribbon to create a new query.
3. Add the **New Drivers** table to the query window and **close** the Show Table dialog box.
4. **Double-click** the asterisk (*) to add all table fields to the query grid.
5. Choose **Design→Query Type→Append** on the Ribbon to open the Append dialog box and follow these steps to set up the append action:

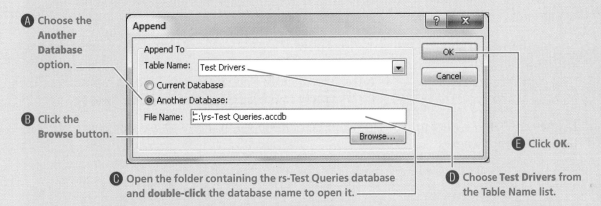

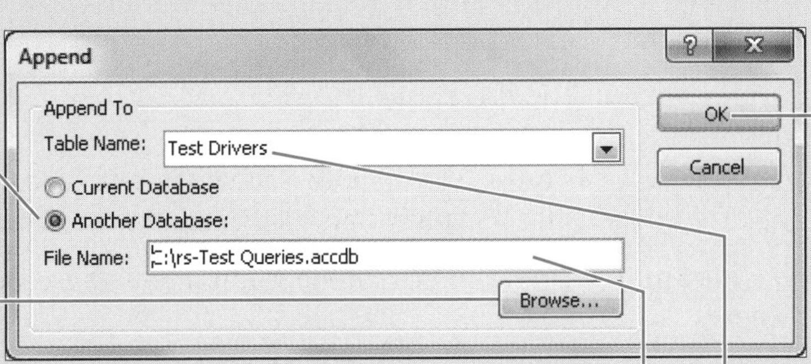

A Choose the **Another Database** option.

B Click the **Browse** button.

C Open the folder containing the rs-Test Queries database and **double-click** the database name to open it.

D Choose **Test Drivers** from the Table Name list.

E Click **OK**.

6. **Save** the query using the query name **`Append New Drivers`**.
7. **Run** the query and click **Yes** to acknowledge that you are appending six rows (records).
8. **Close** the query and the database.

Verify the Append Action

9. **Open** the rs-Test Queries database and open the Test Drivers table.
   The table now contains 17 records instead of the 11 you started with.
10. **Close** the Test Drivers table.
11. If you are continuing with additional Reinforce Your Skills exercises, leave the database **open**. If you have completed your work, **close** the database and **exit** Access.

REINFORCE YOUR SKILLS 6.4

Create a Make Table Query

Daily records are required by some states to report all accidents and violations to different state divisions. The report should contain the driver ID, last name, date of the accident and/or violation, the officer ID, and whether or not a ticket was issued. It should also report data for the current date only and store the data in a table outside the main database.

In this exercise, you will add a new record to the Test Driving Records table and then create a Make-Table query that sends data to a new table to hold the data.

Before You Begin: Your rs-Test Queries database should be open.

1. **Open** the Test Driving Records table and edit the dates in the Accident Date and Violation Date columns to reflect the current date.
2. **Close** the table and choose **Create→Queries→Query Design** on the Ribbon to create a new query.
3. Add the **Test Driving Records** table to the query and **close** the Show Table dialog box.
4. Add the following **fields** to the query grid: DriverID, AccidentDate, AccidentReportID, ViolationDate, ViolationCode, OfficerID, and Ticket?.
5. Choose **Design→Query Type→Make Table** on the Ribbon and follow these steps to set Make Table options:

Ⓐ Choose the **Another Database** option.

Ⓑ Click **Browse** and locate and open the rs-Append Drivers database.

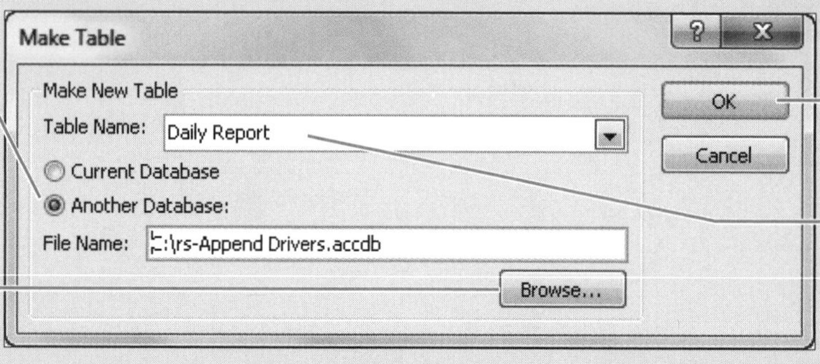

Ⓓ Click **OK**.

Ⓒ Type **`Daily Report`** in the Table Name box.

6. Follow these steps to set criteria for the Make Table query:

Ⓐ Enter the **criteria** for the AccidentDate column: **`Date()`**.

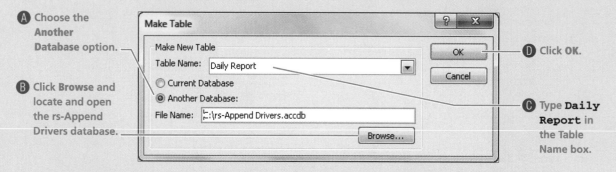

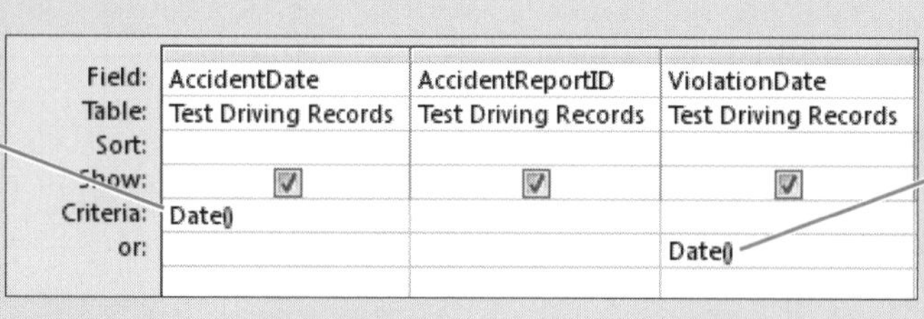

Ⓑ Enter the **criteria** in the *or* row for the ViolationDate column: **`Date()`**.

The Date() criteria tells Access to look for the current date.

7. **Save** the query using the query name **`Daily Report`**.
8. **Run** the query and click **Yes** to acknowledge the message about pasting four rows into a new table.

Verify the Action

9. **Close** the query and **close** the database.
10. **Open** the rs-Append Drivers database and **open** the Daily Report table to view the records.
11. **Close** the table and the database.

REINFORCE YOUR SKILLS 6.5

Use an Aggregate Function in a Query

Valley Hospital obtains reports from the drivers license bureau that reports the number of organ donors registered for drivers. Because the OrganDonor field in the srs-Test Queries database is a Yes/No field type, you can create a new query and display Totals to count the number of organ donors. Saving the query as part of the database enables users to run the query each time the hospital and other health agencies request a report.

In this exercise, you will create a new query in the rs-Test Queries database to count the number of organ donors and show the name and state of each donor.

1. **Open** the rs-Test Queries database and choose **Create→Queries→Query Design** on the Ribbon to create a new query.
2. Add the **Test Drivers** table to the query and **close** the Show Table dialog box.
3. Add the FirstName, LastName, StateIssued, and OrganDonor **fields** to the query grid.
4. **Run** the query.
5. Choose **Home→Records→Totals** on the Ribbon to count the number of donors.
6. **Save** the query using the query name **`Organ Donors`**.
7. Print a copy of the query results.
8. **Close** the query and the database.

Apply Your Skills

APPLY YOUR SKILLS 6.1

Create a Query Containing a Calculated Field

The Homestead realty company currently has listings for single-family homes ranging in price from the low $100,000s to more than $2 million. Their listings show square footage for each home along with the number of bedrooms and bathrooms. Recently, clients looking for homes are requesting the price per square foot of listed homes. As a result, the local manager of the company has requested that you add a field to the listings table to show the price.

In this exercise, you will review the data stored in the Properties table and then create a query containing a calculated field so square footage is calculated each time the price of homes increases.

1. **Open** the as-Homestead Properties database from the Lesson 6 folder and save the file as a new database named **`as-Homestead Properties Queries`**.
2. Open the **Properties** table, review the data, and then **close** the table.
3. Create a new **query** in Design View that contains all fields from the Properties table added individually in the order in which they appear in the table.
4. **Save** the query using the query name **`Square Foot Values`**.
5. Create a **calculated field** named **`SqFtPrice`** in the next available query grid column and include the following formula for calculating price per square foot: **`[Price]/[SqFeet]`**.
6. Click the **top border** of the SqFtPrice expression column and **drag** the column so that it appears between the SqFeet and Beds columns.
7. Format the calculated field to **Currency**.
8. **Save** changes to the query, **run** the query, and **print** a copy the first page of the query results datasheet.
9. **Close** the query.

APPLY YOUR SKILLS 6.2

Create a Parameter Query

The records in the as-Homestead Properties Queries database represent only a portion of the real estate listings available for sale in the area. Most people looking for homes want to view homes selling within a certain range of values. Others are looking for homes in a particular subdivision, and others want a home with a specific number of bedrooms or square footage. Before the remaining records are added to the database you are developing, the manager of the local office wants you to develop queries that make it easier for agents to locate homes by entering data for any of these features.

In this exercise, you create parameter queries to meet these needs.

1. **Open** the as-Homestead Properties Queries database and create a new query in Design View.
2. Add the **Properties** table to the query window and add all fields from the table individually to the query grid.
3. Type **0** (zero) in the Criteria row for the Sold column to limit the display of properties to those that have not yet been sold.
4. **Type** the following expressions in the Criteria row for the Price column:
   `Between [What is the lower price limit?] And [What is the higher price limit?]`
   Typing two prompt messages in the criteria expression presents two prompts when you run the query so that you can display listings for a range of values.
5. **Save** the query using the query name **`Listings by Price`**.

Test the Query

6. **Run** the query, entering sample values such as 250,000 and 350,000 when prompted.
7. **Review** and **print** the query results datasheet.

Create and Test a New Query Using an Existing Query

8. **Save** the Listings by Price query while in Design View as a new query named **`Listings by Size`**.
9. Display the **Listings by Size** query in Design View, remove the **criteria** for the Price field and **enter** the following expression for the SqFeet column:
   `>[What is the minimum square footage you want?]`.
10. **Save** and **run** the query, entering a sample square footage such as 2000 when prompted.
11. **Review** and **print** the query results datasheet.

Create and Test Query

12. Save the **Listings by Size** query as a new query named **`Listings by Bedrooms`**.
13. Open the **Listings by Bedrooms** query in Design view, and set the appropriate expression to prompt users for the number of bedrooms.
14. **Save** and **run** the query, enter a bedroom number between 1 and 7, and then **review** and **print** the results.
15. **Close** all open queries.

APPLY YOUR SKILLS 6.3

Create Action Queries

Sold properties need to be removed from the Properties table and placed in a new table within the same database. In this exercise, you will create a make table query that copies records for sold properties from the Properties table to a new table. You will then create an append query that appends records for sold properties to the new table as properties are sold.

Before You Begin: *Your as-Homestead Properties Queries database should be open.*

1. Create a new **query** in Design View that contains the **Properties** table.
2. Add all **fields** individually to the query grid and set the criteria for the Sold column to **`Yes`** (one value Access assigns to checked boxes).
3. Change the query to a make **table** query that sends the data to a new table in the current database named **`Sold Properties`**.
4. **Save** the query using the query name **`Make Table Query`**.
5. **Run** the query to add 54 records to the new table.
6. **Close** the query, open the new **Sold Properties** table, and **print** a copy of the first page of the table datasheet.
7. Create a new **query** named **`Append Sold Properties`** using the Make Table Query.
8. Change the query type of the new query to an **append** query and set options for the append query to append records to the Sold Properties table in the current database (but do NOT run the query).
9. **Close** all open windows.

APPLY YOUR SKILLS 6.4

Create a Delete Query

Sold properties need to be removed from the Properties listing so that the data reflects only those properties still on the market. You can delete the records for sold properties from the Properties table after moving them to the Sold Properties table using a delete query. In this exercise, you will create a delete query to accomplish this task.

Before You Begin: *Your as-Homestead Properties Queries database should be open.*

1. Create a new **query** in Design View that contains only the **Properties** table.
2. Add all **fields** from the Properties table individually to the query grid, set the **criteria** for the Sold column to -1, and **save** the query using the query name Delete Sold Properties.
3. Set the query as a **delete** query, **save** changes to the query, and **run** it.
   The message box indicates that you are about to delete 54 records. If your message box shows any other value, click No and check the settings in your query design grid.
4. **Delete** the 54 records indicated and **close** the query window.
5. **Close** the database and **exit** Access.

Critical Thinking & Work-Readiness Skills

In the course of working through the following Microsoft Office-based Critical Thinking exercises, you will also be utilizing various work-readiness skills, some of which are listed next to each exercise. Go to labyrinthelab.com/workreadiness *to learn more about the work-readiness skills.*

6.1 Identify Use of Query Types

Green Clean personnel will need to add many objects and records to the database as time goes on. Review the information contained in this lesson to identify the types of queries you would create or special Access features you would use to accomplish the following tasks. Record your answers along with the reasons for using each query type in a Word document named **ct-Query Types** saved to your Lesson 06 folder.

WORK-READINESS SKILLS APPLIED

- Reasoning
- Solving problems
- Writing

- Display fields from multiple tables for values in one field greater than 1,000.
- Change all records for products acquired from another company.
- Display the total number of items sold by each company.
- Display a list of personnel from a specific town.

6.2 Create an Append Query

Foxy's Tread is a gym and exercise facility that has an agreement with Green Clean to provide wellness and fitness consulting for Green Clean employees. Foxy's Tread recently acquired Easy Up, an independent gym. A table containing the list of Easy Up employees is stored in the ct-Easy Up Personnel database (Lesson 06 folder). Save the ct-Easy Up Personnel database (Lesson 06 folder) as a new file named **ct-Easy Up Query**. Save the ct-Foxy's Tread database (Lesson 06 folder) as a new file named **ct-Foxy Queries**. Then, create a query that will append the employees listed in the ct-Easy Up Query database to the Foxy Personnel table in the ct-Foxy Queries database. Print a copy of the personnel table after running the query.

WORK-READINESS SKILLS APPLIED

- Reasoning
- Acquiring and evaluating information
- Organizing and maintaining information

6.3 Create Action Queries

The Sales Department at Green Clean is setting up a database to track sales data by department. A sample of sales records is stored in the Sales Data table in the ct-Green Clean database (Lesson 06 folder). The table consists of all sales data fields, many of which should appear in different tables to eliminate redundant data. Review the data and identify the tables that should hold the different fields. Then, create action queries to distribute the data among various tables and delete the records from the original table. Store the queries in a database named **ct-Green Clean Queries** and print a copy of each table datasheet.

WORK-READINESS SKILLS APPLIED

- Reasoning
- Solving problems
- Interpreting information

Customizing Input Forms

LESSON OUTLINE

7.1 Customizing Form Design
7.2 Creating Forms
7.3 Modifying Form Controls
7.4 Modifying Form Layout
7.5 Creating Multiple Items Forms
7.6 Printing Forms
7.7 Concepts Review
Reinforce Your Skills
Apply Your Skills
Critical Thinking & Work-Readiness Skills

LEARNING OBJECTIVES

After studying this lesson, you will be able to:

- Use Form Design and Layout Views
- Add, delete, format, and modify form controls
- Apply Themes and design elements to forms
- Set form properties and tab order
- Create a multiple item form
- Print forms

By now, you have most likely created simple forms using tools in the Forms section of the Ribbon. Some of those forms may have contained fields and data from one table, while others contained fields and data from multiple tables that were part of a query. When you create simple forms, the forms include all fields contained in a table or query grid, and Access places the fields on the form in the order in which they appear in the datasheet.

Because forms serve as an input object, many forms—those used to process customer orders, calculate payroll, and locate data—often call for fields from multiple tables that are organized logically on the form. In this lesson, you will use Form Design View to place selected fields on the form, format fields and the form, and arrange and group fields to streamline data entry. In addition, you will enhance elements of the forms and set print options for printing forms individually or in a continuous layout.

Student Resources labyrinthelab.com/acc10

Designing at Green Clean

Isaac Carter, the information technology consultant who maintains the intranet and company website, has accepted the responsibility of designing and formatting forms and reports in the Green Clean database to make them more attractive and user-friendly. Part of the task will be to customize the forms so that they better identify the company. To accomplish this, he plans to add the corporate logo and business name to all forms. The first task is to devise a layout and design that corporate executives approve. The first draft of a sample form design that he plans to create and present to the IT manager is shown here. After the IT manager reviews the design, Isaac can complete a sample form for review by other executives.

The corporate logo is at the top of the form.

The company name appears on each form.

Data fields are arranged and grouped logically.

The first draft of a custom report

7.1 Customizing Form Design

Video Lesson labyrinthelab.com/videos

If you have used the Form Wizard to create a form, you learned that the wizard walked you through the process of selecting the table or query that contained the fields and data you wanted to include on the form. Using the wizard, Access placed all fields contained in the table or query grid on the form.

You can also create and modify forms using Design View. Form Design View enables you to add fields to the form, modify existing fields, arrange fields as you want them to appear, and build the form manually to display just the effect you want to achieve. Access also contains a Form Layout View that enables you to format and modify forms while viewing field data in each form.

Although you can actually create a new form from a blank form palette, many people prefer creating new forms using the Forms Wizard and then use Form Design View to modify the layout and elements on the form. Regardless of which procedure you prefer, the techniques for building and designing the form—working with controls, setting properties, adding pictures, and so forth—are the same.

Examining Form Design View

When you display a form in Form Design View, Access displays a palette on which fields currently contained on a form appear in boxes. The background of the palette, by default, contains dots that you can use to position fields on the form. If you create a form from scratch, the form palette is blank. A Field List similar to the field lists that display in Query Design View can be opened in Form Design View so that you can drag fields from the field list and position them on the form.

As you work in Form Design View, it is important to identify key elements associated with form design. Each form in an Access database organizes data by *sections* and contains *controls* to display data and other items on the form.

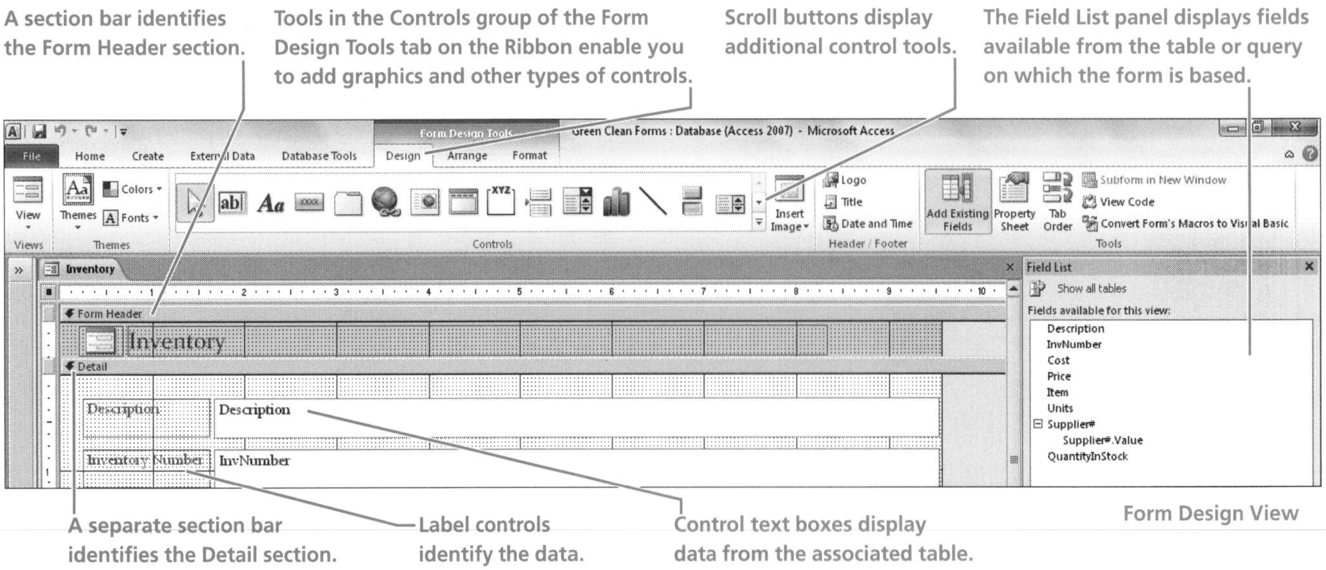

Form Design View

QUICK REFERENCE	USING FORM ELEMENTS
Element	**Description**
Sections	The major parts of the form, such as the Form Header, the Form Footer, the Detail, the Page Header, and the Page Footer. Section bars divide form sections.
Controls	Items on a form that display data, perform actions, and decorate the form. Access uses three main types of data controls on forms—bound controls, unbound controls, and calculated controls. Each data control consists of two parts—control label and control text box—that are tied to a field in a database table.
Bound control	A control that ties, or binds, data displayed on a form to a field in a database table so that the field value appears on the form. Bound controls normally appear in the Detail section of a form.
Unbound control	An item on a form that is independent of data and fields in a database table. Unbound controls can be lines, rectangles, pictures, and so forth. Unbound controls can appear in any form section.
Calculated control	A control that is tied to an expression or calculated field constructed in a query. Calculated controls normally appear in the Detail or Form Footer section of the form.
Control label	The part of a control that contains text to identify the data displayed on the form. Normally, the control label text is the field name or caption set for the field. For example, *Inventory Number* is a label that identifies the *InvNum* field.
Control text box	The part of a control that displays data from a field in an Access table. For example, *545* is the data contained in the *InvNum* field.
Form Header/ Footer	The sections of a form that contain text, pictures, and other items that are repeated at the top (header) or bottom (footer) of each form.
Detail section	The main section of the form, which normally displays data from database tables that varies from record to record.
Page Header/ Footer	The sections of a form that contain text and other items that are repeated at the top (header) or bottom (footer) of every *page* of an individual record displayed in the form.

Identifying Layout View Elements

Although Form Design View provides a tool for designing and modifying new forms, many people think Layout View provides a more intuitive view to use when modifying forms. Most of the tools available in Design View are also available in Layout View. The major difference: In Layout View, the form is actually running, so data displays in the form during editing, making it easier to adjust placement of controls and to size controls so that data displays properly. In Design View, you see the form sections and structure, but no data displays. In addition, tools for adding many additional controls are available in Design View. It is a simple matter to switch between Layout View and Design View when required tools are available only in Design View.

Tools on the Ribbon are much like those in Design view.

Sections display without the section bars.

Label and text box controls show active data.

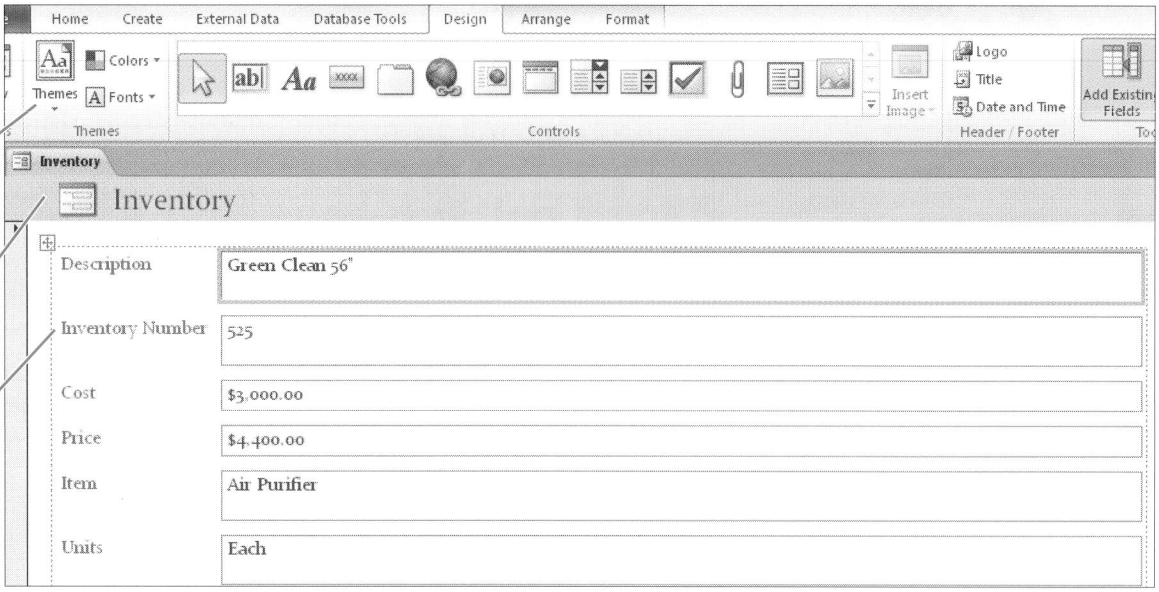

DEVELOP YOUR SKILLS 7.1.1

Display Form Views

In this exercise, you will open an existing form and display the form in Design View and Layout View. In addition, you will select controls on the form and adjust the size of form sections.

1. **Open** the Green Clean database from your Lesson 07 folder and **save** the database using the filename **`Green Clean Forms`**.
2. **Open** the Navigation Pane, **right-click** the Employees form and choose **Design View**.
3. Follow these steps to select a text box control:

Ⓐ Click the **ID** text box to select the control. A solid dark border outlines a selected control. The solid border may appear in a color, such as orange.

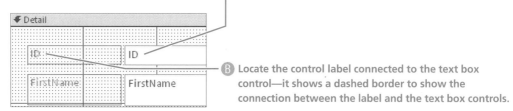

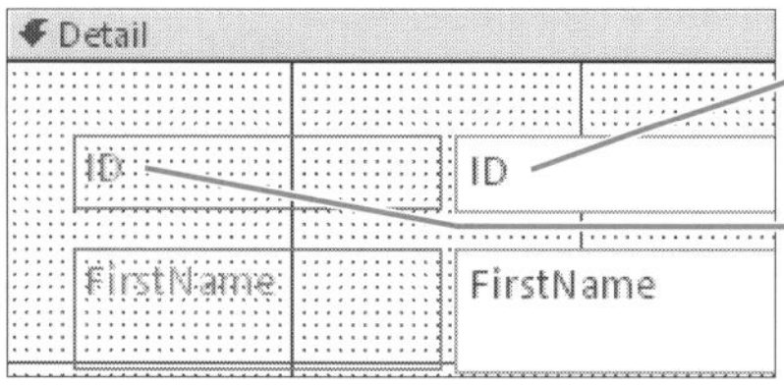

Ⓑ Locate the control label connected to the text box control—it shows a dashed border to show the connection between the label and the text box controls.

4. Click the **ID** label control.
   The solid border appears around the label and the text box control shows a dashed border.

5. Follow these steps to size the form sections:

Ⓐ Point to the upper border of the **Detail** section bar until the mouse appears as a page-sizing mouse shape.

Ⓑ Drag the border **down** the form until the black bar appears at the position shown here.

Ⓒ Release the mouse button to drop the border at about the **1/2** mark on the vertical ruler.

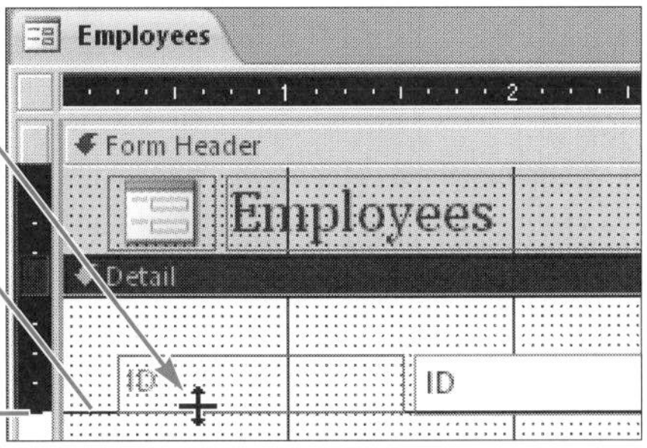

6. Choose **Design→Views→View menu ▾** and choose **Layout View** on the Ribbon to switch views.

7. Follow these steps to select controls in Layout View:

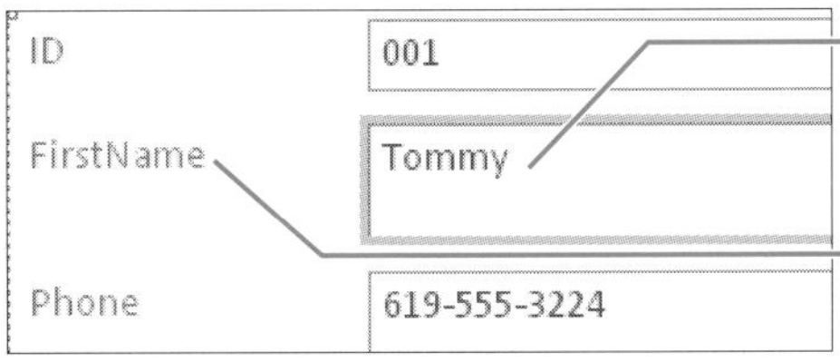

Ⓐ Click the **FirstName** text box control that contains the data Tommy. Access places a colorful bold border around the selected control.

Ⓑ Locate the associated **FirstName** label.

8. Choose **Design→Views→View menu ▾** on the Ribbon.

9. Choose **Design View** to switch views.

10. **Save** changes to the form and then **close** it.

From this point forward, the instructions for switching views will simply instruct you to switch to the appropriate View. For example, switch to Design View or switch to Layout View.

7.2 Creating Forms

Video Lesson labyrinthelab.com/videos

Access, as you have found, provides a number of different alternative procedures for creating forms. Most of you have already created a simple form and a form using the Form Wizard. Now you can concentrate on creating and designing custom forms.

Identifying a Record Source

Every form in an Access database obtains its data from the primary source—a table. Whether you design a form using fields and data displayed directly from a table or from multiple tables contained in a query results datasheet, the data must first be stored in a table. The object that contains the fields and data in a form is called the *record source*—the source of the data records. Normally a form contains fields from one table or query. However, when a relationship exists between two database tables, you can access fields from related tables. Access displays a list of related tables at the bottom of the Field List.

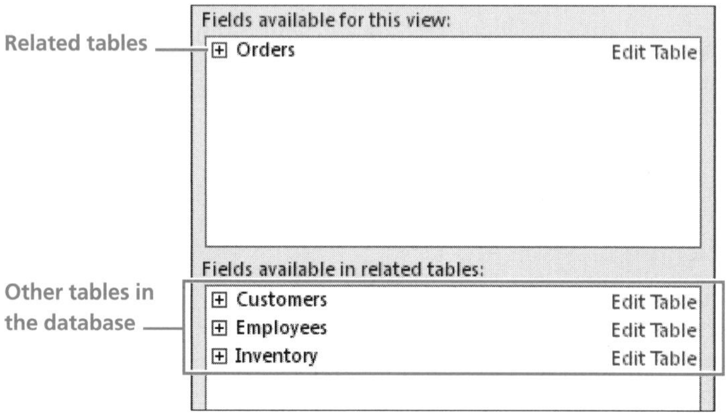

Working with Form Controls

So far, the controls you have selected on the form are bound controls that display data contained in database tables. Access has three basic types of controls that you can add to forms.

- **Bound controls—**Controls that tie, or bind, data displayed on a form to a field in a database table so that the field value (data) appears on the form. Bound controls normally appear in the Detail section of a form.
- **Unbound controls—**Lines and other drawn objects, text for titles, graphics, and so forth—independent items you can add to a form to enhance the appearance of the form.
- **Calculated controls—**Controls that are tied to an expression or calculated field constructed in a query. Calculated controls normally appear in the Detail or Form Footer section of the form.

Adding Bound Controls to Forms

If you start with a blank form, you will have to add all the controls to the form—building the form from scratch. If you work with an existing form and just want to customize it, you will naturally need to add controls to the form. Sometimes these controls will be additional fields required to display additional data. Other times, the controls you add will be descriptive text and graphics. Tools for adding bound controls appear in the Field List pane that opens when you create a new form and display it in Design View. To add a field to the form, you drag it from the Field List panel and drop it on the form.

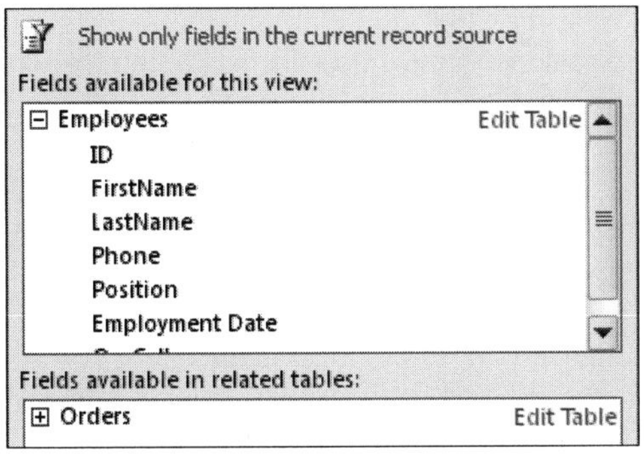

Access displays fields contained in tables and queries on the Field List panel. Use these to create bound controls.

Moving and Sizing Controls

As you position fields on forms, Access sizes the text box control using the Field Size property for the field. You can adjust the size of each control to accommodate the values entered in the field. Sizing controls in Access is similar to sizing drawn objects in other programs. You select the control and Access displays handles on the corners and sides of the control. You can drag the handle to the size you want to set for the control. Because each bound control contains two parts—the label and the text box—you can size each part separately.

Control label

Control text box

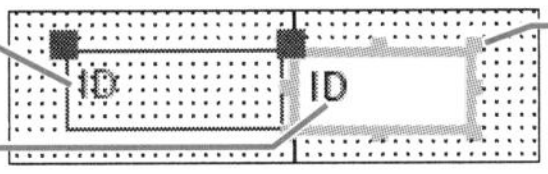

Handles appear on the corners and sides of the selected control. When you point to a handle, the mouse pointer changes to a two-headed black sizing arrow. 

 Moving and positioning controls on a form is similar to sizing the control. The main difference is that the mouse pointer appears as a white arrow with a four-headed black arrow when it is positioned to pick up and move a control.

Selected controls are identified by handles on the sides and corners of each part of the control. You may have noticed that the upper left handle is larger than other handles on the selected control. This handle enables you to separate the label from the text box, moving each part of the control to position it where you want it. When you point to a border of the control, you move both parts of the control together.

FROM THE KEYBOARD
← ↑ → ↓ to move selected controls

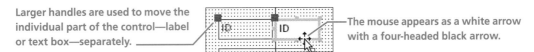

Larger handles are used to move the individual part of the control—label or text box—separately.

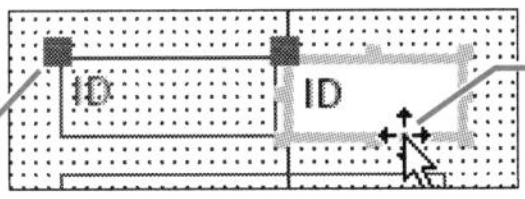

The mouse appears as a white arrow with a four-headed black arrow.

QUICK REFERENCE **CREATING FORMS**

Task	Procedure
Create a simple form	■ Select the table for which you want to create a form. ■ Choose Create→Forms→Form on the Ribbon.
Create a form in Design View	■ Select the table for which you want to create a form. ■ Choose Create→Forms→Form Design on the Ribbon.

QUICK REFERENCE	CREATING FORMS (continued)
Task	**Procedure**
Create a split form	■ Select the table for which you want to create the form. ■ Choose Create→Forms→More Forms→Split Form on the Ribbon.
Create a form using a wizard	■ Select the table for which you want to create the form. ■ Choose Create→Forms→Form Wizard on the Ribbon.
Create a multiple item form	■ Choose Create→Forms→More Forms→Multiple Items on the Ribbon.

DEVELOP YOUR SKILLS 7.2.1

Create a Blank Form and Use Bound Controls

In this exercise, you will create a blank form for the Customers table, add bound controls to the form, and size and move the controls.

1. Select the **Customers** table in the Navigation Pane and then **close** the Navigation Pane.
2. Choose **Create→Forms→Form Design** on the Ribbon.
   Access creates a new form and displays it in Design View.
3. Choose **Design→Tools→Add Existing Fields** on the Ribbon to open the Field List and follow these steps to add a field to the blank form:

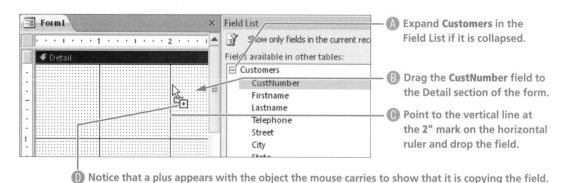

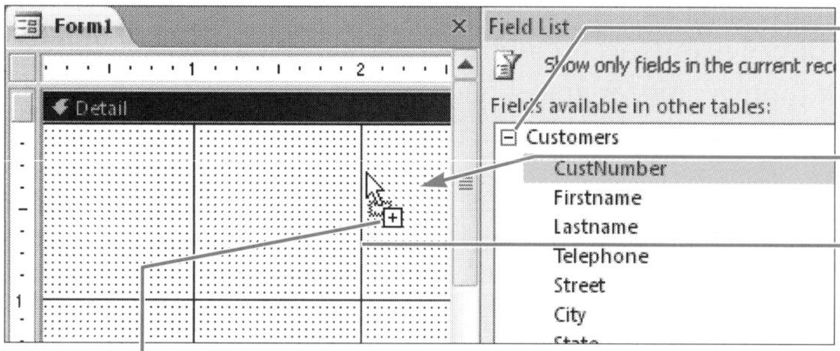

The left side of the text box control aligns at the 2" mark, the spot where the mouse pointed when you dropped the control.

4. Repeat the procedures outlined in **step 3** to add the following fields to the form, dropping them below the CustNumber field: FirstName, LastName, Street, City, State, ZIP, Telephone, and Comments.
5. Follow these steps to separate the control label from the text box:

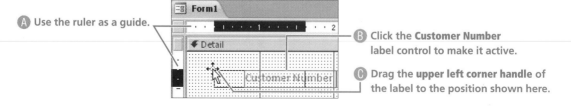

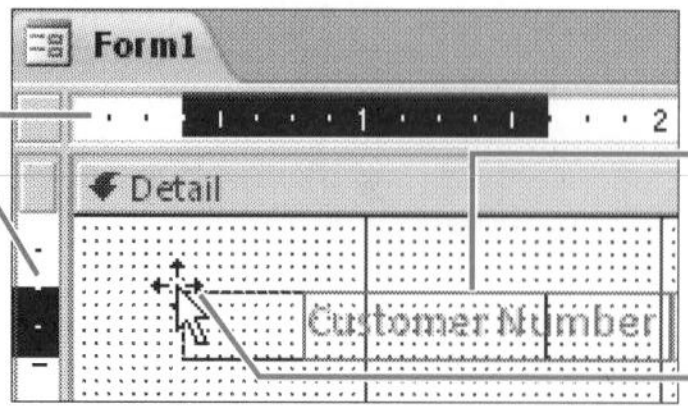

Ⓐ Use the ruler as a guide.
Form1
Fields available in other tables:
Detail
Ⓐ Expand **Customers** in the Field List if it is collapsed.
Ⓒ Point to the vertical line at the **2"** mark on the horizontal ruler and drop the field.
Ⓓ Notice that a plus appears with the object the mouse carries to show that it is copying the field.
Customer Number
Ⓑ Click the **Customer Number** label control to make it active.
Ⓒ Drag the **upper left corner handle** of the label to the position shown here.

6. Repeat the procedures outlined in **step 5** to position the right side of each field label approximately one-half inch from the control text box.

7. Follow these steps to size the CustNumber text box appropriately for the data:

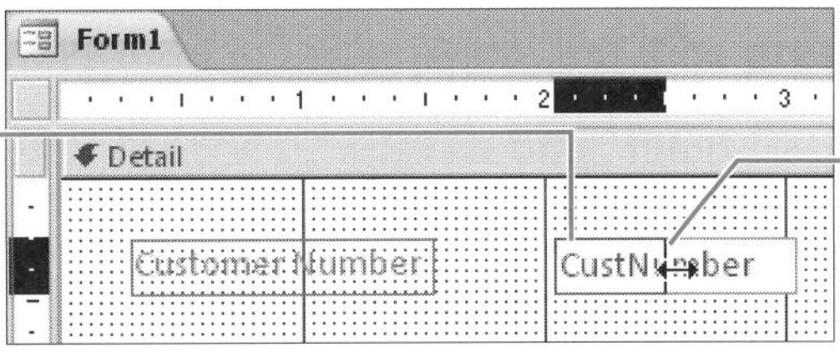
Form1
Detail
Customer Number
CustNumber
A Click the **CustNumber** text box to select it.
B Drag the **right center handle** to the approximate location shown here on the horizontal ruler.

8. Follow these steps to move fields to different positions on the form:

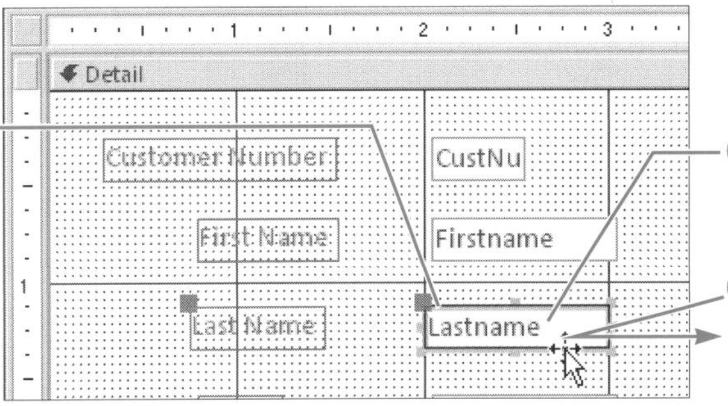
Detail
Customer Number
CustNu
First Name
Firstname
Last Name
Lastname
A Click the **LastName** text box to select it.
B **Point** to an area on the text box border away from all handles.
C Drag the control to about the **5"** mark on the horizontal ruler beside the FirstName text box.

When you drop the control text box, the Last Name label overlaps the FirstName control box. That's okay for now—you'll fix it soon.

9. Repeat the procedures outlined in steps 7 and 8 to size the control text boxes and position them as shown on the following figure:

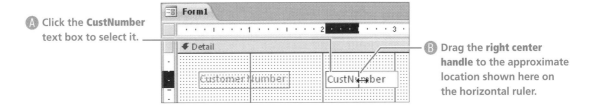

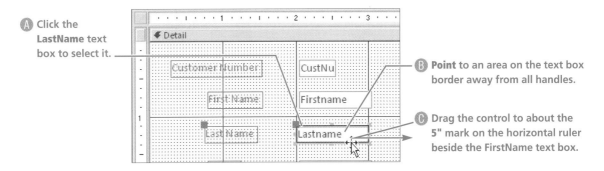

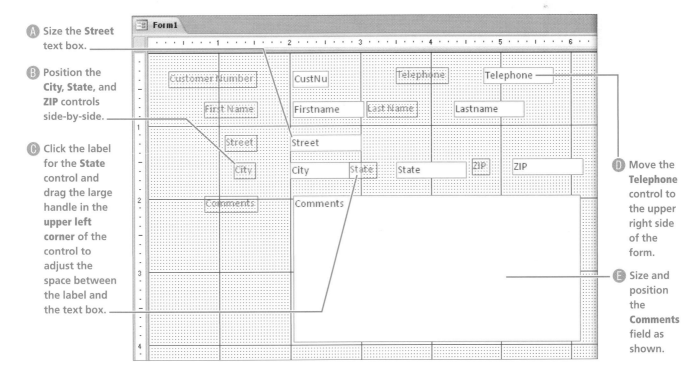

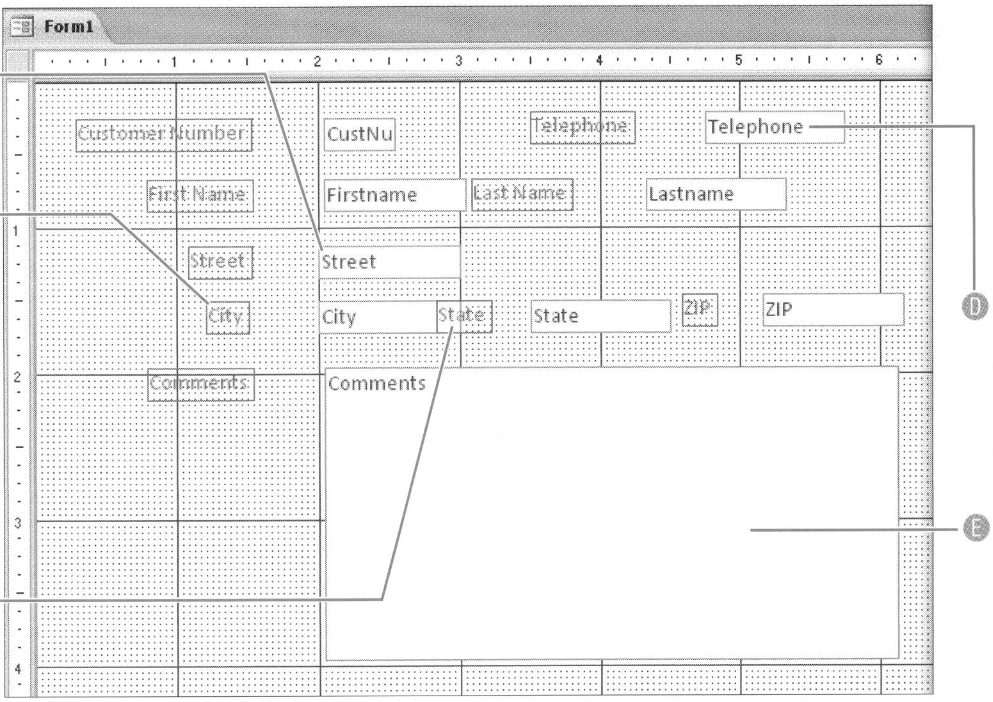
Form1
Customer Number
CustNu
Telephone
Telephone
First Name
Firstname
Last Name
Lastname
Street
Street
City
City
State
State
ZIP
ZIP
Comments
Comments
A Size the **Street** text box.
B Position the **City, State,** and **ZIP** controls side-by-side.
C Click the label for the **State** control and drag the large handle in the **upper left corner** of the control to adjust the space between the label and the text box.
D Move the **Telephone** control to the upper right side of the form.
E Size and position the **Comments** field as shown.

10. Repeat the procedure outline in **step 9C** to position labels closer to their associated textboxes.

11. **Save** the form using the form name **Customers** and then **close** the form.

7.3 Modifying Form Controls

Video Lesson labyrinthelab.com/videos

As you design and work with forms, there will be times when you want to edit the appearance of control labels or remove them from the form. Access contains tools that enable you to change form control labels, change the format of the text box data to display as currency, for example, and to format font and control background color.

Editing Labels

Control labels identify the values contained in control text boxes. As a result, they need to be as descriptive as possible and yet also be concise. You have already learned how to set field captions to change the column headings when field names are somewhat cryptic or contain text run together. When you add field controls to forms, you can edit the text contained in labels directly in the label control box.

Deleting Controls

Some controls on a form stand by themselves without the need for a label. You can delete unnecessary labels to allow better arrangement and format on forms and also remove controls completely. Because each bound control contains two parts, removing labels and controls depends on the part of the control selected:

QUICK REFERENCE — DELETING CONTROLS AND LABELS

Task	Procedure
Delete an entire control	■ Select the text box part of the control. ■ Press [Delete].
Delete a label	■ Select the label part of the control. ■ Press [Delete].

DEVELOP YOUR SKILLS 7.3.1

Delete Labels and Edit Label Text

In this exercise, you will delete control labels and change the control label text on the Customers form.

1. Display the **Customers** form in Design View.
2. Follow these steps to delete a control label:

Ⓐ Click the **Last Name** label to select it.

Ⓑ **Press** Delete.

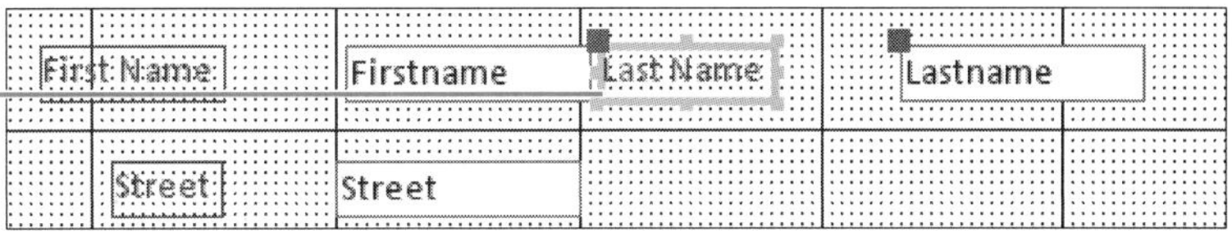

TIP If you accidentally delete the wrong part of the control, click the Undo button on the Quick Access toolbar to reverse the action and then try again.

Access removes the control label, leaving the control text box.

3. Repeat the procedures outlined in **step 2** to delete the following labels: City, State, ZIP.

Edit Control Labels

4. Follow these steps to edit the First Name label on the form:

Ⓐ Click the **First Name** label to make it active.

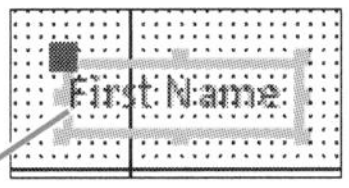

Ⓑ **Double-click** the word First in the label to select it.

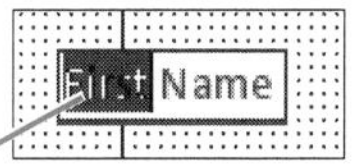

Ⓒ **Press** Delete twice to remove the selected word and the space after it.

5. Repeat the procedures outlined in **step 4** to select text in the Street label and type **`Address`**.
6. Size and position the **FirstName** and **LastName** text box controls closer together, and then adjust the position and size of the **City**, **State**, and **ZIP** fields.
   Leave the database and form open for the next activity.

Using Design Font Tools

Tools for formatting controls appear on the Format tab of the Ribbon when Form Design and Layout views are active. Using these tools, you can change the font format, design, size, color, and alignment as well as the fill color of the control box.

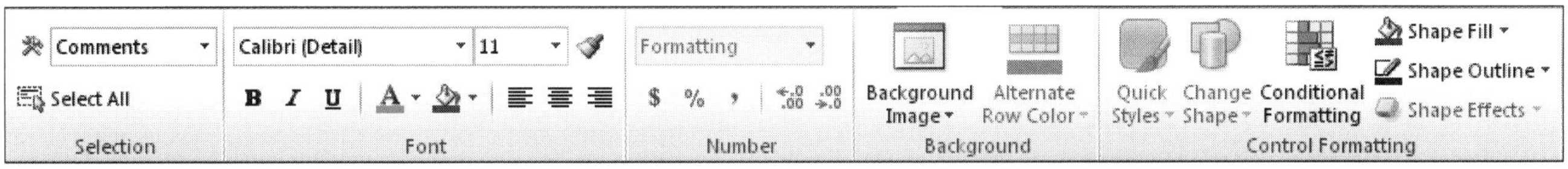

The Format tab of the Ribbon contains tools for formatting form controls.

Applying Conditional Formatting

In addition to formatting controls manually using the tools on the Ribbon, you can define and set conditional formatting for Access to use when the data in a control meets the criteria you set. For example, suppose you want the font for amounts of orders greater than $1,000 to display in red text and the values between $500 and $1,000 to appear in blue text. You can define the format you want to apply and set the criteria that must be true for the format to go into affect, and Access applies the format when the conditions are met.

The Conditional Formatting Rules Manager lists rules that you want Access to apply to fields on a form.

The New Formatting Rule dialog box presents the tools used to set criteria for each rule.

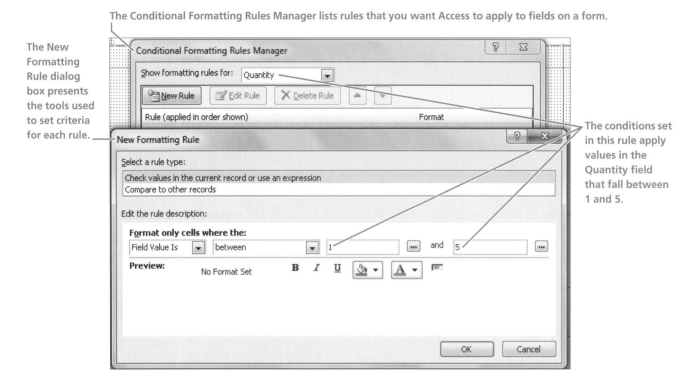

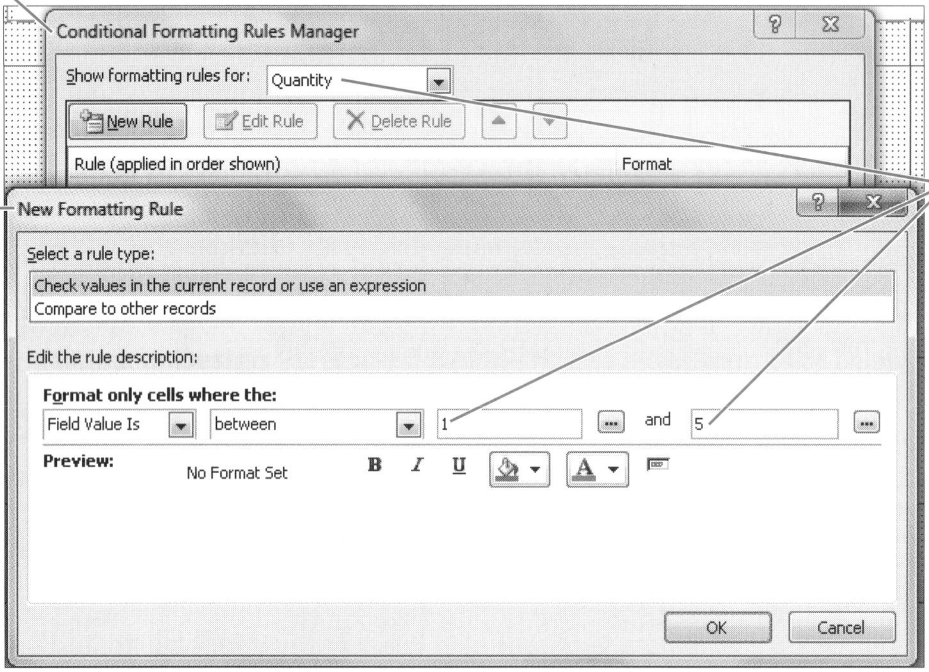

The conditions set in this rule apply values in the Quantity field that fall between 1 and 5.

Another way conditional formatting is useful is when you want to highlight the active field on a form to more easily locate the insertion point. You can set conditional formatting to tell Access to change the format of the control when it is active.

Using the Property Sheet

FROM THE KEYBOARD
F4 to open or close the Property Sheet

The Property Sheet is also available for formatting controls you add to forms. When you display the Property Sheet in Design View, it opens as a panel down the right side of the design window. The Property Sheet provides access to properties such as the field format (general number, currency, etc.), font format, alignment, and many others. The properties displayed vary depending on which control is selected and whether the label or the text box part of the control is selected.

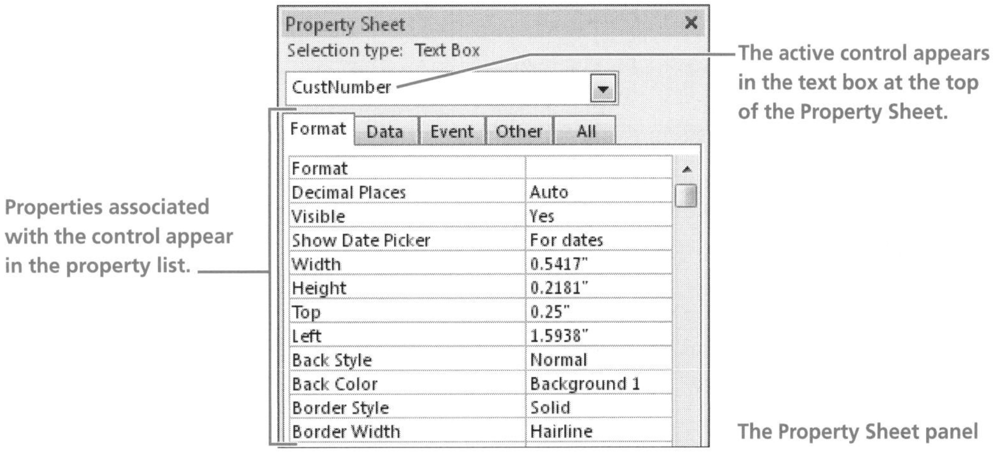

The Property Sheet panel

Using the Fill Color Palette

Whether you are formatting text or background fill color, the techniques for using the color palette are the same. Access identifies the color names in three parts:

Color Name, Color Type, Percent Light or Dark

So if you are formatting text or fill and the instructions say Dark Red, Accent 4, 20% Darker, you will be able to locate the appropriate color. Review the following figure to learn more about locating the right color.

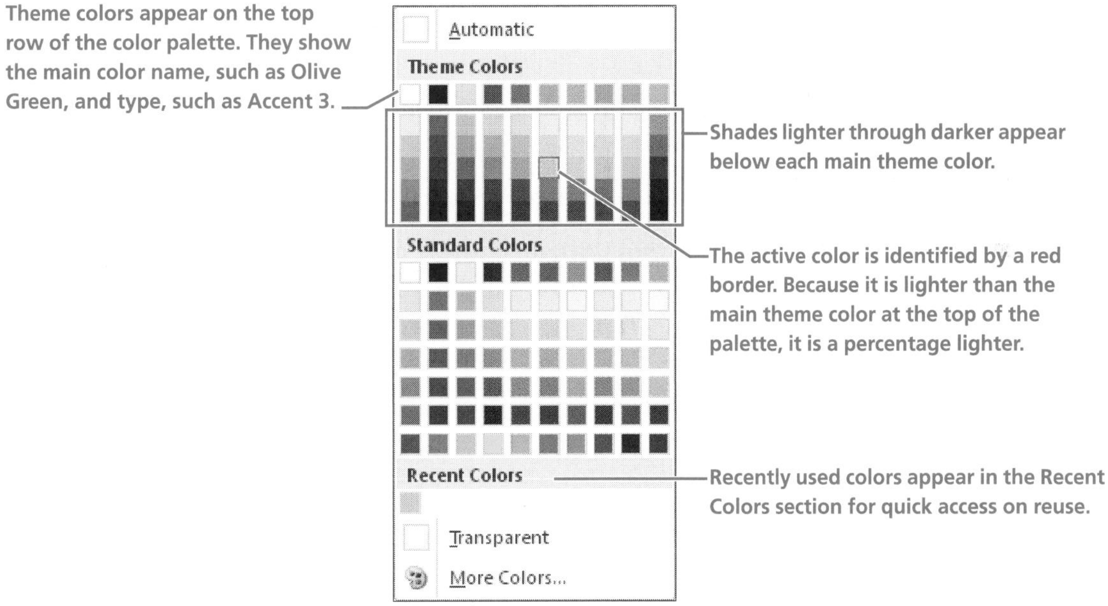

Theme colors appear on the top row of the color palette. They show the main color name, such as Olive Green, and type, such as Accent 3.
Automatic
Theme Colors
Shades lighter through darker appear below each main theme color.
Standard Colors
The active color is identified by a red border. Because it is lighter than the main theme color at the top of the palette, it is a percentage lighter.
Recent Colors
Recently used colors appear in the Recent Colors section for quick access on reuse.
Transparent
More Colors...

DEVELOP YOUR SKILLS 7.3.2

Apply Formatting to Controls

In this exercise, you will format labels, set conditional formatting, and use properties to format controls on the Customers form.

Before You Begin: The Customers form in the Green Clean Forms database should be open in Form Design view.

1. Follow these steps to format label text:

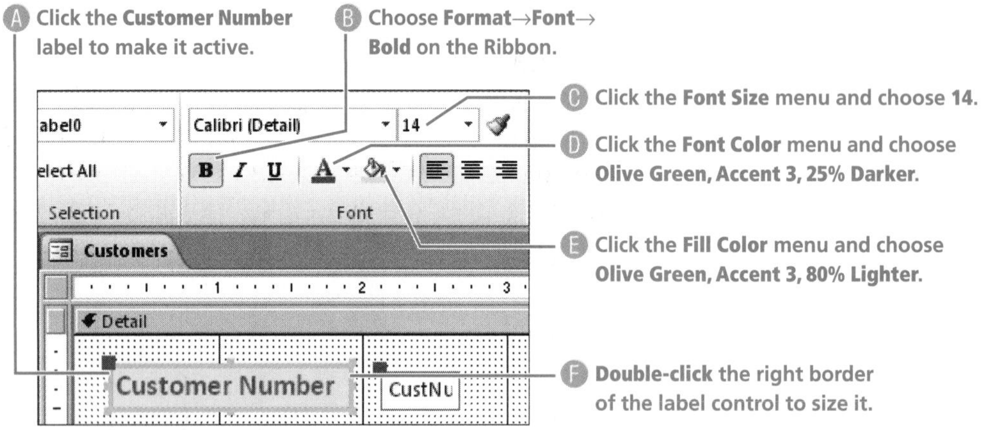

A Click the **Customer Number** label to make it active.
B Choose **Format→Font→Bold** on the Ribbon.
C Click the **Font Size** menu and choose **14**.
D Click the **Font Color** menu and choose **Olive Green, Accent 3, 25% Darker.**
E Click the **Fill Color** menu and choose **Olive Green, Accent 3, 80% Lighter.**
F **Double-click** the right border of the label control to size it.
abel0
Calibri (Detail)
14
elect All
Selection
Font
Customers
Detail
Customer Number
CustNu

Access formats the control label as shown in the preceding illustration.

Apply Conditional Formatting

Now you will apply conditional formatting that will identify those records for international customers or customers who have no ZIP Code entered.

2. Click the **ZIP** control text box to make it active.
3. Choose **Format→Control Formatting→Conditional Formatting→** on the Ribbon to open the Conditional Formatting dialog box.

4. Follow these steps to assign a conditional format to the ZIP text box:

A Ensure that the **ZIP** field appears in the Show formatting rules for: box.

B Click the **New Rule** button.

C Select *not between* from the drop-down list.

D Type **1** in the first field.

E Type **99999** in the last field.

F Click **OK** to close the New Formatting Rule dialog box and click **OK** to close the Conditional Formatting Rules Manager dialog box to complete the rule.

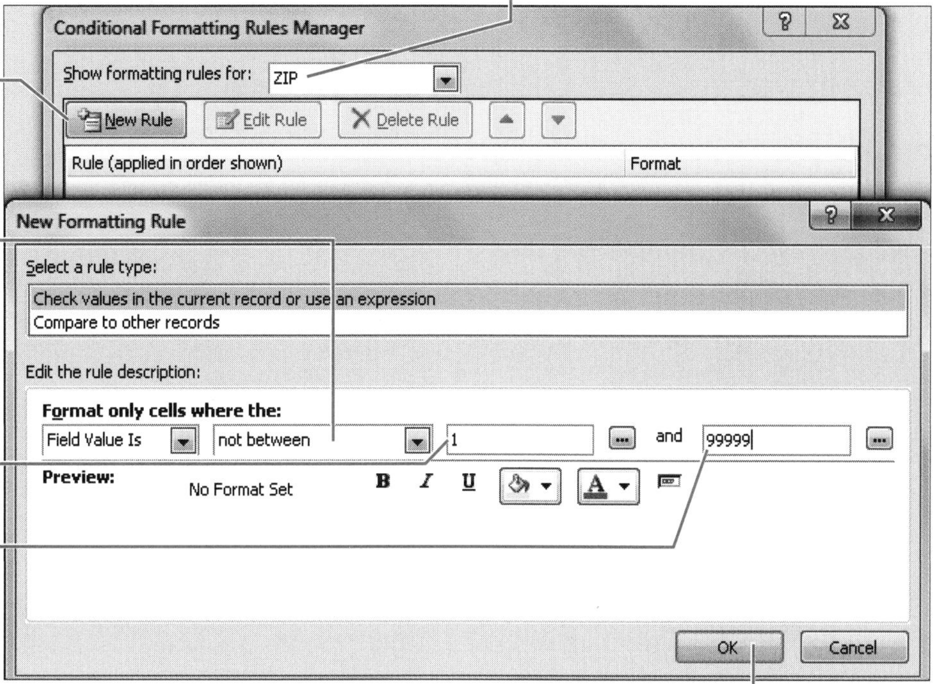

Use the Property Sheet

To format the text in the Comments memo field, you will use the property sheet.

5. Click the **Comments** control text box to make it active.

6. Choose **Design→Tools→Property Sheet**  on the Ribbon to open the Property Sheet panel.

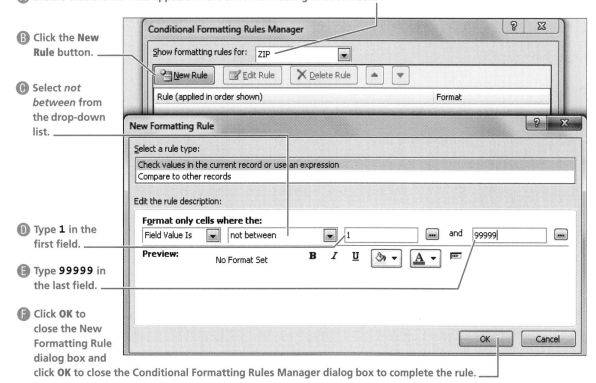

7. Follow these steps to set the Fore Color property for the control:

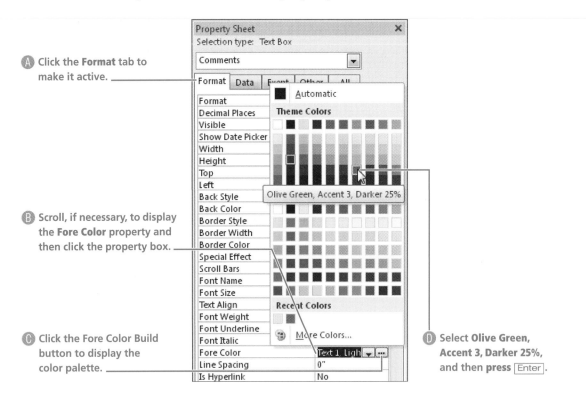

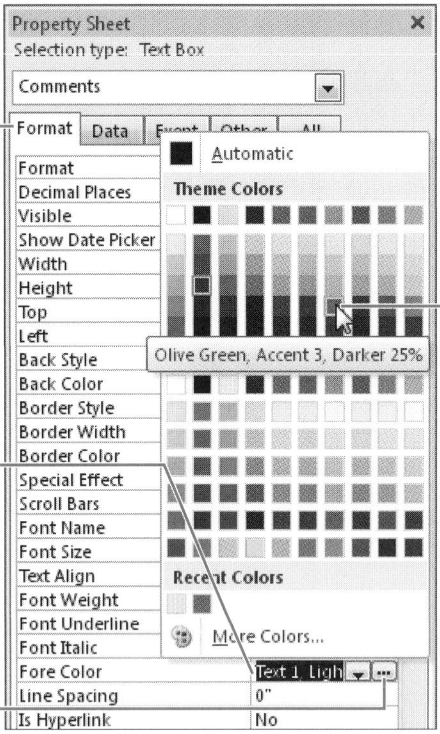

A Click the **Format** tab to make it active.

B Scroll, if necessary, to display the **Fore Color** property and then click the property box.

C Click the Fore Color Build button to display the color palette.

D Select **Olive Green, Accent 3, Darker 25%,** and then **press** [Enter].

Paint Formats

Use the Format Painter to apply formats to other labels.

8. Click the **Customer Number** control label to make it active.
9. Choose **Format→Font** on the Ribbon and double-click **Format Painter** to collect the formats applied to the Customer Number label.
   Access picks up the format of the label, and the mouse pointer appears to carry a paint brush so that you can paint the format onto other labels.
10. Click each of the four additional **control labels** on the form to apply the format to the label.
11. **Press** [Esc] to drop the paint brush and then adjust the size of each label to show all text.
12. **Save** changes to the form and then **close** it.

Arranging Controls

Video Lesson labyrinthelab.com/videos

You have already positioned controls on the form in the area of the form you want them to appear. Access also contains tools that enable you to align the controls and then group them so that controls relating to the same general topic appear together and move together when you move one control. Tools for aligning, grouping, and distributing controls appear on the Arrange tab of the Ribbon.

Selecting Multiple Controls

Selecting, moving, positioning, and aligning each form control individually can be tedious and time-consuming. By selecting multiple controls and then moving or sizing them, you reduce the amount of time needed to position them or format them. You will also select multiple controls in order to group them on a form.

QUICK REFERENCE — SELECTING MULTIPLE CONTROLS

Task	Procedure
Select controls individually	■ Click the first control. ■ Press and hold [Shift] and click each additional control.
Select controls in a horizontal or vertical line	■ Point to the vertical ruler on the left side of the form until the mouse pointer appears as a right-pointing black arrow and click to select all controls horizontally. ■ Point to the horizontal ruler at the top of the form until the mouse pointer appears as a down-pointing black arrow and click to select all controls vertically.
Select controls in a general area of the form	■ Point to a position slightly outside the area of the top left control and then drag the mouse pointer to a position slightly outside the area of the bottom right control.

Aligning Controls

As you move and position controls on forms, it is sometimes challenging to position them so that they align properly. Access alignment tools help with aligning multiple controls.

QUICK REFERENCE — ALIGNING SELECTED CONTROLS

Task	Procedure
Align controls using the Ribbon	■ Select multiple controls. ■ Choose Arrange→Sizing & Ordering→Align and click the alignment that represents the alignment you want to apply—Left, Right, Top, Bottom, To Grid.
Align controls using the shortcut menu	■ Select multiple controls. ■ Right-click one of the selected controls and choose the Align menu. ■ Choose the alignment you want to apply—Left, Right, Top, Bottom, To Grid.

Anchoring Controls

You can also anchor controls—tie them to a section or to other controls so that moving or sizing a section adjusts the size and position of the anchored control as well. Access provides nine different anchor positions that range from top left to bottom right. Although you anchor controls in Design View and Layout View, the results of the anchor show only in the Layout View and Form View.

FROM THE KEYBOARD

Press and hold [Alt] and drag selected controls to position the control more precisely
or
Press and hold [Ctrl] and tap the arrow keys to nudge the control into place

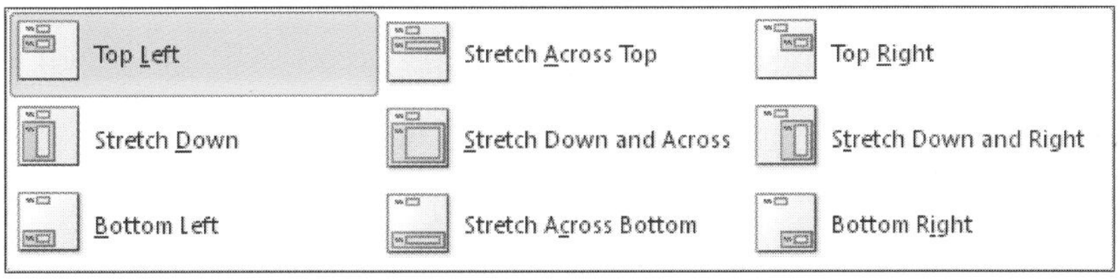

Anchor positions

DEVELOP YOUR SKILLS 7.3.3

Arrange, Group, and Anchor Form Controls

In this exercise, you will select multiple controls, align, group, and anchor controls on the Customers form in your Green Clean Forms database.

1. Display the **Customer** form in Design View and follow these steps to select multiple controls:

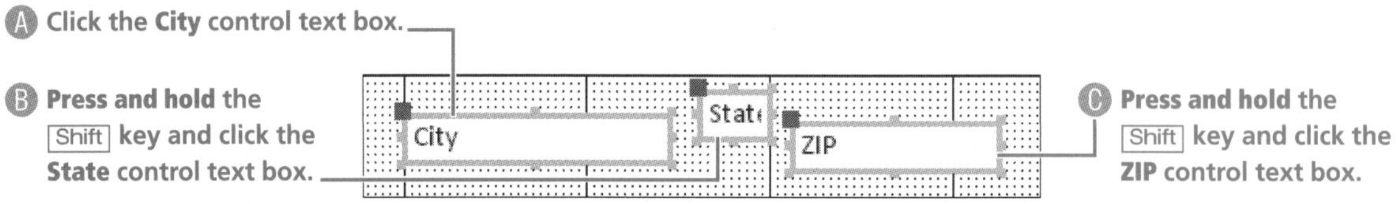

A Click the City control text box.
B Press and hold the Shift key and click the State control text box.
City
State
ZIP
C Press and hold the Shift key and click the ZIP control text box.

2. Choose **Arrange→Sizing & Ordering→Alignment→Bottom** on the Ribbon to align the controls.
3. Follow these steps to select control labels:

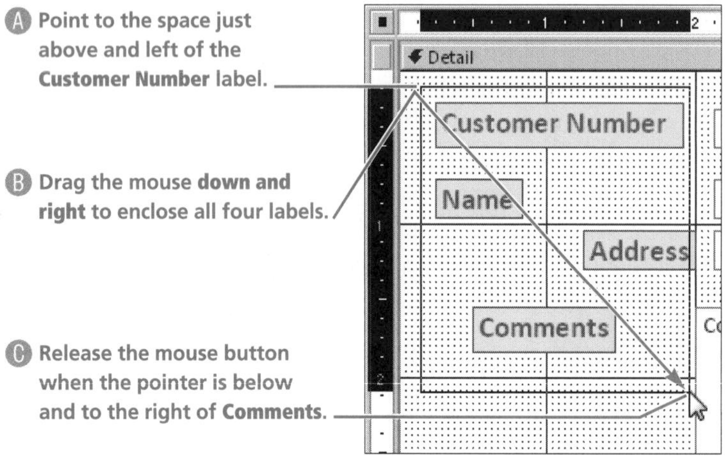

A Point to the space just above and left of the Customer Number label.
B Drag the mouse down and right to enclose all four labels.
C Release the mouse button when the pointer is below and to the right of Comments.
Detail
Customer Number
Name
Address
Comments

Access selects all four label controls.

TIP

If control text boxes are also selected, click a neutral area of the form and try again. Be certain to avoid extending the marquee area onto the control text boxes.

4. Choose **Arrange→Sizing & Ordering→Align→Right** on the Ribbon to align the controls.

Group Controls

5. Select the following controls using the technique you prefer: Address label, Street, City, State, and ZIP text boxes.
6. Choose **Arrange→Sizing & Ordering→Size/Space→Group** on the Ribbon to group the selected controls.

Anchor Controls

7. Select both parts of the **Comments** control.
8. Choose **Arrange→Position→Anchoring** menu on the Ribbon.
9. Choose **Stretch Across Bottom**.
10. Choose **Home→Views menu→Form View** on the Ribbon to display the form as users will see it.
11. **Save** changes to the form and then **close** it.

7.4 Modifying Form Layout

Video Lesson labyrinthelab.com/videos

So far, you have added, edited, arranged, and formatted controls on a new form and saved the form. These changes had no effect on the form layout and design itself. For example, the form palette is still white and the Detail section is the only section displayed. Formatting a form, as distinguished from formatting controls, involves such additional tasks as:

- Displaying and editing Form Header and Form Footer sections.
- Formatting section backgrounds.
- Adding design elements to sections.

Displaying Form Header and Form Footer

It is important to display data that remains consistent for each record in a separate section of the form to avoid having to repeat the controls over and over again. Controls such as page number, title, logos, and so forth, that you place in the header or footer sections of the form repeat on forms as they do on pages of a Word document. As a result, you can add them one time and they will display on each form. By default, Access hides the Form Header and Form Footer of a new form until you are ready to display them. To display the Form Header and Form Footer, you select an element that you want to add to the sections from tools on the Design tab of the Ribbon.

Form Headers contain controls you want repeated at the top of each form.

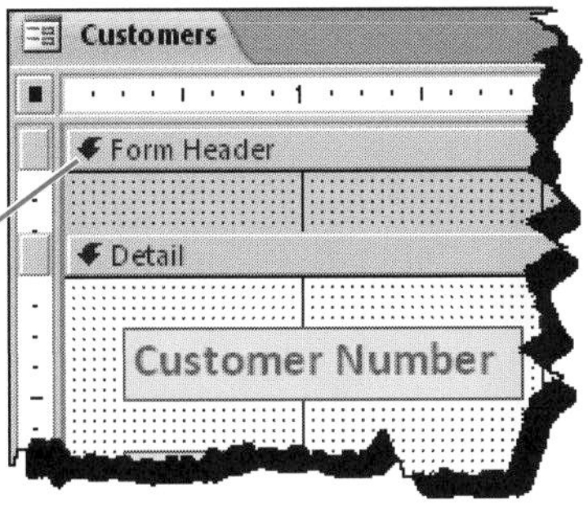

Form Footers contain controls you want repeated at the bottom of each form.

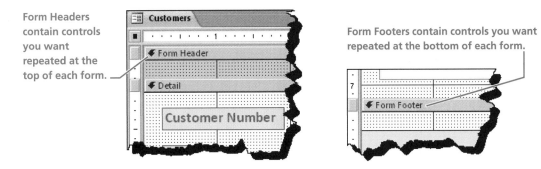

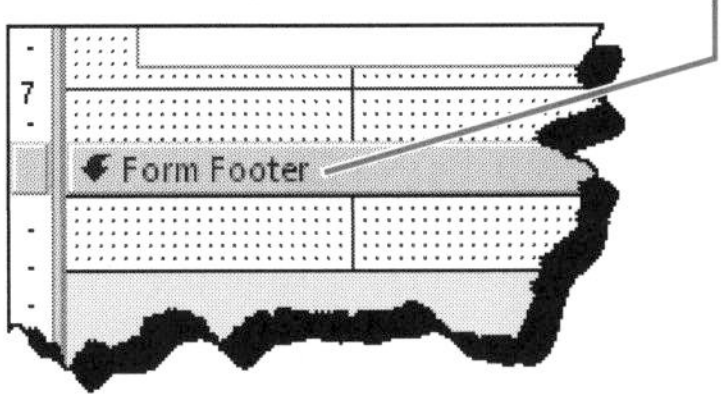

Sizing Form Sections

When you size form sections, keep in mind that you size a section by dragging the bottom of the section up or down. As a result, you often need to drag the bar for the section that appears below the section you want to enlarge. For example, to make the Form Header section larger, drag the Detail section bar down. To make the Form Header section smaller, drag the Detail section bar up.

The mouse pointer appears as a two-headed arrow with a bar when positioned appropriately for sizing a section.

Formatting Form Section Background

The background of the Form Footer section appears the same as the detail section. The Form Header section is, by default, shaded to distinguish it from the other parts of the form. As you may recall, each section of a form is separated from other sections by a section bar that contains the title of the section. Many database designers format the background of the Form Header section to display a company color and then add a title and a company logo to the section.

The Form Header section is formatted with a background color, title, and logo.

DEVELOP YOUR SKILLS 7.4.1

Display and Format a Form Header

In this exercise, you will display Form Header and Footer sections and format the header background on the Customers form in your Green Clean Forms database.

1. Display the **Customers** form in Design View.
2. **Right-click** the Detail section bar and select **Form Header/Footer** to display the sections.
3. Follow these steps to make the Form Header section larger:

A Point to the upper border of the **Detail** section bar until the mouse pointer appears as a two-headed black arrow with a bar between the points.

B Drag the **Detail** section bar down to about the 1" mark on the vertical ruler.

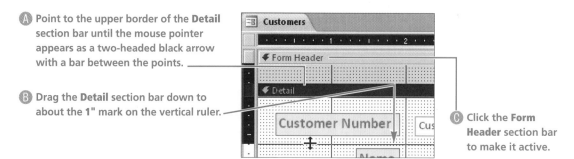

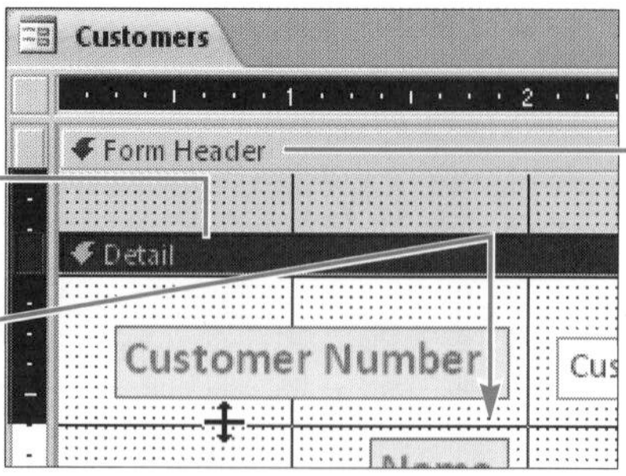

C Click the **Form Header** section bar to make it active.

4. Choose **Format→Font→Fill Color** ▾ menu on the Ribbon, and then choose the **Olive Green, Accent 3, 40% lighter** color to format the Form Header with a pale olive background.
5. **Save** changes to the form and leave it **open** for the next exercise.

Adding Design Elements to Forms

Video Lesson labyrinthelab.com/videos

Design elements—drawn shapes, logos, graphics, and titles—improve the appearance of a form. Because these elements need no access to data contained in database tables, they are considered unbound controls—controls that are bound to no data. Tools for adding unbound controls appear on the Design tab of Ribbon. Point to a control on the Ribbon and use the tool tip to identify the control.

The expanded Controls group on the Design tab of the Ribbon displays controls you can add to any form section.

The Header/Footer group on the Design tab of the Ribbon contains tools for adding the most commonly used header/footer elements.

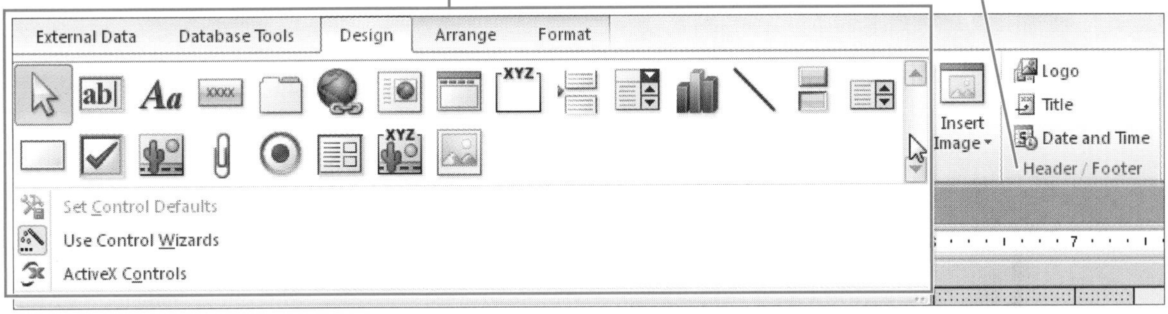

When you use most of the unbound controls to add design elements to any database object, the mouse pointer appears as a plus symbol (+) called a *crosshair*. Sometimes the character or symbol on the control icon appears with the crosshair of the mouse pointer to identify the shape or control you are adding to the form. A few of these mouse pointers are shown below.

Crosshair mouse appears above the symbol.

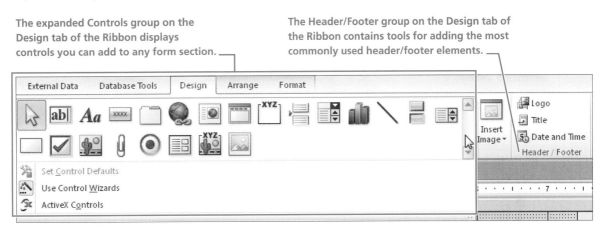

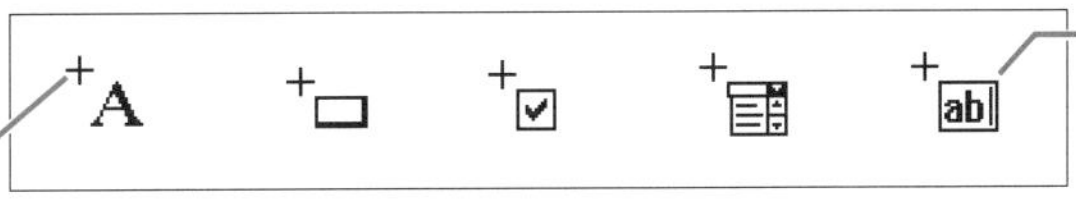

Symbols represent (left to right) label, button, checkbox, combo box, and text box.

DEVELOP YOUR SKILLS 7.4.2

Add Unbound Controls to Forms

In this exercise, you will add a title and image to the Form Header section of the Customers form in the Green Clean Forms database using unbound controls.

1. Choose **Design→Header/Footer→Title** on the Ribbon to add the form title to the Form Header section.
   Access adds the title to the Form Header section and selects the Customers text so that you can edit it.
2. Type **`Green Clean Customers`** and **press** [Enter].
   Access sizes the label control to fit the text, when necessary.

3. Follow these steps to size the new title:

Ⓐ Click the **faint-dotted border** of the additional control shown here and **press** [Delete] on the keyboard.

Ⓑ Drag the **lower right corner handle** on the title control.

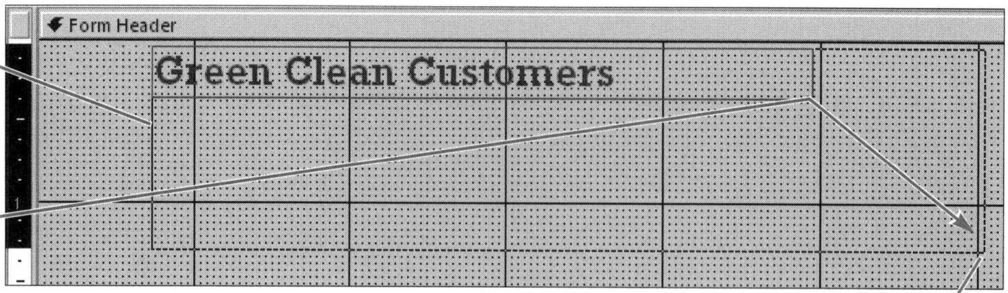

Ⓒ **Release** the mouse button when the control is about the size shown here.

When you add a title control to the form, Access automatically places a label with the control. Because you don't need that control, deleting it will ensure that the logo you are going to place appears in the correct location on the form.

4. **Press** [F4] to display the Property Sheet and set the following properties for the label control to format the label text:

Property	Setting
Special Effect	Raised
Border Color	Olive Green, Accent 3, Lighter 40%
Fore Color	Olive Green, Accent 3, Darker 50%
Font Name	Mistral
Font Size	40 (Type 40 in the Font Size box and press [Enter].)
Text Align	Right

5. Adjust the size of the title, if necessary, by dragging the right border of the control and then move it to the right to allow room for the logo; then **save** changes to the form.

Add a Logo Image to a Form Header

6. Choose **Design→Header/Footer→Logo** on the Ribbon and follow these steps to add a logo to the form:

Ⓐ Navigate to your Lesson 07 folder.

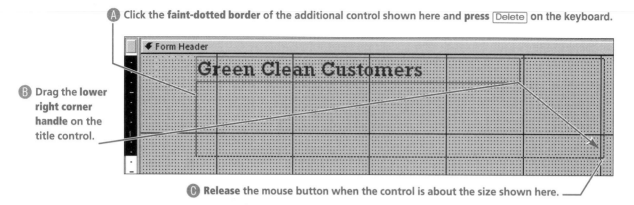

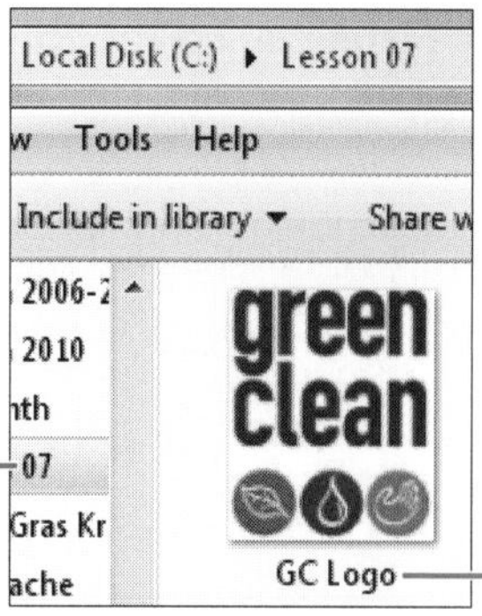

Ⓑ **Double-click** the GC Logo.bmp file in the Lesson 07 folder.

Access places the picture file in the image control box on the form and sizes the box to fit the image.

7. Adjust the position and size of the image appropriately in the **Form Header** section.
8. Switch to **Form View** and review the form changes.
   Your form should be similar to the one shown here.

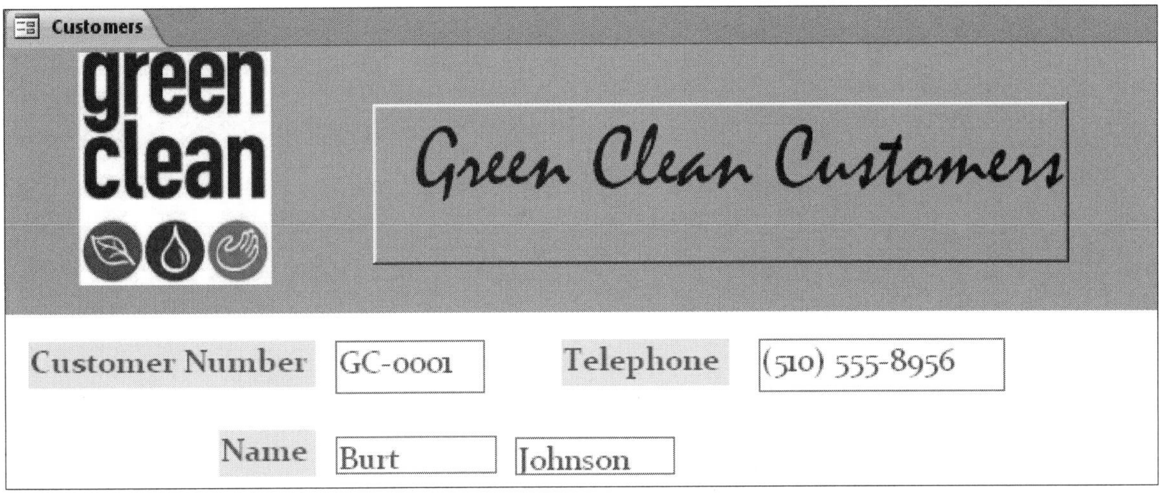

9. **Save** changes to the form and then **close** it.

Setting Additional Form Properties

Video Lesson labyrinthelab.com/videos

You have already used the Property Sheet to format controls and sections on the form. Now that you have the visual elements of the form set, you can focus on the functional elements of the form itself. Form properties include those form items that affect the whole form, such as the record selector bar, scroll bars, and navigation buttons.

Choosing Items to Show on Forms

For most forms, the navigation buttons that appear at the bottom of the form window are important to display different form records. Scroll bars can be useful when the form and data extend beyond the boundaries of the monitor. When the form can be sized to display the complete form onscreen at the same time, there is no need for scroll bars, and they can be removed from view. However, because the entire form appears onscreen on one computer does not necessarily mean the entire form will appear onscreen on every computer. Allowances must be made for individual screen size and resolution.

The record selector bar can also be useful. However, many businesses find that their employees inadvertently click the record selector bar and delete records when they really want to delete data in a form field. As a result, many businesses remove the record selector bar from their forms to prevent accidental data loss.

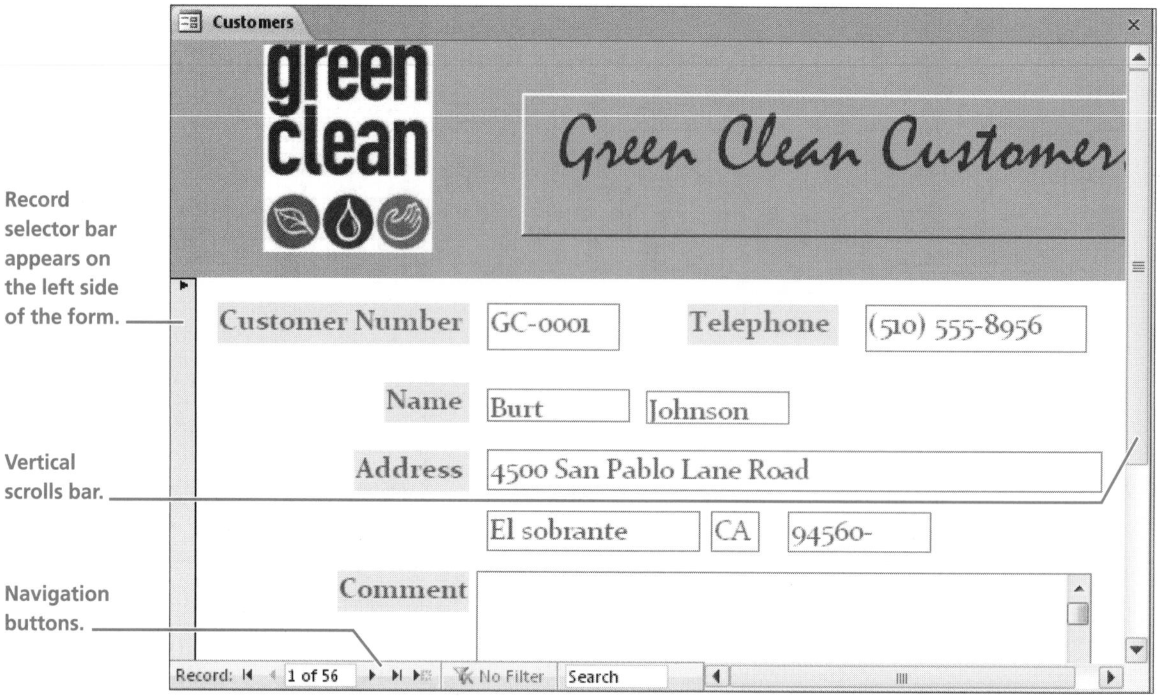

Displaying the Form Property Sheet

FROM THE KEYBOARD

Shift+Spacebar to select an entire form when no form selection bar is displayed

As you have already discovered, the properties displayed in the Property Sheet vary, depending on the item that is selected or active on the form. To access properties that affect the whole form, no item on the form can be selected. You can click a blank area of the form to display Form properties or select Form from the Property Sheet Selection Type list. The Property Sheet is available in both Design and Layout Views.

TIP

The Property Sheet contains numerous properties, some that will be familiar to you—such as caption—and many that are unfamiliar—Allow PivotTable View, for example. Some of these properties will be covered in later lessons. However, if you would like to know more about them, use Access Help to get yourself up to speed on what they do.

DEVELOP YOUR SKILLS 7.4.3

Set Form Properties

In this exercise, you will use the Property Sheet to set properties for the Customers form.

1. Display the **Customers** form in Design View and then **press** F4 to display the Property Sheet.
2. Follow these steps to set Form properties:

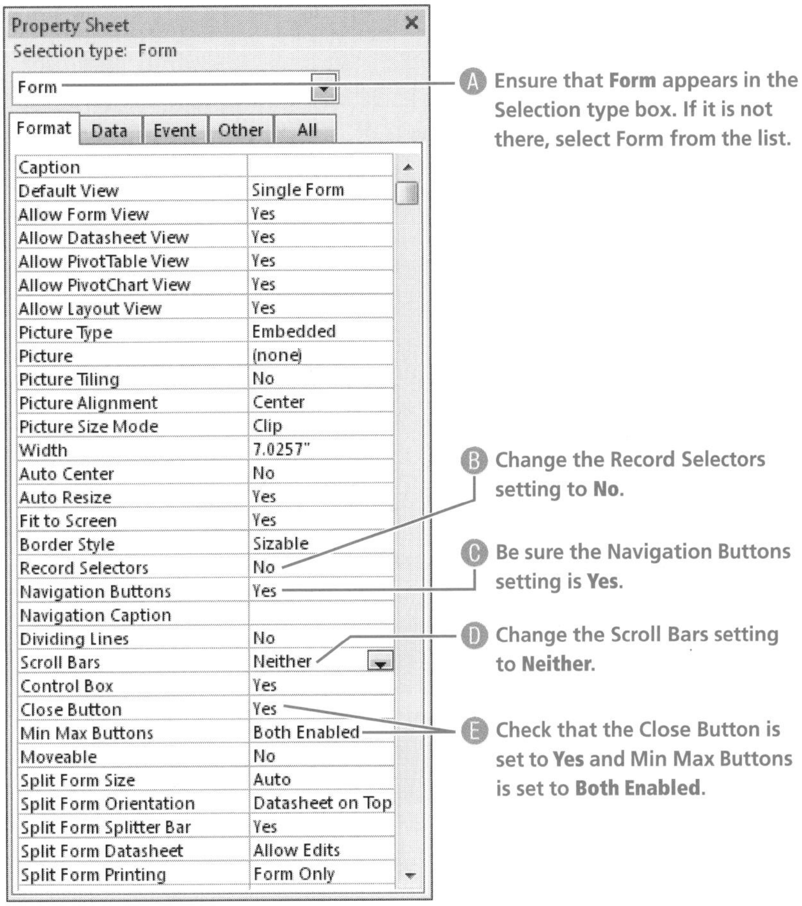

3. **Save** changes and switch to Form View to display the form. Leave the form **open** for the next exercise.

Setting a Form Tab Order

Video Lesson labyrinthelab.com/videos

Regardless of the arrangement of bound and unbound controls on a form, when you use a form to enter records, Access moves from one field to the next each time you press Tab or Enter. Access moves among fields on a form in the order in which the fields appear in the table datasheet or query grid on which you base the form. When you design custom forms, the order in which you position controls may be significantly different from the order in which they appear in a table datasheet. As a result, pressing Tab sometimes makes it appear as if Access is just randomly hopping from control to control all over the form.

You can control the order in which Access moves among form fields by changing the tab order—the order in which Access moves among onscreen fields. Setting a tab order enables you to view data on the form and access each field in the order it appears onscreen. In addition, you may want to set a tab order to skip fields containing data that should not be changed, move onscreen to fields in the order in which fields appear on a printed form, or move to fields in a more logical order than the current setting. The Tab Order dialog box contains the setting to control tab order:

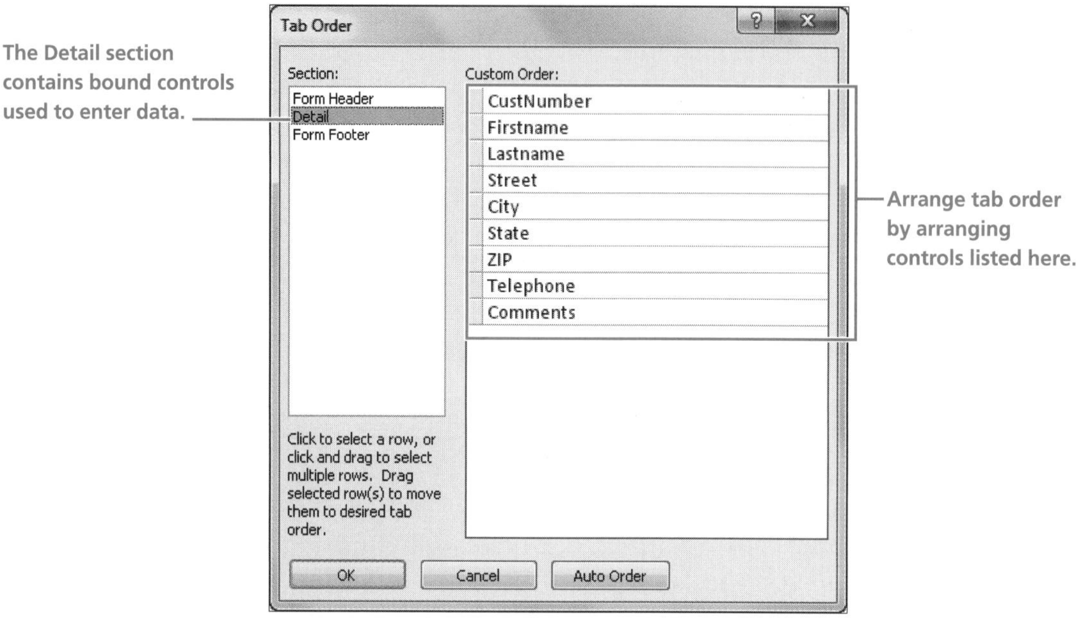

DEVELOP YOUR SKILLS 7.4.4

Set Tab Order

In this exercise, you will set the tab order for the Customers form.

1. Display the **Customers** form in Form View and **press** [Tab] to advance through all fields on the form.
2. Switch to **Design View**.
3. Choose **Design→Tools→Tab Order** on the Ribbon to open the Tab Order dialog box.
4. Follow these steps to move the Telephone field to a new position in the order:

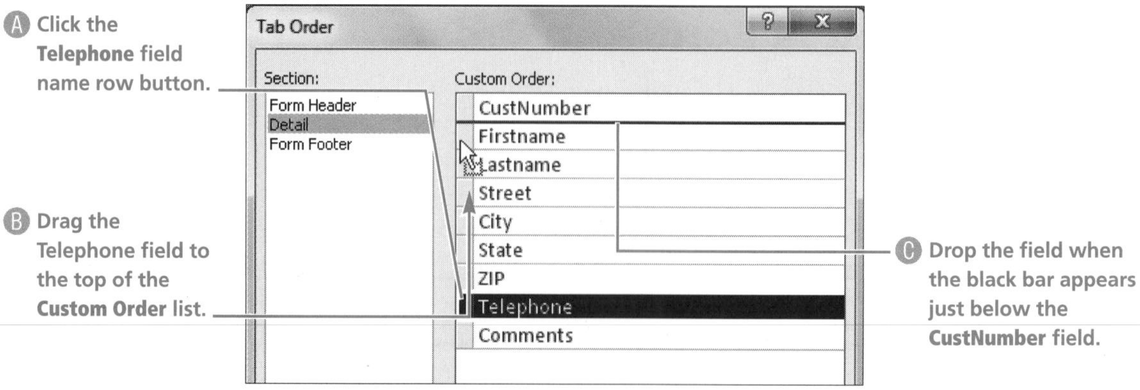

5. Repeat the procedures outlined above to move the ZIP field and place it after the State field; then click OK.

Test the Tab Order

6. Display the form in **Form View** and **press** Tab to move through all fields.
   Access now moves from field to field, starting at the top left of the form and stopping at each field to the Comments field.
7. **Save** changes to the form and then **close** it.

7.5 Creating Multiple Items Forms

Video Lesson labyrinthelab.com/videos

Custom designing a form or creating simple forms are good ways to format forms when you want to be able to display or print a copy of each record individually. Sometimes, however, you will want to print a list of multiple items in a table using a layout that is more appropriate for printing and distributing than a table datasheet. The Multiple Items form is used to create and format a form for those occasions.

When you create a Multiple Items form, Access creates a form that resembles a datasheet because data appears in rows and columns. However, you can customize a Multiple Item form using the same tools and procedures you used to create the custom form in this lesson. For example, you can adjust the size of control text boxes, add graphic elements to the form, and enhance the form with color.

Applying Themes to Forms

Themes are form designs that were developed by a group of professional design specialists and are similar to templates in Word and PowerPoint. Themes contain color, font, and control settings to enhance the form. You can use the Themes to quickly and efficiently format all sections of a form as well as form controls. Point to a Theme to identify the Theme name in the ScreenTip and scroll down the Themes palette to display additional Themes.

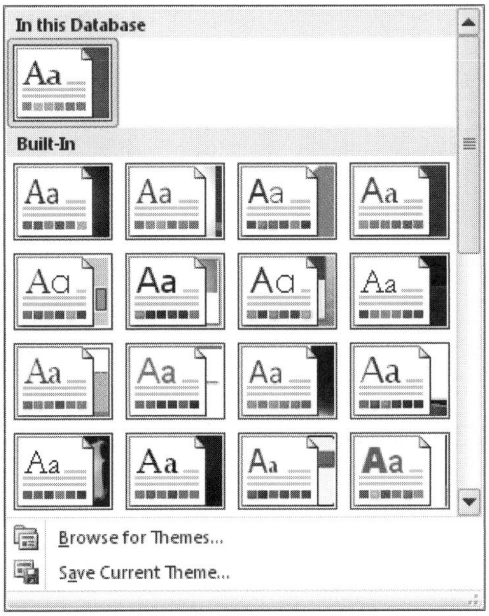

The palette of Themes available for formatting Access database forms are arranged alphabetically.

QUICK REFERENCE	APPLYING THEMES TO A FORM
Task	**Procedure**
Apply Themes to a form	■ Display the form to which you want to apply the Theme in Design View. ■ Choose Design→Themes→Themes on the Ribbon. ■ Choose the Themes design to apply.

DEVELOP YOUR SKILLS 7.5.1

Create a Multiple Item Form and Apply Themes

In this exercise, you will create a new form for the Inventory table and apply a Theme to the form.

1. Select the **Inventory** table in the Navigation Pane.
2. Choose **Create→Forms→More Forms→Multiple Items** on the Ribbon.
   Access creates a new form and displays the form in Layout View.
3. Drag the **right borders** of each column heading to a size appropriate to the data; then **scroll down** the form to ensure that data is displayed properly for all records.
4. Switch to **Design View** and click a blank area of the form pane below the form palette to ensure that the theme you select applies to the entire form.
5. Choose **Design→Themes→Themes** **menu ▾** on the Ribbon.

TIP: Themes are arranged alphabetically.

6. Choose the **Paper Theme** and then select the graphic in the Form Header section and **press** Delete to remove it.
7. Switch back for **Form View** and review the form.
8. **Save** the form using the form name **`Inventory`** and leave it **open**.

7.6 Printing Forms

Video Lesson labyrinthelab.com/videos

Procedures for printing forms are basically the same procedures you would use to print files in other programs, such as Word, Excel, and PowerPoint. As with each different program, print options in Access vary with different objects. For example, you can print individual forms—one for each record—or print forms so that they print continuously, one after another, on standard sheets of paper.

FROM THE KEYBOARD

[Ctrl]+[P] to open the Print dialog box

Printing All Record Forms

The default setting in Access for printing forms is to print all records with multiple records (forms) on each sheet. The easiest way to determine how forms will look when you print them is to display them in Print Preview before printing.

The File→Print→Quick Print command sends all records directly to the printer without opening the Print dialog box.

Printing Selected Record Forms

When you want to print selected records, you would first select the record and then display it in Print Preview. When you click the Print button on the Ribbon in Print Preview, the Print dialog box opens so that you can choose the option to print all records, the records numbers you want to print, or the selected records.

QUICK REFERENCE **PRINTING RECORD FORMS**

Task	Procedure
Print all records	■ Choose File→Print→Quick Print.
Print specific records	■ Press [Ctrl]+[P] and set the print options for the records to print. *or* ■ Choose File→Print→Print and set the print options for the records to print.

DEVELOP YOUR SKILLS 7.6.1

Print Forms

In this exercise, you will print a copy of one customer record form and the inventory using the Inventory form.

1. Display the **Inventory** form and choose **File→Print→Quick Print** to print all records in the Multiple Items form.
2. **Close** [X] the form and open the Customers form.
3. **Press** [Ctrl]+[P] to open the Print dialog box and follow these steps to print record 5:

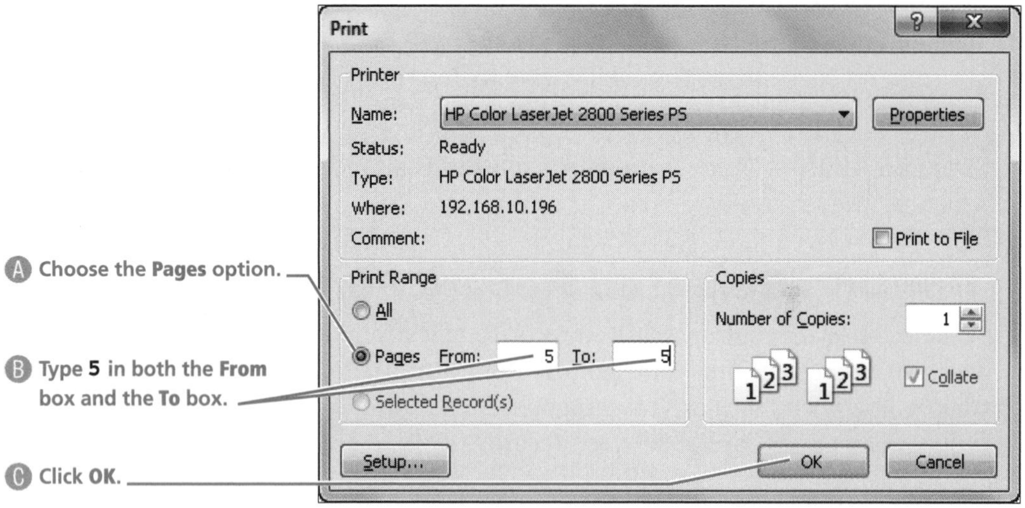

4. **Close** [X] all open database objects, **close** the database, and **exit** Access.

7.7 Concepts Review

Concepts Review labyrinthelab.com/acc10

To check your knowledge of the key concepts introduced in this lesson, complete the Concepts Review quiz by going to the URL listed above. If your classroom is using Labyrinth eLab, you may complete the Concepts Review quiz from within your eLab course.

Reinforce Your Skills

REINFORCE YOUR SKILLS 7.1

Create a Multiple Item Form and Apply a Theme

Raritan Clinic East has initiated a plan to improve the looks of the data entry forms for their database. The datasheet that displays Ana Mills' schedule can be formatted to display the data more attractively using a Multiple Items form. In this exercise, you will create a new Multiple Items form using the Ana Mills Schedule query and apply a Theme to the form.

1. **Open** the rs-Raritan Clinic database from the Lesson 07 folder and **save** the file in the current format using the filename **`rs-Raritan Clinic Forms`**.
2. Open the **Navigation Pane** and select the **Ana Mills Schedule** query.
3. Choose **Create→Forms→More Forms→Multiple Items** to create the new form.
4. Switch to **Design View**.
5. Choose **Arrange→Themes→Themes** on the Ribbon and then choose **Concourse** from the Themes palette.
6. **Save** the form using the default form name Access assigns and **print** a copy of the form in Form View.

REINFORCE YOUR SKILLS 7.2

Add a Form Header Graphic and Adjust Control Position

The generic graphic that appears at the top of the Multiple Items form needs to be replaced by a more appropriate image. In this exercise, you will replace the generic graphic with a new image in your rs-Raritan Clinic Forms database using techniques different from those used in the Develop Your Skills exercises. You will also size and position controls and set the image Size Mode property to control how the image appears in the control box.

1. Open the **Ana Mills Schedule** form in Design View.
2. Click the **graphic** in the Form Header section and **press** [Delete] to remove it.
3. Drag the **Detail** section bar down on the form to make the Form Header section larger.
4. Point to the **ruler** at the position even with the column headings in the Form Header section and **click** to select all three headings.
5. **Tap** the [↓] key on the keyboard to move the control labels down closer to the Detail section bar.
6. Click the **Ana Mills Schedule** title and then drag it to the right edge of the form.
7. Choose **Design→Controls→Image** on the Ribbon and **click** close to the upper left corner of the Form Header section to create the image box.
   Access opens the Insert Picture dialog box.
8. **Open** the Lesson 07 folder and **double-click** the rs-Staff Logo file to insert it into the image box.

Size the Image Control and Set Properties

9. **Drag** the handles on the image control to size the image to about 1" by 1" on the form rulers.
10. **Press** [F4] to open the Property Sheet, choose the **Format→Size Mode** property and choose **Stretch** from the Size Mode list.
11. Adjust the position of other controls in the Form Header appropriately for the form.
12. **Save** the changes, **print** a copy of the form in Form View, and then **close** it.

REINFORCE YOUR SKILLS 7.3

Create a Form in Design View

Another form that Raritan Clinic East administrators would like you to customize is a form to enter new resources. In this exercise, you will create a new form using Design View for the Resources table in your rs-Raritan Clinic Forms database.

1. Choose **Create→Forms→Form Design** on the Ribbon to create the new form.
2. Choose **Design→Tools→Add Existing Fields** on the Ribbon to open the Field List panel, if necessary.
3. **Expand** (+) the Resources table in the Field List to display all fields in the table.
4. Drag the fields from the Field List and position them as shown:

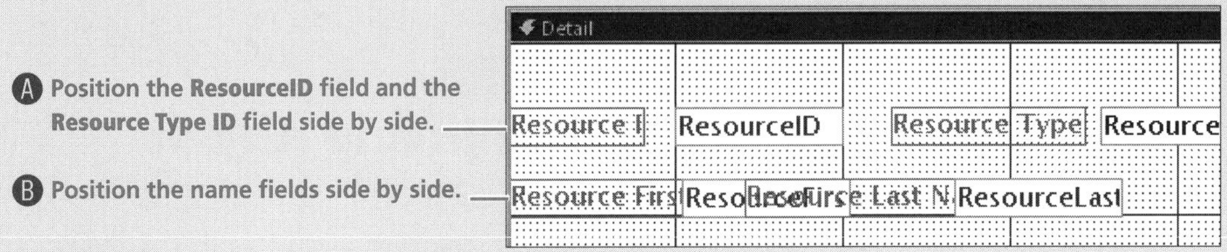

5. **Close** the Field List and then select the **Resource Last Name** control label and **press** [Delete] to remove it.
6. Click the **Resource First Name** control label and edit the text to read **`Name`**.
7. **Save** the form using the form name **`Resources`** and leave it **open**.

REINFORCE YOUR SKILLS 7.4

Format and Enhance Form Controls

The Resources form now needs to be formatted to enhance its appearance. In this exercise, you will modify the Resources form, apply font formats and control backgrounds, and size and arrange controls on the form.

1. Display your **Resources** form in Design View and **press** [F4] to open the Property Sheet.
2. Click each of the following controls to select them and make changes to the properties identified:

Control	Property	Value
Resource ID Label	Caption	Staff ID:
	Fore Color	Dark Blue 5
	Back Color	Light Blue 2
	Font Name	Comic Sans MS
	Font Size	14
Resource ID Text Box	Fore Color	Light Blue 2
	Back Color	Dark Blue
	Font Name	Comic Sans MS
	Font Size	14
	Special Effect	Raised

3. **Size** the control boxes to fit the format of the labels and data.

Use the Format Painter

4. Click the **Staff ID** label.
5. Choose **Format→Font** on the Ribbon and double-click the **Format Painter** to turn it on.
6. Click the two additional **control labels** on the form to paint the format onto it; then **press** [Esc] to turn off the Painter.
7. Repeat the procedures outlined in **steps 5 and 6** to paint the format of the ResourceID text box onto the three additional control text boxes on the form.
   Recognize that the form needs additional work. You will complete the form in the following exercises.
8. **Save** changes to the form and **print** a copy of the form.

REINFORCE YOUR SKILLS 7.5

Size, Align, and Distribute Controls

The Resources form is coming along nicely. After you formatted the controls in the previous exercise, you may have noticed that the alignment was off, the size of the text in the labels is too large to show completely, and the spacing between the controls is off. In this exercise, you will use tools on the Arrange *tab of the Ribbon to correct these problems. As you work, you will use additional alignment and distribution controls available on the Ribbon.*

1. **Press** [Ctrl]+[A] select all controls on the form.
2. Choose **Arrange→Sizing & Ordering→Size/Space→To Tallest** on the Ribbon to size the controls uniformly.
3. Select the **Name**, **ResourceFirstName**, and **ResourceLastName** controls.
4. Choose **Arrange→Sizing & Ordering→Align→Bottom** on the Ribbon to align the controls.
5. Repeat the procedures outlined in **step 4** to align the controls on the top row of the form.
6. Size and position individual control labels and text boxes appropriately on the form.
7. Select the four controls on the **top** row.
8. Choose **Arrange→Sizing & Ordering→Size/Space→Equal Horizontal** on the Ribbon.
9. **Save** changes to the form and **print** a copy of the form.

REINFORCE YOUR SKILLS 7.6

Format Form Sections

The Resources form is almost complete. In this exercise, you will add a Form Header to the form, format sections of the form, and set a tab order for the form.

1. Display the **Resources** form in Design View, **right-click** the Detail section bar, and select **Form Header/Footer**.
2. Drag the **Detail** section bar down to about the 1" mark on the vertical ruler to make the Form Header section larger.
3. Click the **Form Header** section bar to select the section and **press** [F4] to open the Property Sheet.
4. Click the **Back Color** property and select **Dark Blue** from the color palette, and then press [Enter].
5. Choose **Design→Header/Footer→Title** on the Ribbon and type `Staff Resource` in the title box.
6. **Delete** the small box to the left of the title.

7. Select the title control again and set the following properties for the control:

Property	Setting
Fore Color	Light Blue 2
Font Name	Comic Sans MS
Font Size	36

8. **Resize** controls as necessary to display values completely.
9. Choose **Design→Header/Footer→Logo** on the Ribbon to place a logo box on the Form Header.
10. **Open** your Lesson 07 folder and **double-click** the rs-Raritan Clinic Logo.jpg file to add it to the form.
11. Set the **Size Mode** property for the image control to **Stretch** and size the control.
12. Click the **Detail** section bar and set the Back Color property to **Light Blue 2**.
13. Choose **Design→Tools→Tab Order** on the Ribbon and drag the ResourceTypeID field up in the Custom Order list so that it appears second in the list.
14. Switch to **Form View** and review the form. Your form should resemble the one shown here:

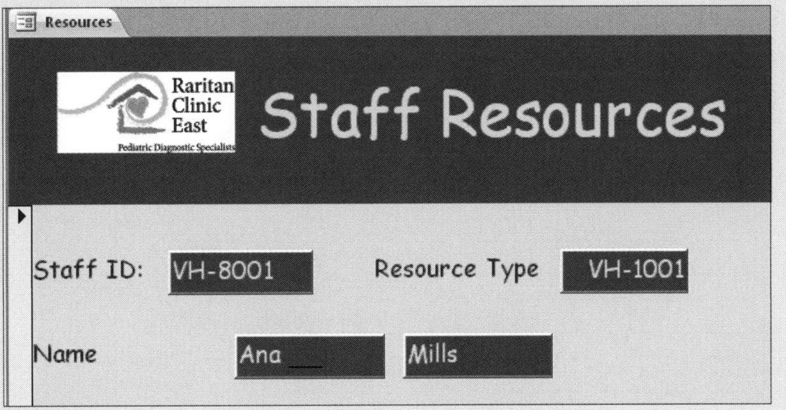

15. **Save** changes to the form and **print** a copy of the form.
16. **Close** the database and then **exit** Access.

Apply Your Skills

APPLY YOUR SKILLS 7.1

Create a Form in Design View

Lagniappe Cruises has just purchased five new ships from another cruise line. They are updating the database to enter the ship descriptions prior to scheduling and entering cruises for the new year. Before they start their update, they have asked you to create custom forms for the database. In this exercise, you will create the shell of two forms for the Lagniappe Cruises Forms database.

1. **Open** the as-Lagniappe Cruises database from the Lesson 07 folder and **save** the database using the file name **`as-Lagniappe Cruises Forms`**.
2. Create a new form using **Design View** and add fields from the Ships table to the form.
3. Position and size the field controls on the form so that they appear similar to the following illustration:

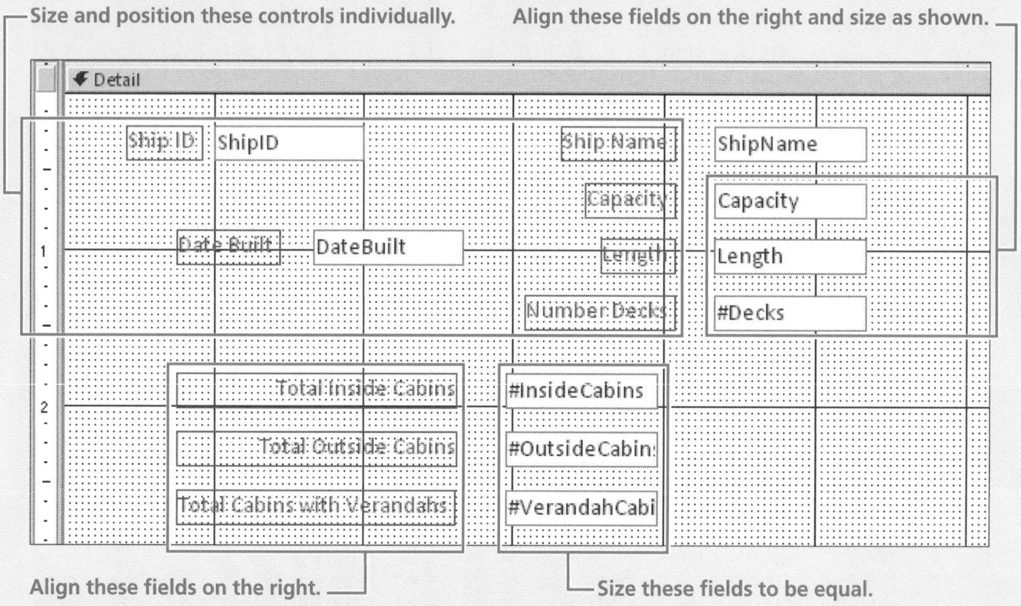

4. **Save** the form as **`Ships`** and **print** a copy of the form.
5. Create another new form and add fields from the **Cruises** table.
6. **Size**, **align**, and **position** fields so that they display all table data.
7. Use **alignment** and **distribution** tools to set the controls.
8. **Save** the form as **`Lagniappe Cruises`** and **print** a copy of the form.

APPLY YOUR SKILLS 7.2

Edit Labels, Format Controls, and Set Properties

You now have the shells for the forms you want to create and they have been approved by management. In this exercise, you will format the controls, edit form labels, and set properties for the as-Lagniappe Cruises Forms database using two different design color schemes to submit so that management can identify the format they prefer.

1. Display the **Ships** form in the as-Lagniappe Cruises Forms database in Design View and open the **Property Sheet**.
2. Select all of the control labels and set the following properties:

Property	Value
Back Color	Orange
Fore Color	Aqua Blue 5
Font Name	Lucida Handwriting
Font Size	12
Font Weight	Extra Bold

3. Adjust the **size** and **position** of the controls after formatting the labels.
4. Select all the control text boxes and set the following properties:

Property	Value
Back Color	Aqua Blue 5
Fore Color	Orange
Font Size	12
Font Weight	Extra Bold

5. Set the **Detail** section background color to **Green 3** and **save** changes.
6. Display the **Lagniappe Cruises** form in Design View and apply a theme to each section of the form.
   Select the theme you prefer—no restrictions here.
7. Adjust the **sizes** and **positions** of the controls.
8. Set the following captions for associated labels:

Label	Caption
Inside Cabin	Inside Cabin Cost:
Outside Cabin	Outside Cabin Cost:
Verandah	Verandah Cost:

9. Select all controls and size the height of all controls to display all text.
10. **Save** changes to the form, **print** a copy, and then **close** it.

APPLY YOUR SKILLS 7.3

Add and Format Form Headers

Adding a header that contains a logo to the top of the forms will further enhance the form. In this exercise, you will create a header for one form in the as-Lagniappe Cruises Forms database.

1. Display the Lagniappe Cruises form in **Design View** and display the **header** and **footer** sections.
2. Add a **title** to the Form Header and type **`Lagniappe Cruises`** in the title box.
3. Format the **header title** by selecting appropriate properties.
4. Make the **Form Header** section larger and add a label below the main title to serve as a subtitle to the header that contains the text **`Annual Schedule`**.
5. Use the **Format Painter** to copy the format from the main title to the subtitle and change the font setting for the subtitle to distinguish it from the main title.
6. Add the as-Lagniappe Cruises Logo.gif file from the Lesson 07 folder to the **Form Header** section and anchor it to stretch down and right.
7. **Save** the form, **print** a copy, and then **close** it.

APPLY YOUR SKILLS 7.4

Set a Tab Order

The arrangement of fields on the forms in the as-Lagniappe Cruises Forms database is positioned in such a way that the natural tab order is out of order. In this exercise, you will set the tab order for both forms in the database.

1. Display the **Lagniappe Cruises** form in **Design View** and select the Detail section.
2. Display the **Tab Order** dialog box.
3. Position the fields in the **Custom Order** list to move through the fields on the form following this path:
   Ship Name→Sail Date→Destination→Inside Cabin Cost→Outside Cabin Cost→Verandah Cost→Itinerary
4. **Save** the changes and **close** it.
5. Repeat the procedures outlined in **steps 1–4** to set the tab order for fields in the Ships form.
6. **Save** the changes and **close** it, **close** the database, and **exit** Access.

Critical Thinking & Work-Readiness Skills

In the course of working through the following Microsoft Office-based Critical Thinking exercises, you will also be utilizing various work-readiness skills, some of which are listed next to each exercise. Go to labyrinthelab.com/workreadiness *to learn more about the work-readiness skills.*

7.1 Design a Database Form for a Company Coffee Shop

Green Clean has a privately-owned coffee shop named First Perk, which uses a separate database. The database contains several tables and queries but needs forms for data entry. At the request of the manager, you will create a form for the Orders table in the First Perk database and graphically enhance the form using features you learned in this lesson. As you work, explore additional features and tools, and apply them as you like. Use the ct-First Perk database and logo (Lesson 07 folder) to complete your form and save the database as a new file named **`ct-First Perk Forms`**. Name the form appropriately and then print a copy of it.

WORK-READINESS SKILLS APPLIED

- Organizing and maintaining information
- Serving clients/customers
- Solving problems

7.2 Design a Database Form for A Company Gift Shop

The Flower Pot, a local florist, rents space in the Green Clean corporate offices. Green Clean purchases fresh floral arrangements from The Flower Pot and sends them to new corporate customers. The owner of The Flower Pot has asked for your help designing a form for the Customers table in The Flower Pot database. Use the ct-The Flower Pot database (Lesson 07 folder) to create a new database named **`ct-The Flower Pot Forms`**. Create a custom form for the Customers table in the new database. Explore additional features as you customize the form and be creative in your design. Be sure to add a graphic to the form—use either the graphic contained in the **`Lesson 07`** folder or one you find on your own. Name the form appropriately and print a copy of it.

WORK-READINESS SKILLS APPLIED

- Organizing and maintaining information
- Serving clients/customers
- Solving problems

7.3 Design and Create Forms for Green Clean

Green Clean has additional tables for which they would like custom forms. Use the Green Clean Forms database that you created at the beginning of this lesson and create a new form for each table for which there is currently no form. Customize the forms using your creativity and print a copy of each form.

WORK-READINESS SKILLS APPLIED

- Organizing and maintaining information
- Serving clients/customers
- Seeing things in the mind's eye

Creating Custom Reports

LESSON OUTLINE

LEARNING OBJECTIVES

After studying this lesson, you will be able to:

- Create a report using Report Design View
- Modify reports
- Add report sorting and grouping levels
- Add graphics and other design elements to reports
- Add calculated controls to a report and calculate totals
- Create a labels report using the Labels Wizard

Reports summarize data into meaningful information for printing. As a result, reports serve as output objects for Access databases. Although reports often summarize data from a single database table, they can display data from multiple tables and queries. Whether you are customizing forms or reports, you can use many of the same techniques to position fields, group date, and add pictures and titles. One important feature of customized reports includes the capability of adding calculated controls to generate report subtotals and totals. In this lesson, you will create a report in Design view, modify the report, format the report, and create calculated and total controls on the report.

Student Resources labyrinthelab.com/acc10

Reporting Data

Customized input forms are great database objects for entering data, displaying data, and printing raw data for records contained in database tables. Most businesses, however, want to summarize data, filter it, or sort it using one of the fields contained in a database table. Green Clean is no exception—the company wants a new report that summarizes the sales for each employee and prints the data with sales totals. Allen Sedgwick, manager of Computer Information Systems, has agreed to create a custom report to meet these needs. The first draft of the report design is shown here. After the CEO reviews the design, he completes a sample report for review by other executives.

green clean

Sales Report

Order ID	Number Ordered	Price	Item Total	Sales Totals
Adams				
GC-24	10	$65.82	$658.24	
GC-35	10	$64.57	$645.70	
GC-5	2	$59.58	$119.15	
GC-5	2	$55.43	$110.86	
GC-5	2	$59.58	$119.15	
GC-10	1	$6.50	$6.50	
GC-10	1	$91.42	$91.42	
	28	57.5567		$1,751.02

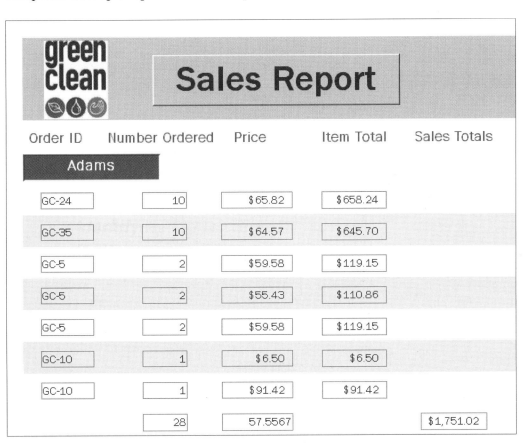

8.1 Using Report Design View

Video Lesson labyrinthelab.com/videos

Report Design View displays the sections of each report, identifies each control contained in the report, and holds the basic layout and design elements for the report. If you have explored Form Design View, you know that it enabled you to view different form sections such as Form Header, Detail, and Form Footer. Report Design View displays numerous sections as well, and each is identified by a section bar. In addition to the Detail section, the report sections used most frequently include the Report Header/Footer sections and Page Header/Footer sections.

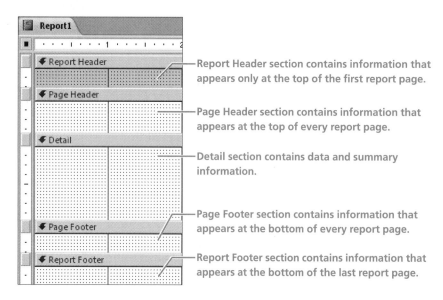

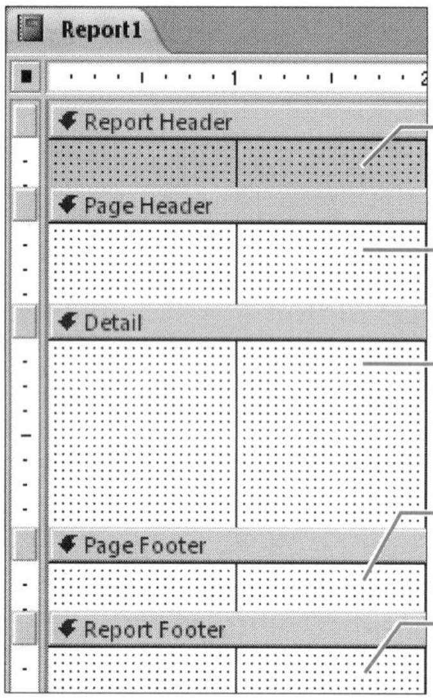

Report Header section contains information that appears only at the top of the first report page.

Page Header section contains information that appears at the top of every report page.

Detail section contains data and summary information.

Page Footer section contains information that appears at the bottom of every report page.

Report Footer section contains information that appears at the bottom of the last report page.

Identifying Report Design View Elements

The design elements you will see as you work with Report Design View resemble those that were available for designing forms. If you have customized forms, many of these elements will be familiar to you.

Tools in the Controls group of the Report Design tab on the Ribbon enable you to add graphics and other types of controls.

Four tabs appear in the Report Design Tools area of the Ribbon.

Scroll buttons display additional control tools.

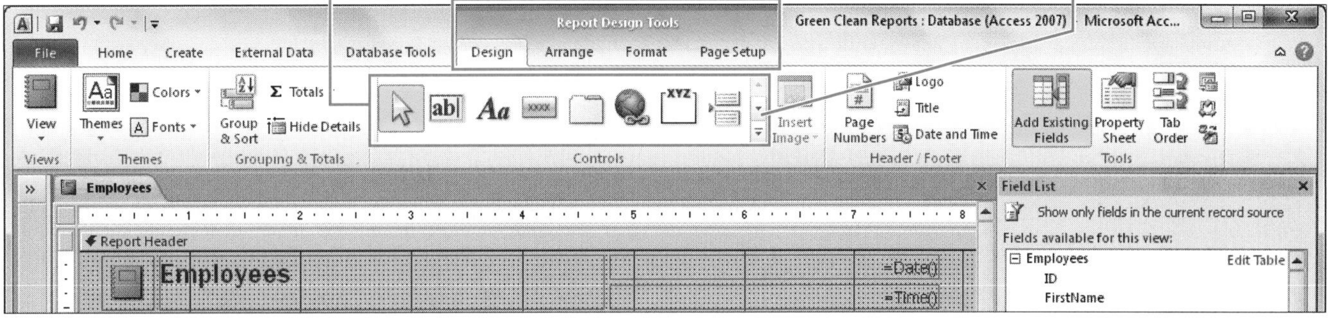

Section bars identify the report sections.

The Report Header section holds the report title, date, and time the report was compiled.

The Field List panel displays fields available from the table or query on which the form is based.

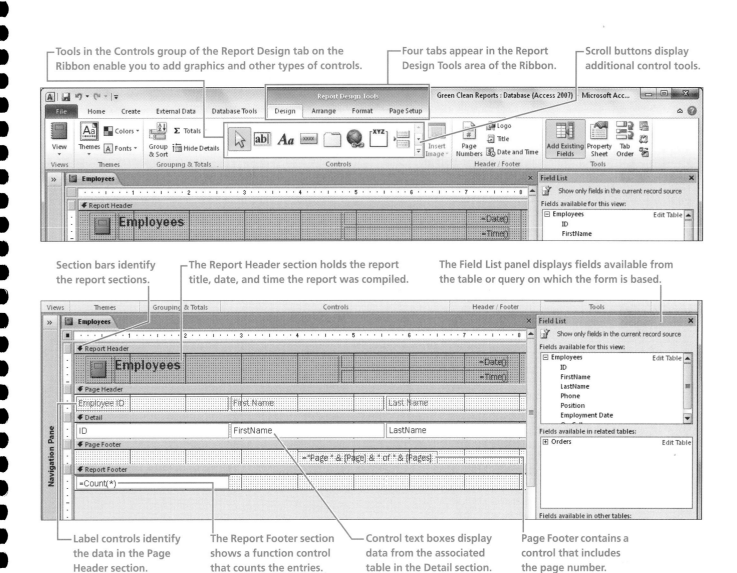

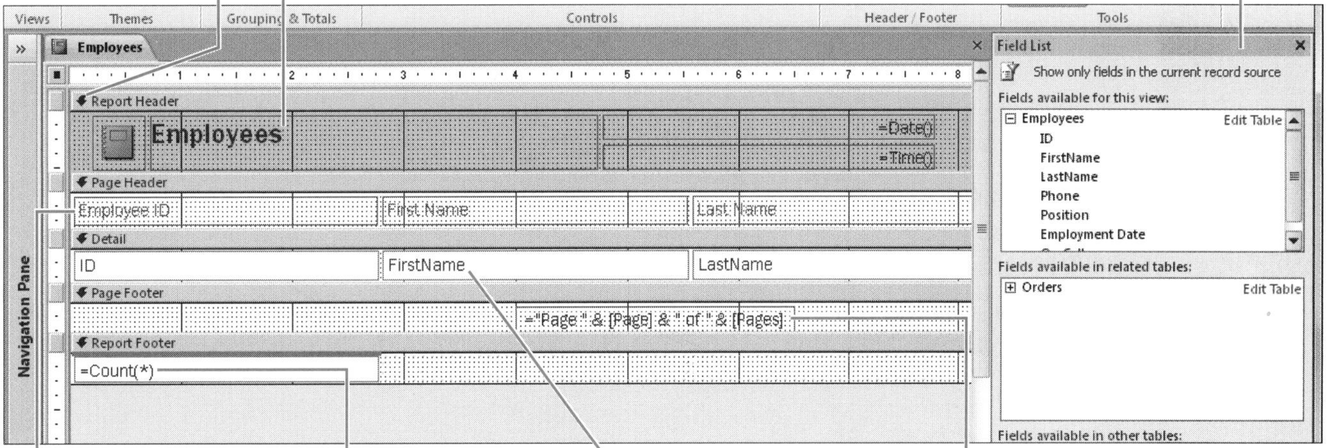

Label controls identify the data in the Page Header section.

The Report Footer section shows a function control that counts the entries.

Control text boxes display data from the associated table in the Detail section.

Page Footer contains a control that includes the page number.

QUICK REFERENCE — IDENTIFYING REPORT DESIGN ELEMENTS

Report Element	Description
Sections	The major parts of the report, such as the Report Header, the Report Footer, the Detail, the Page Header, and the Page Footer. Section bars divide report sections.
Controls	Items on a form or report that display data, perform actions, and decorate the object. Access uses three main types of controls on reports—bound controls, unbound controls, and calculated controls. Each control consists of two parts—control label and control text box—that are tied to a field in a database table.
Bound control	A control that ties, or binds, data displayed on a report to a field in a database table so that the field value appears on the report. Bound controls normally appear in the Detail section of a report.
Unbound control	An item on a report that is independent of data and fields in a database table. Unbound controls can be lines, rectangles, pictures, and so forth. Unbound controls can appear in any report section.

QUICK REFERENCE — IDENTIFYING REPORT DESIGN ELEMENTS (continued)

Report Element	Description
Calculated control	A control that is tied to an expression created for the report or to a calculated field constructed in a query. Calculated controls normally appear in the Detail or Report Footer section of the report.
Control label	The part of a control that contains text to identify the data displayed on the report. Normally, the control label text is the field name or caption set for the field. For example, *Employee Number* is a label that identifies the *Employee#* field.
Control text box	The part of a control that displays data from a field in an Access table. For example, *ToliP01* is the data contained in the *Employee#* field.
Report Header/ Footer	The sections of a report that contain text, pictures, and other items that are repeated at the top (header) or bottom (footer) of the report.
Detail section	The main section of a report, which normally displays data from database tables that varies from record to record.
Page Header/ Footer	The sections of a report that contain text and other items that are repeated at the top (header) or bottom (footer) of every *page* of the report.
Group Header/ Footer	The sections that identify a field on which data in the report is grouped (*Group* Header) and enables you to report summary data for the group (*Group* Footer). The name of the grouped field appears in the *Group* Header and Footer bars.

Displaying Report Views

As you design reports, you will find that there are three views available—Report View, Layout View, and Design View. Working with these views is similar to working with views in Form design. Each view has its own distinct purpose:

QUICK REFERENCE — USING REPORT VIEWS

View	Description	Use this view to . . .
Report	Displays when you open a report. Report View does not permit modification of formatting or data. Report View presents the report as it will print.	▪ Preview a report layout before printing. ▪ View summarized data.
Layout	Displays a "run" of a report layout with sample data displayed so that you can size and position controls appropriately. You can modify formatting in this view as well as use many of the same design tools that are available in Design View.	▪ Preview a report with data. ▪ Size and position controls and ensure that all data contained in a field displays properly on a report. ▪ Add a limited number of controls to a report.
Design	Displays the design palette containing sections and section bars, controls, labels, design elements, and other report features. In addition, tools for adding many additional controls are available in Design View.	▪ Format and design a report. ▪ Add summary data and controls. ▪ Add design elements.

Switching Between Views

It is a simple matter to switch between Layout View and Design View when required tools are available only in Design View. The Home and Design tabs on the Ribbon both contain controls that allow you to switch the View.

QUICK REFERENCE	SWITCHING AMONG REPORT VIEWS
Task	**Procedure**
Display Report View	■ Open a report. ■ From Layout View, choose Design→Views→View menu ▼ and choose Report View. *or* ■ From any view, choose Home→Views→View menu ▼ and choose Report View.
Display Design View	■ Right-click a report name in the Navigation Pane and choose Design View. *or* ■ From Layout View, choose Design→Views→View menu ▼ and choose Design View. *or* ■ Open a report and choose Home→Views→View menu ▼ and choose Design View.
Display Layout View	■ Right-click a report name in the Navigation Pane and choose Layout View. *or* ■ From Design View, choose Format→Views→View menu ▼ and choose Layout View. *or* ■ Open a report and choose Home→Views→View menu ▼ and choose Layout View.

DEVELOP YOUR SKILLS 8.1.1

Display Report Views

In this exercise, you will open an existing report and display it in all three report views.

1. **Open** the Green Clean database from your Lesson 08 folder and **save** the file using the filename **`Green Clean Reports`**.
2. Open the **Employees** report to display the report in **Report View**.
3. Choose **Home→Views→View menu ▼** on the Ribbon and choose Design View.
4. Follow these steps to locate associated controls:

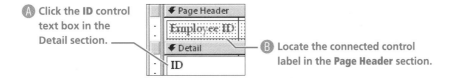

Ⓐ Click the **ID** control text box in the Detail section.

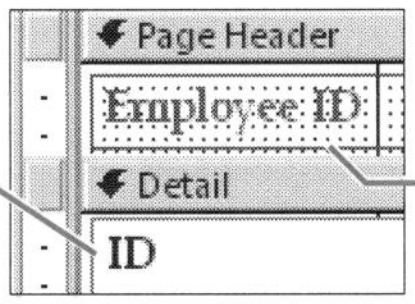

Ⓑ Locate the connected control label in the **Page Header** section.

5. Choose **Home→Views→View menu ▼** on the Ribbon and choose **Layout View**.

NOTE

From this point forward, the instructions for switching views will simply instruct you to switch to the appropriate view. For example, switch to Design View or switch to Layout View.

6. Follow these steps to identify features in Layout View:

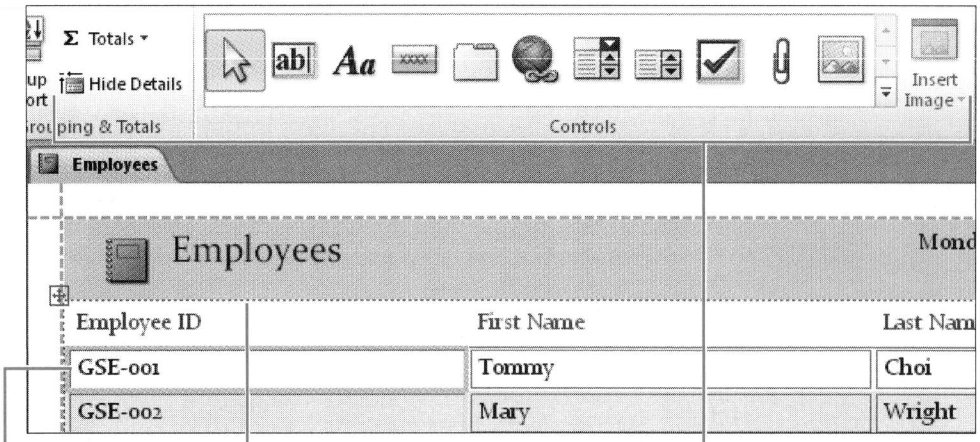

Ⓐ Click EmployeeID value **GSE-001**.

Ⓑ Locate the associated column heading that displays a **dotted border**.

Ⓒ Review the tools on the Design tab of the Ribbon.

7. **Close** the report without saving changes.

NOTE The appearance of buttons on the Ribbon may be different from those shown here due to screen resolution and monitor size.

8.2 Creating a Report in Design View

Video Lesson labyrinthelab.com/videos

Now that you are familiar with many of the features found in reports and Report Design View, you may find building a report from scratch using Design View more efficient—especially when you want to include only a few fields from a table in the report. When you create a new report in Design View, you select the table that contains the fields you want to include in the report, drag fields to report sections, and insert group sections. When the basic structure of the report is complete, you can add controls to create titles, add graphics, and insert footer controls. Many of the tools you use to build a report in Design View appear on the Design tab of the Ribbon.

Working with Report Controls

The controls you selected on the report when it was displayed in both Layout View and Design View are bound controls that display data contained in database tables. Access has three basic types of controls that you can add to reports—and these controls parallel those you can add to forms.

- **Bound controls**—Controls that tie, or bind, data displayed on a report to a field in a database table so that the field value (data) appears on the report. Bound controls normally appear in the Detail section of a report.
- **Unbound controls**—Lines and other drawn objects, text for titles, graphics, and so forth—independent items you can add to a report to enhance the appearance of the report.

- **Calculated controls**—Controls that are tied to an expression, aggregate function, or calculated field constructed in a query or built directly on the report. Calculated controls normally appear in the Detail or report Footer section of the report.

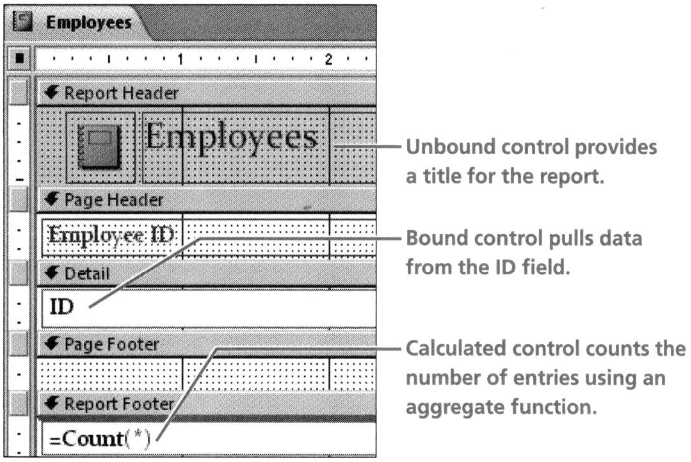

Adding Controls from Field Lists

The Field List contains a list of all tables that appear in the database. You can expand a table to display all fields contained in the table. In addition, when you add a field from one table to the list, a section of the Field List panel shows tables that are related to the selected table. As a result, you can expand related tables and use fields from related tables in the report.

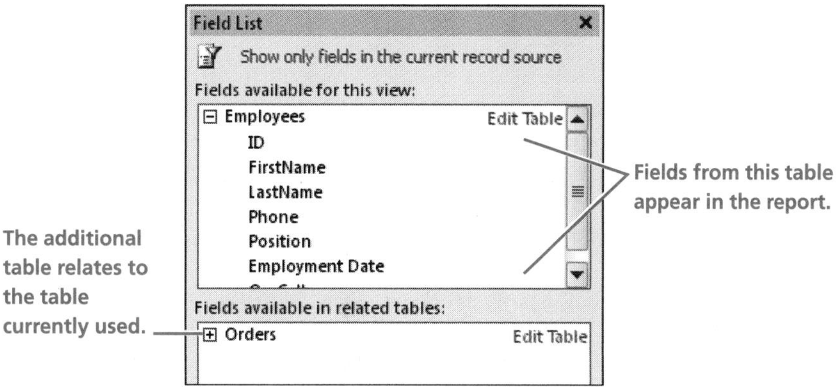

Dragging Controls from the Field List

Adding bound controls from the available field list to a section of a report is as simple as dragging the control and dropping it into the appropriate report section. When you add a field from the field list to the report page, Access places both the control label and control text box for a bound control on the report. Because most reports display the control label in the Page Header section, you can cut it from the Detail section and paste it into the Page Header section or delete it from the Detail section and add a new label control to the Page Header section. If you try to drag the field to the Page Header section and then move the control text box to the Detail section, Access moves both parts of the control to the Detail section.

FROM THE KEYBOARD

Ctrl+X to cut an object

Ctrl+V to past an object

Adding Controls from the Ribbon

When you display a report in Design View, Access displays control tools on the Ribbon used to add unbound controls to reports. Tools used to change font and add color to reports are also available in Layout View. As a result, working in Design View as you design and set controls on reports is essential.

QUICK REFERENCE	ADDING CONTROLS TO A REPORT
Task	**Procedure**
Drag controls	■ Display the report in Layout or Design View. ■ Choose Design→Tools→Add Existing Fields to open the Field List. ■ Expand the table containing the field you want to add. ■ Drag the field onto the report and position it where you want it.
Add controls from a Ribbon	■ Display the report in Design View. ■ Choose Design→Controls and click the control type button you want to add to the report. ■ Click or drag a control in the position and size you want on the report.

NOTE A limited number of controls is available in Layout View. As a result, most people use Design View to add controls to reports because more controls are available when Design View is displayed.

DEVELOP YOUR SKILLS 8.2.1

Create a Report in Design View

In this exercise, you will create a report in Design View, add bound controls to the report, and position control labels in the Page Header.

1. Choose **Create→Reports→Report Design** on the Ribbon.
   Access creates a new blank report and displays it in Design view. The Field List should also be displayed.

TIP If the Field List is closed, choose Design→Tools→Add Existing Fields on the Ribbon to open it.

2. Follow these steps to add a field to the report:

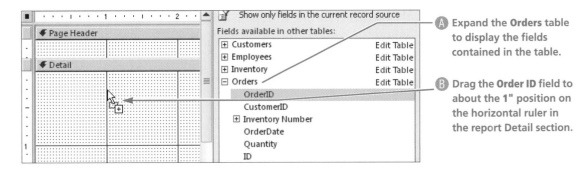

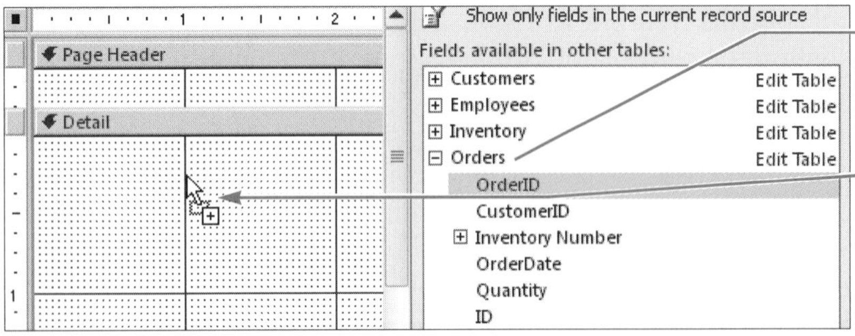

Ⓐ Expand the **Orders** table to display the fields contained in the table.

Ⓑ Drag the **Order ID** field to about the **1"** position on the horizontal ruler in the report Detail section.

3. Follow these steps to move the Order ID control label to the Page Header section:

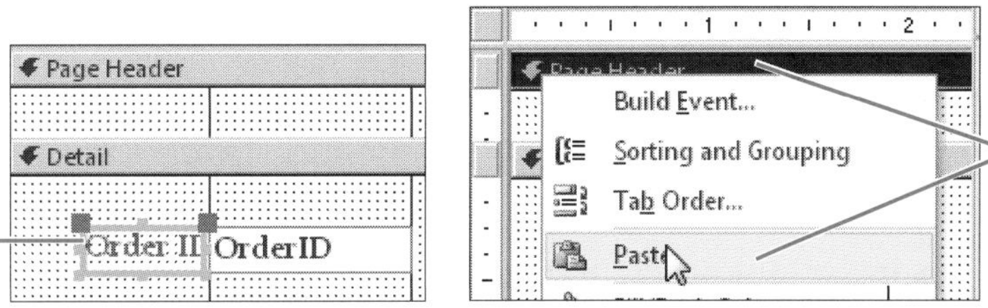

Access places the label at the left edge of the Page Header section.

4. Drag the **Order ID** control text box to the left and position it below the Order ID label.
5. Repeat the procedures outlined in **steps 2–4** to add fields, position labels, and move text boxes to the positions shown in the following figure.

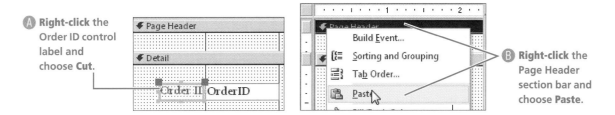

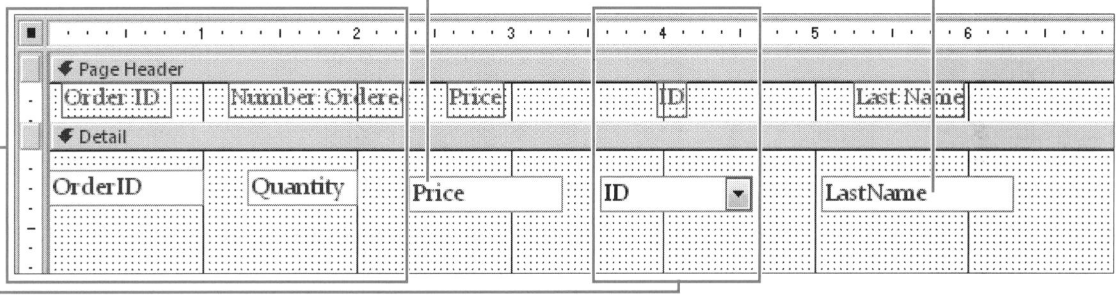

6. **Save** the report using the Report name `Sales Report` and leave it **open**.
After saving the report, Access places the name of the table from which each control text box came before the field name and separates the table name from the field name using a period (.). For example, you will notice Orders. OrderID in the first control text box in the Detail section of the report after saving it.

8.3 Modifying a Report in Design View

Video Lesson labyrinthelab.com/videos

As you work in Report Design View, you can use many of the techniques and features used to customize forms to format and enhance data controls on the report and set background colors, etc. One important difference between customizing forms and reports is the general layout of the object. Reports normally display control labels in the Report Header section so that they serve as column headings. Control text boxes appear in the Detail section. In addition, when you group summary data in a report, Access displays Group sections that hold group titles, group field control labels, and group summary data.

Adding Report Sorting and Grouping Levels

The report you have created is relatively sparse—it currently contains only five fields and column headings. If you printed the report now, it would resemble a table datasheet. However, by grouping the data using the *Employee* field, you create a report that provides information that is easier to locate. A *group* is a collection of records that has at least one data element in common. For example, if you want to display all vendors with offices in the same state, you could group on the State field. A group consists of a Group Header, records, and a Group Footer. Grouping records enables you to separate records visually on a report and display introductory and summary data for each group.

Order ID	Number Ordered	Price	Item Total	Sales Totals
Navarro				
GC-30	2	$65.82	$131.65	
GC-30	2	$74.57	$149.14	
GC-20	50	$6.50	$325.05	
GC-7	7	$83.55	$584.82	
GC-4	6	$55.90	$335.41	
	67	57.2682		$1,526.06
Riso-Neff				
GC-12	5	$48.47	$242.33	
	5	48.466		$242.33

Data records are grouped for each employee.

Using the Group, Sort, and Total Panel

To view the grouping and sorting settings, you display the Group, Sort, and Total panel at the bottom of the Access window. You can then use the panel to add groups and sorting settings or review them after you set them. You can also set up groups using commands on the shortcut menus and then study the effect in the Group, Sort, and Total panel. You can set properties in the Group, Sort, and Total panel to display or hide group headers and footers. Additional properties enable you to tell Access how to group data, set a grouping interval, and set group properties for keeping items in a group together on a page.

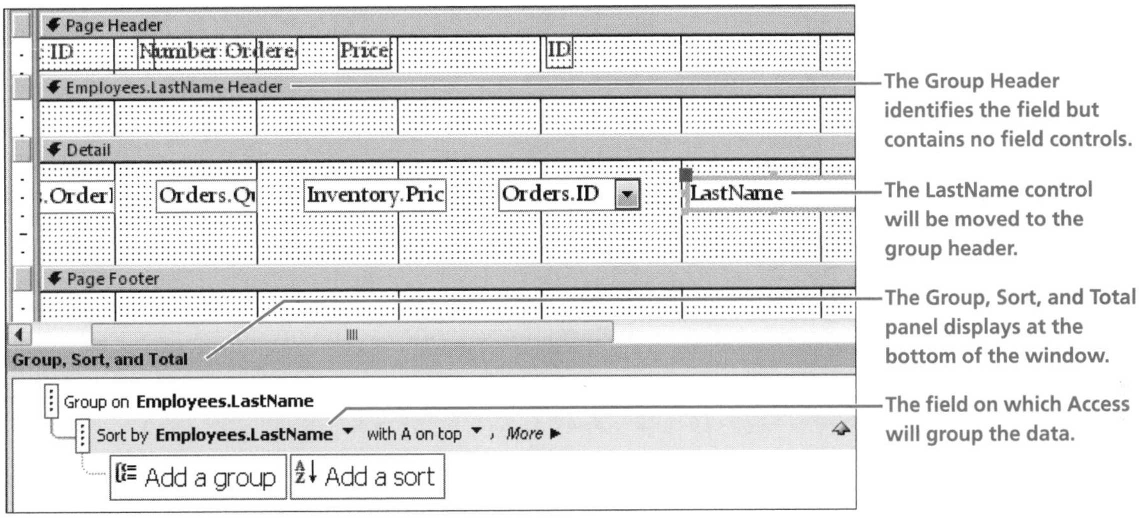

Page Header
ID
Number Ordered
Price
ID
Employees.LastName Header
Detail
Orders.Q
Inventory.Pric
Orders.ID
LastName
Page Footer
Group, Sort, and Total
Group on Employees.LastName
Sort by Employees.LastName with A on top, More
Add a group
Add a sort
The Group Header identifies the field but contains no field controls.
The LastName control will be moved to the group header.
The Group, Sort, and Total panel displays at the bottom of the window.
The field on which Access will group the data.

Working with Group Sections

Setting a group and sort order does not automatically place the column heading or field control text box on the report. It simply sets the grouping and sorting order and creates a section on the report to hold the controls. After you set up the groups, it is important to either move the group field from the Detail section to the Group section or add it to the Group section. By placing the field text box control in the Group Header section, Access groups all entries by the field you choose and each item in the Group Header section prints only one time—at the start of a new group value.

Creating Multi-Level Groupings

Access provides multi-level grouping for records on a report. If, for example, you want to print invoices that group items ordered by type or category for each customer, you would use two-level grouping. You can set multiple groups using the Sort, Group, and Total panel or by choosing the command from the shortcut menu.

QUICK REFERENCE	ADDING SORT AND GROUP LEVELS
Task	**Procedure**
Display the panel using the Ribbon in Layout or Design View	■ Display the report is Design View. ■ Choose Design→Grouping & Totals→Group & Sort on the Ribbon.
Add group level	■ Right-click the field on which you want to group data records. ■ Choose Group On *Field Name*.
Add sort order	■ Right-click the field on which you want to sort data or groups. ■ Choose Sort A to Z or Smallest to Largest *or* ■ Choose Sort Z to A or Largest to Smallest .

NOTE

The command you see when you right-click a field name to group or sort depends on the data type of the field.

DEVELOP YOUR SKILLS 8.3.1

Add a Group and Sort Level to a Report

In this exercise, you will add a group and sort level to the Sales Report in your Green Clean Reports database that groups records by sales person.

1. Display the Sales Report in **Design View**.
2. **Right-click** the Employees.LastName text box control in the Detail section of the report and choose **Group On**.
   Access displays a group header for the new group.
3. Choose **Design→Grouping & Totals→Group & Sort** on the Ribbon to open the Group, Sort, and Total panel.
4. **Right-click** the LastName text box control in the Detail section again and choose **Cut**.
5. **Right-click** the Employee.LastName Header section bar and choose **Paste** to place the text box control in the group header section.
6. Follow these steps to set a sort order using the Group, Sort, and Total panel:

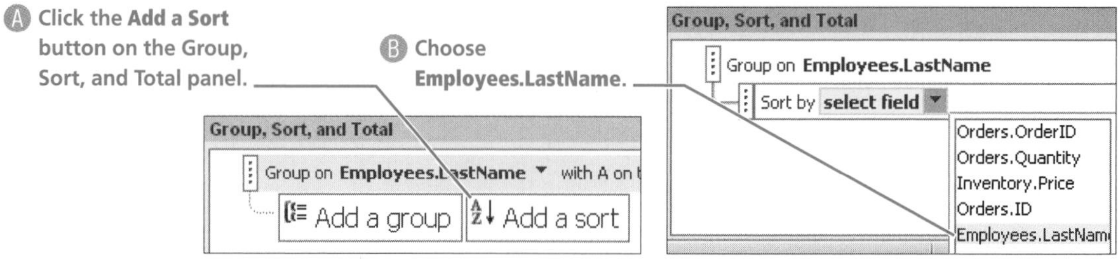

7. **Right-click** each of the following controls in the sections identified and choose **Delete** to remove them:

Section	Control
Page Header	ID label and Last Name label
Detail	Orders.ID ID

8. Scroll **down** to the bottom of the report palette and follow these steps to size the Detail section:

Ⓐ Drag the **Page Footer** section bar up.

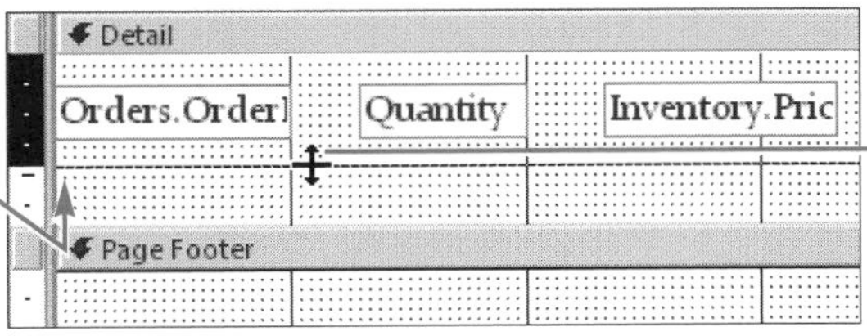

Ⓑ Drop the section bar just below the **Detail** section controls.

9. Switch to **Report View** and compare your report to the one shown here:

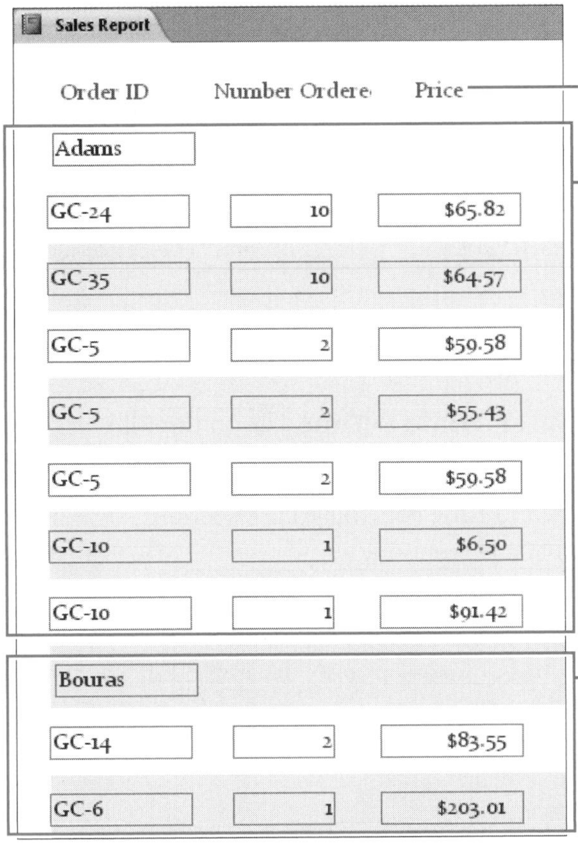

Notice that the column headings need to be fixed.

All orders for Adams display first.

Orders for Bouras start.

10. **Save** changes to the report, and then **close** it.

Adding Date and Time Data to a Report

Video Lesson labyrinthelab.com/videos

When reports change frequently and are printed regularly, keeping track of the most current report can be a challenge. You can add a date and/or time to the footer section of a report to help you track the reports. When you add the date and time controls, Access places the controls in the Report Header section by default. You can move them to the section in which you want them to appear or leave them in the Report Header section.

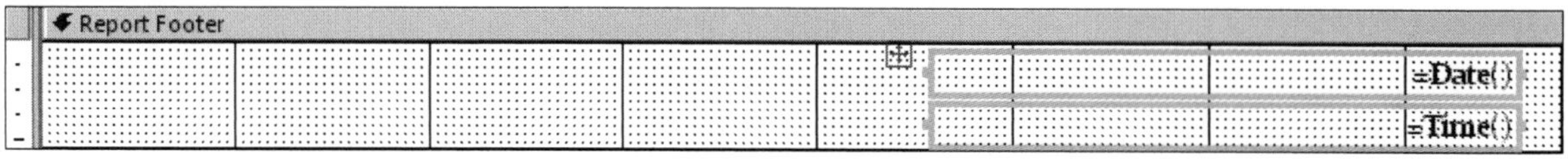

The Date and Time controls in the Report Footer section.

QUICK REFERENCE **ADDING DATE AND TIME FIELDS TO A REPORT**

Task	Procedure
Add a date field to a report	■ Choose Design→Header/Footer→Date & Time on the Ribbon. ■ Check the Include Date checkbox, select the format option, and click OK.
Add a time field to a report	■ Choose Design→Header/Footer→Date & Time on the Ribbon. ■ Check the Include Time checkbox, select the format option and click OK.

DEVELOP YOUR SKILLS 8.3.2

Add Date and Time to the Page Footer Section

In this exercise, you will add the date and time to the Page Footer section of your report.

1. Display the Sales Report in **Design View**.
2. Choose **Design→Header/Footer→Date & Time** on the Ribbon to open the Date and Time dialog box.
3. Follow these steps to add date and time controls to the section:

Ⓐ Check the **Include Date** checkbox.

Ⓑ Choose the **mm/dd/yyyy** format option.

Ⓒ Check the **Include Time** checkbox.

Ⓓ Choose the **hh:mm time** option and then **press** Enter.

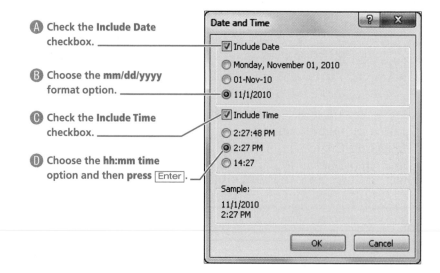

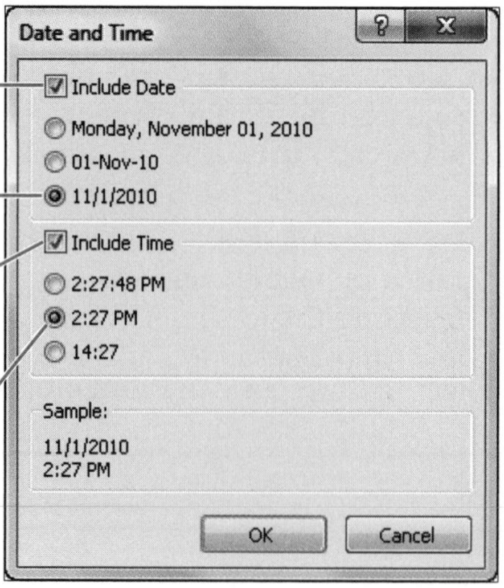

4. Click the **=Date()** control and **press** [Shift] and click **=Time()** control to select both controls in the Report Header section.
5. **Right-click** one selected control and choose **Cut**; then **right-click** the Page Footer section and choose **Paste**.
6. Drag the controls to the right side of the **Page Footer** section.
7. **Save** changes to the report and then **close** it.

Adding Graphics to Reports

Video Lesson labyrinthelab.com/videos

Adding a graphic to a report that identifies the business can be an effective way to associate a corporate logo with a company. Graphics also dress up a report to make it more interesting to those who use the report. Access contains two basic tools for adding a graphic to a report or form:

- The Image or Insert Image control: Enables you to position a graphic on any report or form section
- The Logo control: Places a logo in the Report Header section of a report and the Form Header section of a form

QUICK REFERENCE	ADDING A GRAPHIC TO A REPORT OR FORM
Task	**Procedure**
Add a logo to a report or form	■ Display the form or report in Design View. ■ Choose Design→Header/Footer→Logo on the Ribbon.
Add a picture to a report or form:	■ Display the report or form in Design View. ■ Choose Design→Controls→Insert Image *or* ■ Choose Design→Controls→Image.

Applying Themes

When you build the report in Design View, you add design elements to the report manually. Formatting a report using the Themes feature enables you to create a report using color schemes available in Access. Themes contain design elements such as background color, font and font size, and so forth that quickly dress up a report without the tedious formatting of controls and background manually and individually. Applying a Theme improves the readability of the report and can make it look more professional. However, caution should be used when applying a Theme to a report because applying Access Themes reformats all objects in the active database with the color scheme defined in the Theme. Because reports are designed for printing, the formatting Themes apply is much more subtle for reports than it is for forms. As a result, you may wish to apply additional formatting controls after you apply the Theme.

QUICK REFERENCE	APPLYING THEMES TO FORMS AND REPORTS
Task	**Procedure**
Apply a Theme	■ Prepare the report or form to which you want to apply the Theme. ■ Display the report or form in Design View or Layout View. ■ Choose Design→Themes→Themes on the Ribbon. ■ Select the Theme to apply.

DEVELOP YOUR SKILLS 8.3.3

Add a Logo and Apply Themes to a Report

In this exercise, you will add a logo to the Report Header section and apply a Theme to the report.

1. Display the Sales Report in **Design View**.
2. Choose **Design→Header/Footer→Logo** on the Ribbon to open the Insert Picture dialog box.
3. **Open** the Lesson 08 folder and **double-click** the GC Logo.jpg filename.
   Access places the logo in the upper left corner of the Report Header section, as shown. Notice, too, that there is a long narrow box immediately to the right and attached to the logo. This box is used to type a title on the report. You can delete the title box or use it to add a title to the report.

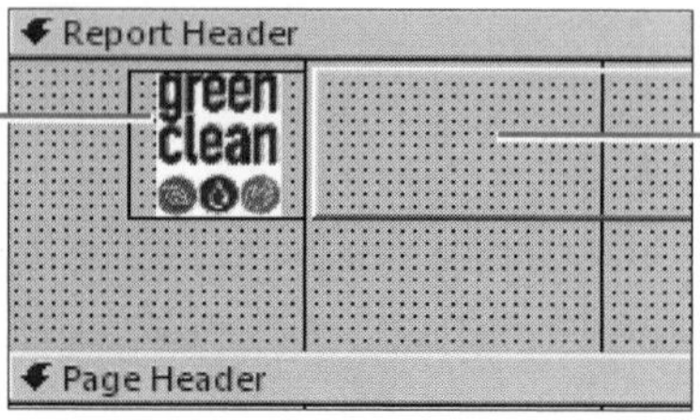

4. Choose **Design→Themes→Themes** on the Ribbon and choose the **Trek Theme** from the palette.
   Although you have selected a different format, you may see no difference in the report until you display the report in Layout or Report View.
5. **Save** changes to the report and then **close** it.

Formatting Controls

Video Lesson labyrinthelab.com/videos

Now that you have the elements you want to include on the report set, you can format the controls to make them visually effective. Aligning controls to ensure that the column headings appear where you want them, adding a title, and formatting the text and sizes of each control are just a few of the edits you can make. The procedures you use to format, align, size, and position the controls are the same procedures you used to format controls on forms.

Selecting Controls

Each control, as you are aware, contains two parts: the control label and the control text box. When you add a field control to a report, Access places both parts of the control on the report and you can reposition the label as you did earlier in this lesson. To select multiple controls at the same time, you have several options: Clicking each control individually, selecting all controls along a horizontal or vertical line, or outlining an area of the report to select all controls within the area.

Sizing Controls

An important part of any report is reporting and summarizing accurate data. Another part of reporting data is ensuring that the data is fully displayed in the report. To accomplish that, you need to size controls on the report so that they are large enough to display the longest data value for each field. Sizing controls is often more efficient in Layout View because the report is running and data displays as you size the control. As a result, you can be certain that data for all records has adequate space.

As you work in Layout View, you will find that active controls display a heavier border than inactive controls. Use the borders to size the control just as you used handles on active controls while working in Design View—drag the border. As you drag the border for the active record, the controls for that field on all records also resize, just as they would if you resized the control in Design View. The main difference is that in Design View, you only see one control—not multiple controls that represent multiple records.

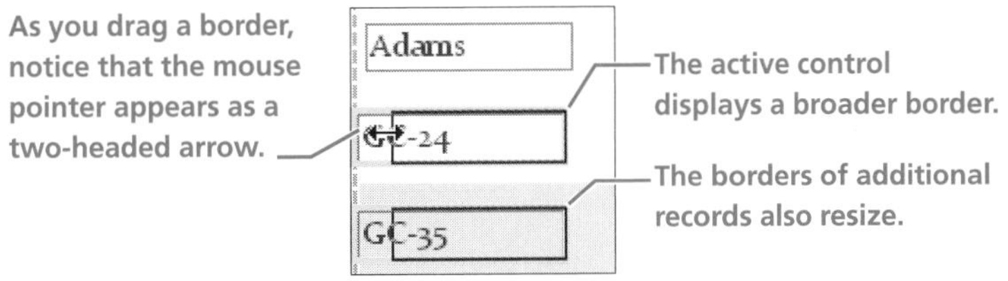

Identifying Mouse Shapes

The mouse pointer shape is important as you work with Design as well as Layout View. You've already seen how the mouse pointer appears when you are sizing a control. In addition to the sizing mouse shape, you will see the white pointer arrow accompanied by a four-headed black arrow that you use to move a control.

DEVELOP YOUR SKILLS 8.3.4

Set, Size, and Align Report Controls

In this exercise, you will use Layout View to reposition controls on the Sales Report, align the controls, and size the controls to fit the data.

1. Display the Sales Report in **Layout View** and follow these steps to size the control:

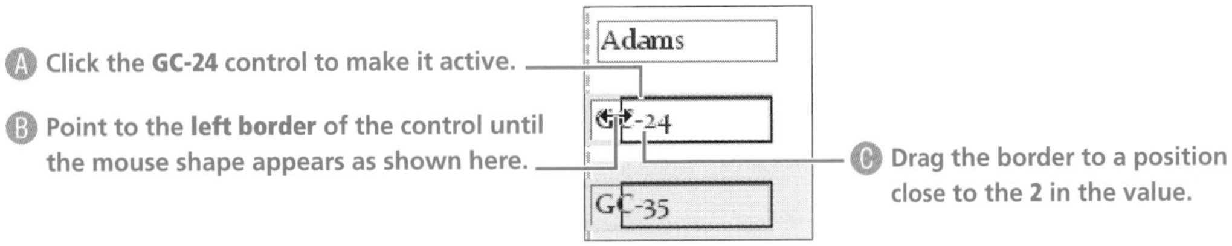

A Click the GC-24 control to make it active.
B Point to the left border of the control until the mouse shape appears as shown here.
Adams
GC-24
GC-35
C Drag the border to a position close to the 2 in the value.

2. Follow these steps to position and align the column headings:

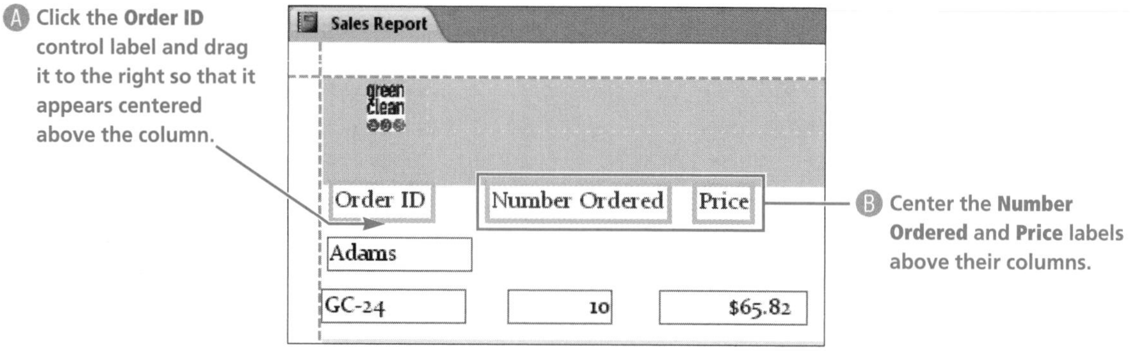

A Click the **Order ID** control label and drag it to the right so that it appears centered above the column.
Sales Report
green clean
Order ID
Number Ordered
Price
Adams
GC-24
10
$65.82
B Center the **Number Ordered** and **Price** labels above their columns.

3. **Save** changes to the report and then **close** it.

Adding a Title to the Report Header

Video Lesson labyrinthelab.com/videos

Titles identify the purpose of forms and reports and often contain only the name of the company. You can use Design View to add a Label control containing the title to the report or use the Title tool that is designed to specifically add and format a title. Both tools are available in both Design and Layout Views. When you use the Title tool to create a title for a form or report, Access places the report name as the title, positions it in the appropriate section of the form or report, and formats the text using the default settings. You can then change the text format if desired, using tools on the Ribbon and the Property Sheet. Because you have already applied a *Theme* to the report in this lesson, Access will format the title using settings that are active in the Theme.

Using the Property Sheet

The Property Sheet contains property settings that control the way many elements of database objects function and look. You have already used the Property Sheet to set data format in tables and form properties. Many of the same properties are available for controlling data display in reports.

DEVELOP YOUR SKILLS 8.3.5

Add a Report Title and Format Text

In this exercise, you will use Layout View to add a report title and format text using the Property Sheet and Ribbon.

1. Display the Sales Report in **Layout View**.
2. Choose **Design→Header/Footer→Title** on the Ribbon.
   Access places a title with the text Sales Report beside the logo at the top of the report.
3. Click the **Sales Report** title and choose **Design→Tools→Property Sheet** on the Ribbon.

4. Change the following property settings to format the title control:

Property	Setting
Special Effect	Raised
Font Size	36
Width	3.5"
Text Align	Center
Font Weight	Semi-bold

5. Drag the **lower-right corner** of the logo and size it to the height of the title.
6. **Save** changes and display the report in **Design View**.

Format Label Controls

7. Click the **vertical ruler** on the left in the Page Header section to select all column headings and choose **Format→Font→Bold** and set the size to **14**.
8. Size each **column heading** so that all text displays and then adjust the positions of the column headings appropriately.
9. Select the **Employees.LastName** text box in the Group Header section and set the following properties in the Property Sheet:

Property	Value
Back Color	Brown, Accent 2
Special Effect	Sunken
Fore Color	White
Font Size	16
Text Align	Center

10. Adjust the size of the **Employees.LastName** control and the height of each report section.
11. **Save** changes to the report, view the report in **Layout View** and make additional adjustments, and then **close** it.

8.4 Performing Report Calculations

Video Lesson labyrinthelab.com/videos

By now, you have most likely learned how to create a calculated field in a query grid. You can also create *calculated controls* in reports that calculate values for each record based on data contained in table or query fields. When you position the calculated control in the Detail section, Access calculates the value for each record in the report each time you open and print the report. As a result, each time you update a value used in a calculated control, Access updates the report the next time you open and print it. The Text Box control is one tool you can use to create a control on the report to hold the calculated expression.

Using the Expression Builder

You can create a calculated control by typing control field names and operators (multiply, divide, add, subtract, etc.), symbols such as square brackets, and so forth, directly in the Control Source property in the Properties dialog box. However, many people find it easier to use the Expression Builder dialog box to build the expression. The Expression Builder dialog box contains features that enable you to paste field names and operators required for the expression right into the dialog box so that you can review the expression. You can use the Expression Builder to create expressions in queries, on forms, or on reports.

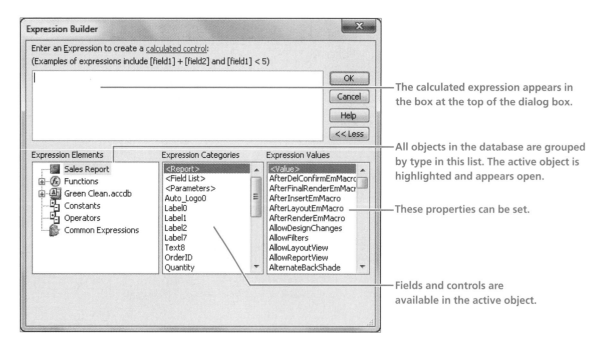

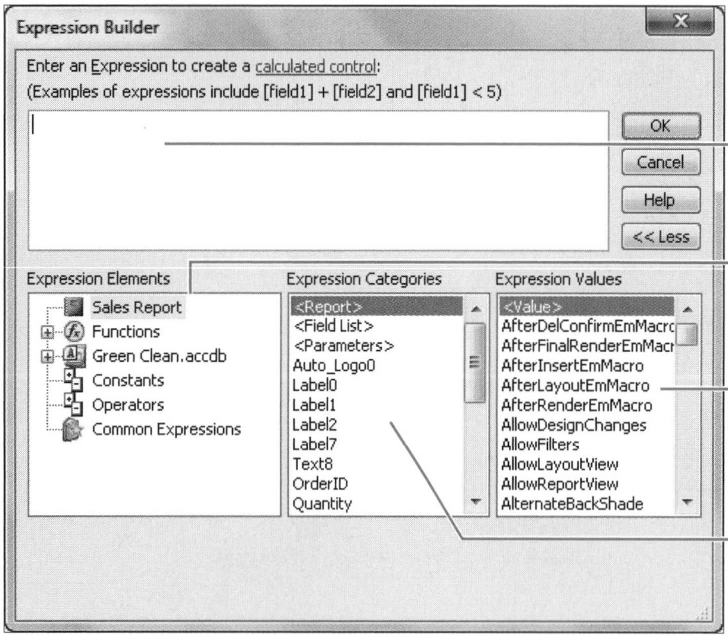

The calculated expression appears in the box at the top of the dialog box.

All objects in the database are grouped by type in this list. The active object is highlighted and appears open.

These properties can be set.

Fields and controls are available in the active object.

QUICK REFERENCE	USING THE EXPRESSION BUILDER
Task	**Procedure**
Create a calculated control using the Expression Builder	■ Display the form or report in Design View. ■ Choose Design→Controls→Text Box [ab] on the Ribbon. ■ Click or draw the control on the form or report palette where you want it to appear. ■ Press [F4] to display the Property Sheet and click the Data tab. ■ Click the Control Source property and then click the Build [...] button. ■ Add fields, operators, and other elements to the expression and then click OK.

DEVELOP YOUR SKILLS 8.4.1

Add a Calculated Control Using the Expression Builder

In this exercise, you will add a bound calculated control to the report that calculates the total sales for each record. You will use the Expression Builder and Design View.

1. Display the Sales Report in **Design View** and display the right side of the **Detail** section.
2. Choose **Design→Controls→Text Box** [ab] on the Ribbon and follow these steps to create the control to hold the calculation:

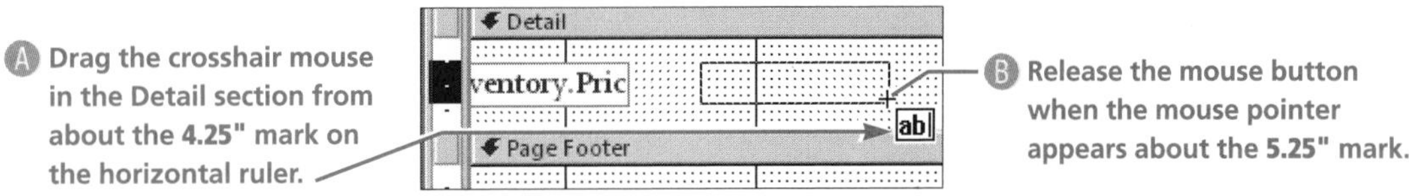

A Drag the crosshair mouse in the Detail section from about the 4.25" mark on the horizontal ruler.
Detail
ventory.Pric
ab
Page Footer
B Release the mouse button when the mouse pointer appears about the 5.25" mark.

Access places a unbound control text box on the report along with a control label.

3. **Press** [F4] to display the Property Sheet and follow these steps to open the Expression Builder:

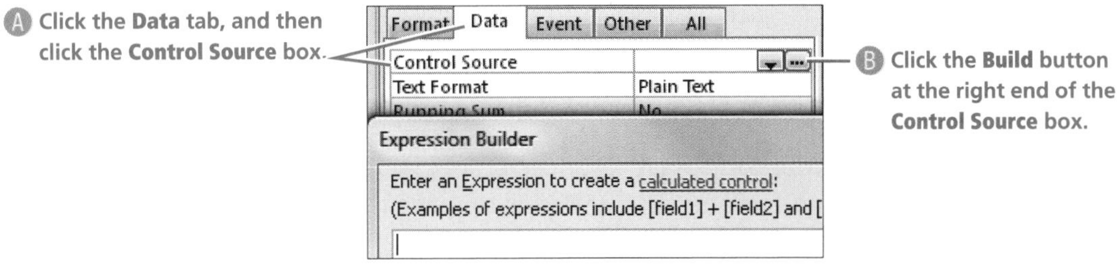

A Click the Data tab, and then click the Control Source box.
Format
Data
Event
Other
All
Control Source
Text Format
Plain Text
Expression Builder
Enter an Expression to create a calculated control:
(Examples of expressions include [field1] + [field2] and [
B Click the Build button at the right end of the Control Source box.

Access opens the Expression Builder dialog box.

4. Follow these steps to create the calculated expression:

Ⓐ **Click Sales Report** in the Expression Elements list.

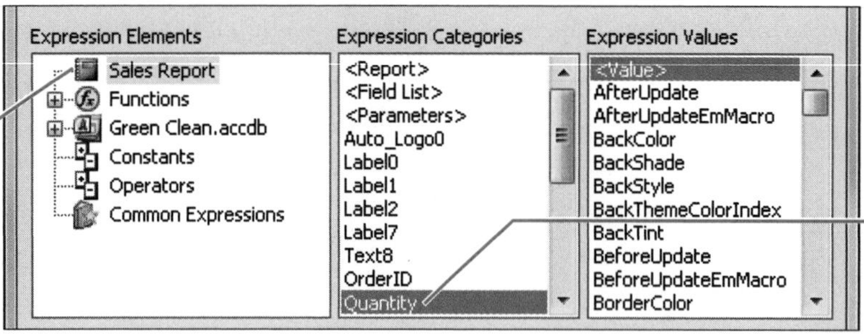

Ⓑ **Double-click** Quantity in the Expression Categories list to add it to the expression.

5. Follow these steps to add the operator to the expression:

Ⓐ Click **Operators** in the Expression Elements list.

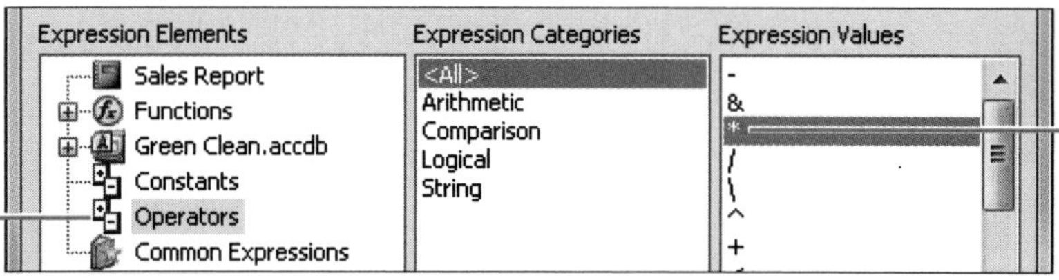

Ⓑ **Double-click** the asterisk (*) in the Expression Values list to add it to the expression.

6. Follow these steps to complete the expression:

Ⓐ Click **Sales Report** in the Expression Elements list.

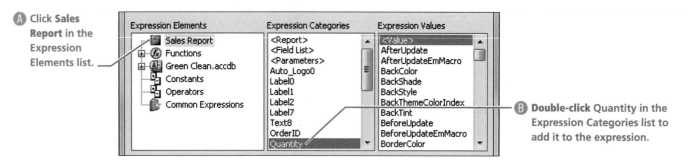

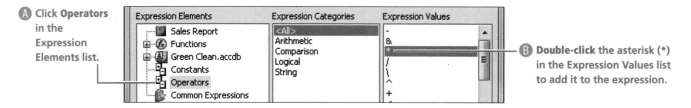

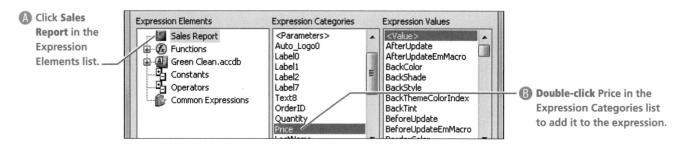

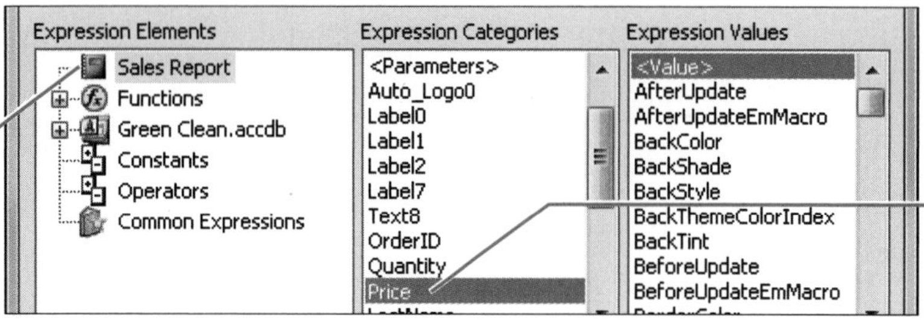

Ⓑ **Double-click** Price in the Expression Categories list to add it to the expression.

Access adds the field to the box at the top of the Expression Builder.

7. Click **OK** to place the expression in the Control Source property box.
8. Click the **Property Sheet Format** tab and set the Format property to **Currency** and the Text Align property to **Right**.
9. **Right-click** the control label on the report and choose **Cut**; then **right-click** the Page Header section bar and choose **Paste** to place the control as a column heading.
10. Position the label above the calculated control text box and then **double-click** the label text and type **`Item Total`**.
11. Click the **Price** column heading (label).
12. Choose **Home→Clipboard→Format Painter** on the Ribbon to pick up the format of the column heading.
13. Click the **Item Total** column heading to paint the format onto it and size the control to display all text.
14. Switch to **Report View** to display the report with totals and then **save** it.

Creating Controls to Calculate Totals

Video Lesson labyrinthelab.com/videos

The calculated control you added to the report calculated a total for each item in the report. The calculated control appeared in the Detail section of the report. You can add calculated controls to other sections of the report so that the control performs a calculation on groups of records. For example, when you have a report that is grouped by sales person, such as the one you are creating, you can add the calculated control to the Group Footer section so that Access calculates a value for each group. And if you want a simple total at the end of a report, you would add the calculated control to the Report Footer section. You can even create a control that calculates sub-totals and then create a control that calculates a grand total at the end of the report.

Displaying the Group Footer Section

You may have noticed, when you set the report to group records by employee last name, that Access displayed the header but left the footer hidden. In most cases, the group footer is used only to display group summary data such as totals and calculations. As a result, before you can add a group total, you must first display the Group Footer section. You display the Group Footer section using the Group, Sort, and Total panel or by setting a function for a field in the Detail section.

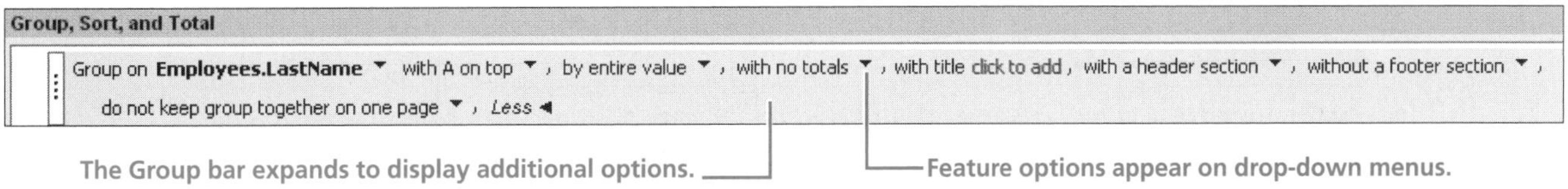

Creating Aggregate Fields

In addition to creating calculated totals in the Group Footer section, you can total values, find averages, and set other aggregate functions directly from the Group bar in the Group, Sort, and Total panel. When you select a field control in the detail section of the report, you can also use the totals button on the Ribbon to set aggregate functions for the field.

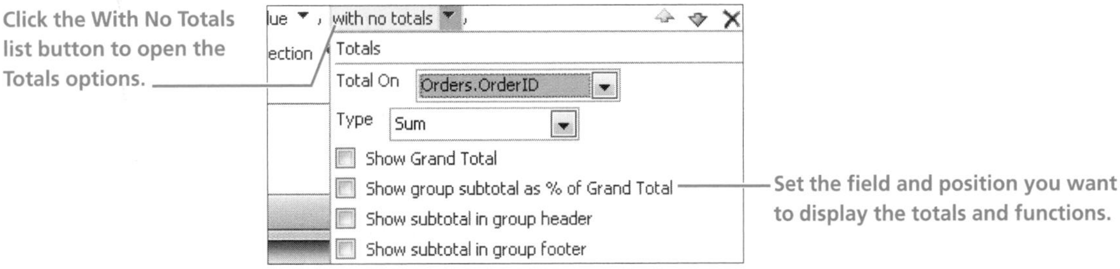

QUICK REFERENCE	USING GROUP, SORT, AND TOTAL FEATURES
Task	**Procedure**
Display the Group Footer section	■ Display the report in Design View. ■ Choose Design→Grouping & Totals→Group & Sort on the Ribbon. ■ Click More on the Group bar for the group for which you want to display a footer. ■ Click the Without a Footer Section list button and choose With a Footer Section.
Set aggregate function totals from the Group bar	■ Display the report in Design View. ■ Choose Design→Grouping & Totals→Group & Sort on the Ribbon. ■ Click More on the Group bar for the group for which you want to display aggregate functions. ■ Click the with no totals list button and set the field, type, and position of the function you want to set.
Set aggregate function totals from the Ribbon	■ Display the report in Design View and click the field control in the Detail section for which you want to set a function. ■ Choose Design→Grouping & Totals→Totals Σ on the Ribbon. ■ Choose the function you want to apply to the field.

DEVELOP YOUR SKILLS 8.4.2

Create Calculated Totals and Set Functions in Group Footers

In this exercise, you will create a calculated total for each sales person and also set a function to calculate the total and average of other columns in the report.

1. Display the Sales Report in **Design View** and select the **Orders.Quantity** control in the Detail section.
2. Choose **Design→Grouping & Totals→Totals** Σ on the Ribbon and choose Sum.
   Access opens the EmployeeLastName Footer section and places the function in the footer.
3. Repeat the procedures outlined in **steps 1 and 2** to set an Average function for the Inventory.Price field in the Detail section.
4. Choose **Design→Controls→Text Box** ab on the Ribbon and create a new text box at about the **5.5"** mark in the Employees.LastName Footer section.
5. Select the **calculated control** in the Detail section and copy and paste it into the Employees.LastName Footer section, positioning it at about the **5.5"** mark.
6. Open the **Property Sheet Data** tab and follow these steps to revise the expression to calculate total sales for each salesperson:

Ⓐ Click the **Control Source** property.

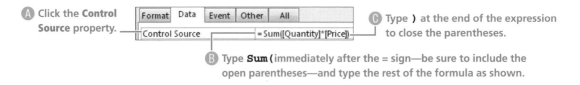

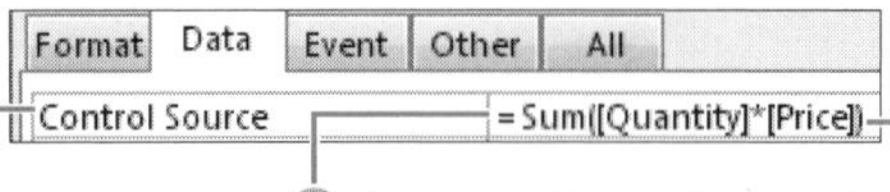

Ⓑ Type **Sum(** immediately after the = sign—be sure to include the open parentheses—and type the rest of the formula as shown.

Ⓒ Type **)** at the end of the expression to close the parentheses.

7. Add a label using the **Label tool** to the Page Header section above the control text box, add the text Sales Totals to the label, and format the label using the **Format Painter** to appear as the other column headings.
8. Switch to **Layout View** and review the report , adjusting the width of any field that displays #####. Pound symbols in a field indicate that the field is not wide enough to display the value.
9. **Save** changes to the report and **close** it.

8.5 Creating Labels Using the Label Wizard

Video Lesson labyrinthelab.com/videos

One common request people have of databases is the capability to print address labels using data contained in a database table. As a result, Access 2007 introduced a new wizard designed specifically for creating labels—it's called the Label Wizard. The Label Wizard steps you through screens from which you can make choices to set up labels using the data from specific tables or queries.

Setting Up the Labels

The procedures for using the Label Wizard are similar to those you have used to create other objects using wizards. The Label Wizard provides options for setting standard labels as well as for creating custom labels. The database object that is active when you start the wizard is the object Access assumes you want to use to create the labels. As a result, it is important to select or open the object before you start.

Adding Fields to the Labels

Adding fields to the labels is similar to adding fields to a Word document when you plan to use the document as a mail merge main document. As a result, it is necessary to add required spacing and punctuation to the label as you insert the fields. In addition, Access places curly braces { } around field names on the labels just as Word does.

A typical label design

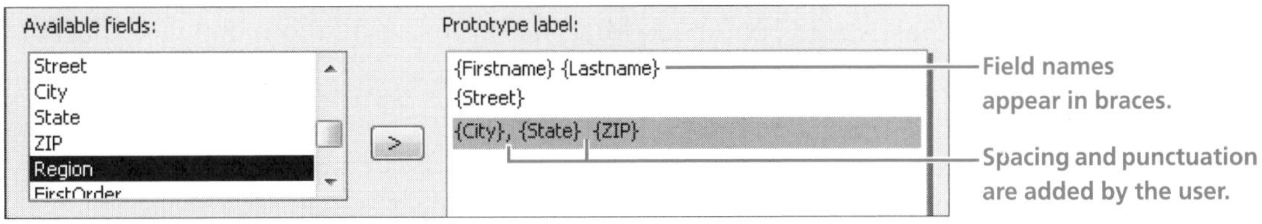

QUICK REFERENCE	CREATING LABELS
Task	**Procedure**
Launch the Label wizard	■ Select the table containing the data you want to use for the labels. ■ Choose Create→Reports→Labels.
Work through wizard screens	■ Select the label type, format, and unit of measure you want to use for the labels and click Next. ■ Set the font, size, and color, and then click Next.
Add fields to a label	■ Double-click the field names in the Available Fields list in the order you want them to appear on the label. ■ Add spacing, punctuation, and hard returns as needed to position the fields properly. ■ Click Next. ■ Select the field on which you want to sort the labels and click Next. ■ Type a label report name and click Finish.

DEVELOP YOUR SKILLS 8.5.1

Create Labels Using the Label Wizard

In this exercise, you will create mailing labels for addressing envelopes for a mass mailing to all customers in the Green Clean Reports database.

1. Click the **Customers** table in the Navigation Pane to make it active.
2. Choose **Create→Reports→Labels** on the Ribbon to launch the Label Wizard.
3. Follow these steps to set the label type and size:

Ⓐ Choose **8463** from the Product number list.

Ⓑ Choose the **English** Unit of Measure.

Ⓒ Choose **Sheet feed** as the Label Type.

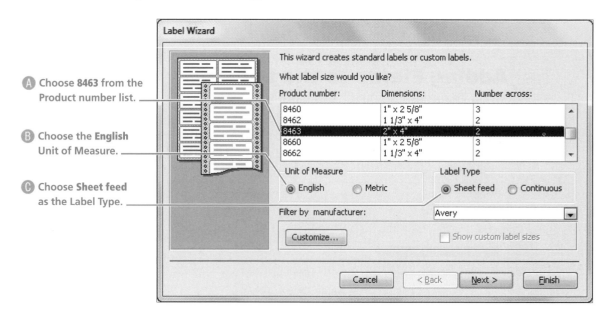

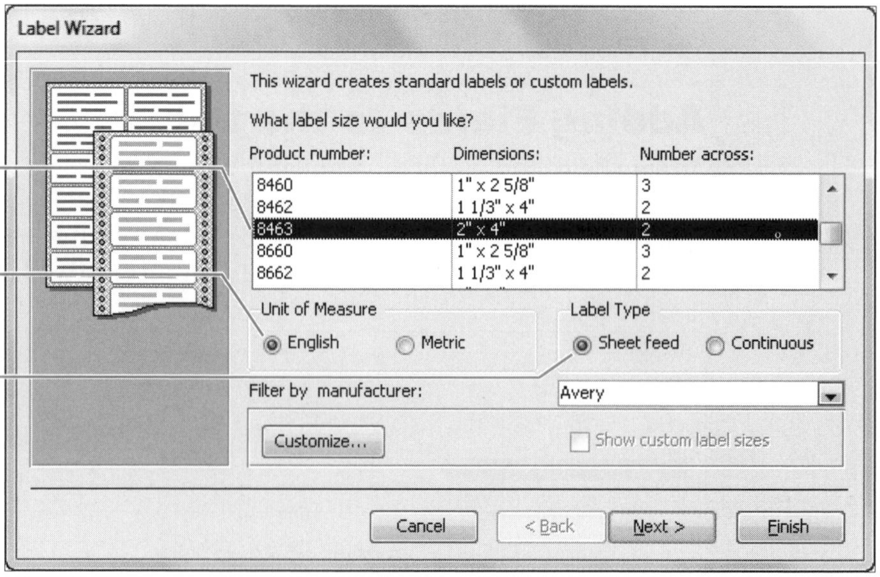

4. Click **Next** and set the Font Size to **10**.

5. Click **Next** and follow these steps to set up the prototype label:

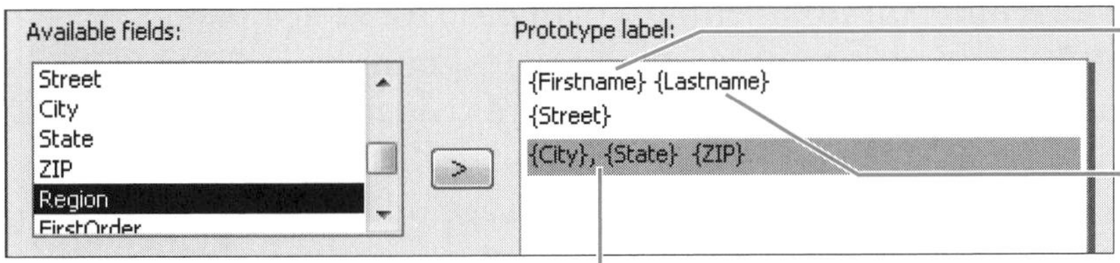

Ⓐ **Double-click** the FirstName field to add it to the label and then **press** the Spacebar to add a space.

Ⓑ **Double-click** the LastName field and then **press** Enter to move to a new line.

Ⓒ **Double-click** additional fields in the Available Fields list to complete this label layout, adding spaces and punctuation you see here.

6. Click **Finish** to complete the labels; click **OK** if Access displays a message about label size. *Access saves the report using the default report name and displays the labels in Print Preview.*

7. **Close** [×] the report.

8.6 Printing Reports

Video Lesson labyrinthelab.com/videos

Reports in Access provide the main output source for disseminating information from the database. As a result, creating meaningful reports is important to the success of the database. After you create and format reports, set grouping and sorting levels, and add summary controls, you are ready to test the report by printing it.

FROM THE KEYBOARD

Ctrl+P to open the Print dialog box

Procedures for printing reports are basically the same procedures you would use to print files in other programs, such as Word, Excel, and PowerPoint. As with each different program, print options in Access vary with different objects. For example, you can print individual pages, all pages, or a set range of pages.

Setting Report Print Layout

Commands on the Page Setup tab of the Ribbon enable you to set up the basic page layout for a report. Using these commands, you can change the paper size and orientation, set margins and columns, and instruct Access to print the data only—leaving the design elements off.

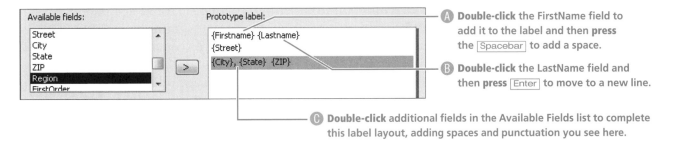

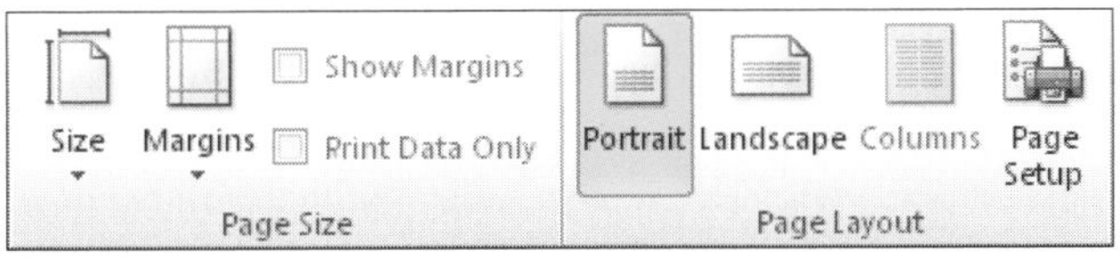

Page Layout tools on the Page Setup tab.

Controlling Page Breaks

If you have used Word to create long documents, you know that controlling page breaks is important to prevent an individual line of a paragraph (often called a widow or orphan) from appearing on a page by itself. The same is true for printing reports. You want to adjust settings so that a group header section stays with at least the first record in the report and also to prevent an individual record or line of a report section from appearing alone. Access contains features that you can set to contain report sections and produce a better organized report.

Setting Page Breaks

Setting a page break on a report is different from setting a hard page break in a Word document or Excel worksheet. Because your report design contains controls for defining the report layout, it can be challenging to determine how many records will appear for each group, and the number of records shown in each group usually varies for each group heading. As a result, setting a page break is an uncertain way to try to control page printouts.

Setting Group Controls

Instead of setting page breaks for printing reports, Access enables you to control how you want to keep groups together on report pages. Setting these controls prevents lone headers on report pages and enables you to keep each group on a single page. Setting these controls also reduces excessive page printouts.

QUICK REFERENCE PRINTING REPORTS

Task	Procedure
Display Print Preview	■ Display Report View. *or* ■ Choose File→Print→Print Preview.
Print specific pages	■ Choose File→Print→Print to display the Print dialog box. ■ Select the Pages option and enter the page numbers you want to print.
Print all report pages	■ Choose File→Print→Quick Print. *or* ■ Choose File→Print→Print to display the Print dialog box. ■ Click OK. *or* ■ Press [Ctrl]+[P] to display the Print dialog box. ■ Click OK.

DEVELOP YOUR SKILLS 8.6.1

Set Print Options

In this exercise, you will set up the report for printing and print the report.

1. Display the Sales Report in **Design View** and display the **Group, Sort, and Total** panel.
2. Follow these steps to set page controls:

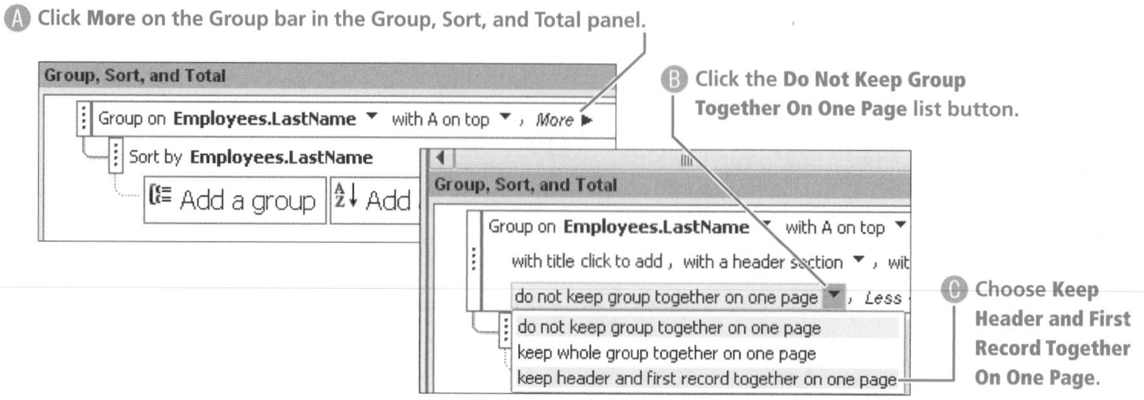

3. **Save** the report and display it in **Print Preview**, navigating to multiple pages.
4. Choose **Print Preview→Print→Print** on the Ribbon to print the report and then **close** it, **close** the database, and **exit** Access.

8.7 Concepts Review

Concepts Review labyrinthelab.com/acc10

To check your knowledge of the key concepts introduced in this lesson, complete the Concepts Review quiz by going to the URL listed above. If your classroom is using Labyrinth eLab, you may complete the Concepts Review quiz from within your eLab course.

Reinforce Your Skills

REINFORCE YOUR SKILLS 8.1

Create a Report in Design View

Lagniappe Cruises is preparing to publish a brochure that describes its cruises for next year. In preparation for this brochure, they would like to have a report that tallies the total cost of each room type based on occupancy. In this exercise, you will create the shell of the report and add fields to the report.

1. **Open** the rs-Lagniappe Cruises database from the Lesson 08 folder and **save** the file using the filename **`rs-Lagniappe Reports`**.
2. Choose **Create→Reports→Report Design** on the Ribbon to create the report.
3. Choose **Design→Tools→Add Existing Fields** on the Ribbon to open the Field List.
4. **Expand** (+) the Cruises table to display the field list for the table.
5. **Drag** the following fields to the report Detail section in the order listed: SailDate, Destination, Ship, InsideCabin, OutsideCabin, Verandah.
6. **Right-click** the SailDate label and choose **Cut**; then **right-click** the Page Header and choose **Paste**.
7. Repeat the procedures outlined in **step 6** to cut and paste the Destination and ShipName labels in the Page Header, dragging the labels to appropriate positions above the field text box control.
8. **Drag** additional fields into the following positions on the report:

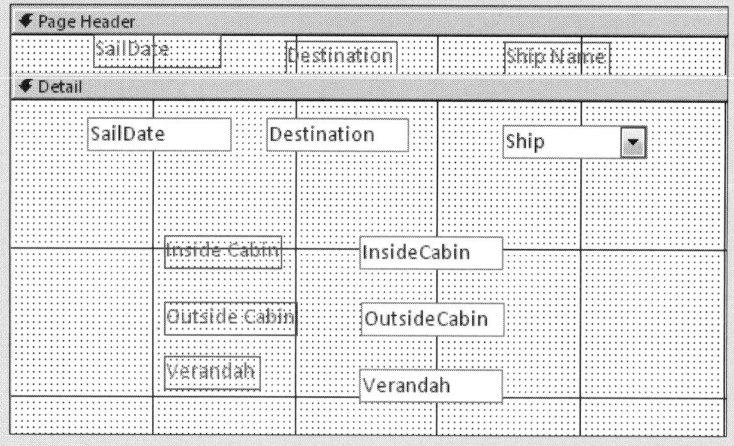

9. **Print** a copy of the report design.
10. **Save** the report using the report name **`Cruise Costs`** and leave it **open**.

REINFORCE YOUR SKILLS 8.2

Add Group Levels, Time, and Date to the Report

Before formatting and enhancing the report you created, you need to better organize the report so that it shows data grouped by date and subgrouped by destination. In this exercise, you will add two group levels to the report and also add time and date controls.

1. Display your Cruise Costs report in **Design View**.

Set Grouping

2. **Right-click** the Destination control in the Detail section and choose **Group On**.
3. **Right-click** the Destination control in the Detail section again and choose **Cut**; then **right-click** the Destination Header section and choose **Paste**.
4. Repeat the procedures outlined in **steps 2 and 3** to create another group using the Sail-Date control in the Detail section.

Align Controls

5. Click the **vertical ruler** even with the first cabin controls and drag the mouse down to select all six cabin controls.
6. Choose **Arrange→Sizing & Ordering→Size/Space→To Widest** to size the controls evenly.
7. Choose **Arrange→Sizing & Ordering→Size/Space→Equal Vertical** to distribute the controls evenly.
8. Select the three cabin labels and choose **Arrange→Sizing & Ordering→ Align→ Left**.
9. Repeat the procedures outlined in **step 8** to align the cabin text boxes on the left.

Add Date & Time Controls

10. Drag the **Page Footer** section bar up and position it just below the **Verandah** controls.
11. Choose **Design→Header/Footer→Date & Time** and set options to add the date and time to the report using a format you prefer.
12. Adjust the positions of additional controls to appear as follows and delete the **Destination** and **SailDate** control labels in the Page Header:

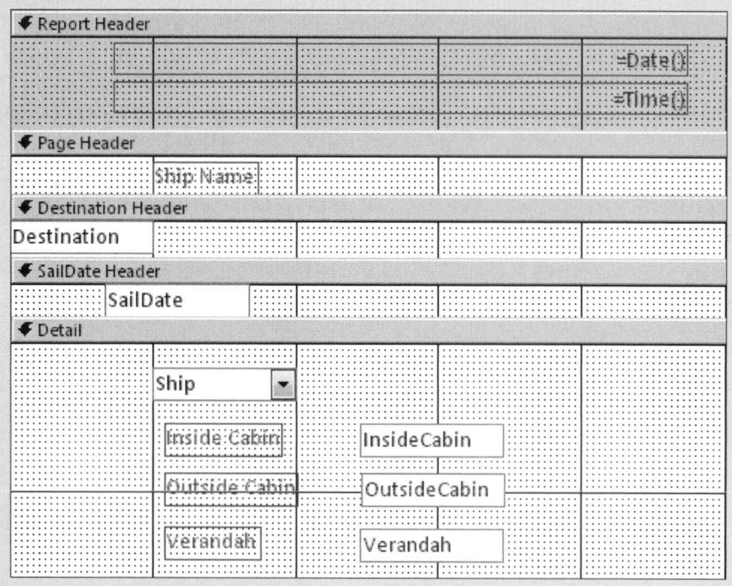

When you group on the Destination and SailDate fields, the labels for the controls no longer appear in the Page Header section of the report.

13. Switch to **Layout View**, review the report, and adjust the size of the destination control to display all text.
14. **Save** changes to the report and **print** a copy of the report.

REINFORCE YOUR SKILLS 8.3

Format and Enhance the Report

You have now established the skeleton of the report. Adding a title and graphics as well as graphic elements to the report will enhance its appearance. In this exercise, you will add a title and logo to the report header section, format text controls, and format the report.

1. Display the Cruise Costs report in **Design View** and drag the border of the **Report Footer** section down to make the section larger.
2. Select both the **Date** and **Time** controls that appear in the Report Header section.
3. **Right-click** the selected controls and choose **Cut**; then **right-click** the Report Footer section and choose **Paste** to move the controls to the footer.

Add and Format a Logo

4. Choose **Design→Header/Footer→Logo** and **double-click** the rs-Lagniappe Cruises Logo.gif file in the Lesson 08 folder to add the logo to the report.
5. Close the **Field List** panel and **press** F4 to open the Property Sheet.
6. Click the **Border Color** property and choose **White** from the color palette.

Add and Format a Title

7. Choose **Design→Header/Footer→Title** and then set the following properties:

Property	Setting
Font Size	72
Fore Color	Orange, Accent 6

8. Size the **title control** to display all text on one line and position the title appropriately.
9. Size the **logo control** appropriately.

Format Detail Section Controls

10. Select all label controls in the **Detail** section, apply the following properties, and drag the left border of the controls to size them appropriately:

Property	Setting
Fore Color	Orange, Accent 6
Font Size	14
Font Weight	Bold

11. Select the **Cabin** text box controls, set the following properties, and then drag the right border of the controls to size them appropriately:

Property	Setting
Fore Color	Accent 6, Darker 25%
Font Size	14
Font Weight	Extra Bold

Format Group Controls

12. Select the **Destination** and **SailDate** controls in the group headers, apply formatting to the controls appropriately, and then size the controls appropriately.
13. Delete the **Ship Name** label in the Page Header section; then select the **Ship** control in the Detail section, set formatting properties of your choice, and size the control appropriately.
14. Display the report in **Layout View** and size the **Destination** group header so that the right edge appears close to the right margin border as shown.

15. Make additional adjustments as necessary to the report, **save** changes to the report, and then **print** a copy of it.

REINFORCE YOUR SKILLS 8.4

Create Calculated Controls

The report you are building is shaping up nicely. Each cabin on the all ships is designed to hold two people. Connecting cabins are designed for families who take a cruise. To report the total cost of each cabin for each cruise, you need to add some calculated controls to the report. In this exercise, you will use the Expression Builder to add the calculated controls to the report.

1. Display the Cruise Costs report in **Design View** and **press** [F4] to open the Property Sheet.
2. Choose **Design→Controls→Text Box** ab| on the Ribbon and then click the **Detail** section beside the Inside Cabin text box.
3. In the Property Sheet, click the **Data** tab, choose the **Control Source** property and click the **Build** button to launch the Expression Builder.
4. Click the **Cruise Costs** report in the Expression Elements list and **double-click** the InsideCabin field from the Expression Categories list to add it to the Expression Builder; then type ***2** to complete the expression and click **OK**.

5. In the Property Sheet, click the **Format** tab and set the Format property to **Currency**.
6. Repeat the procedures outlined in **steps 2–5** to create calculated controls for the Outside Cabin control and the Verandah control, substituting the appropriate field name in the expression and setting both to Currency format.
7. **Delete** the labels for each control you added.

Add a Label Control

8. Choose **Design→Controls→Label** and place a label control containing the text **`Total Cost`** beside the Ship control in the Detail section.

Format the New Controls

9. Click the **Ship** control in the Detail section and choose **Design→Font→Format Painter** to pick up the format applied to the control and then click the Total Cost label to apply the format to the label.
10. Repeat **step 9** to pick up the format of the cabin text boxes and apply it to the calculated controls.
11. **Align** controls appropriately and then **save** changes to the report.
Your report should appear similar to:

REINFORCE YOUR SKILLS 8.5

Create Count Totals

The number of cruises to each destination is a value that is also required for this report. In this exercise, you will create a total count of cruises for each destination.

1. Display the Cruise Costs report in **Design View** and click the **Destination** control in the Destination Header section.

2. Choose **Design→Grouping & Totals→Group & Sort** and click More on the Group on Destination bar.

3. Follow these steps to show a count of each destination in the footer section:

Ⓐ Click the **With No Totals** list button.

Ⓑ Choose **Destination** from the Total On list.

Ⓒ Check the **Show Subtotal In Group Footer** checkbox.

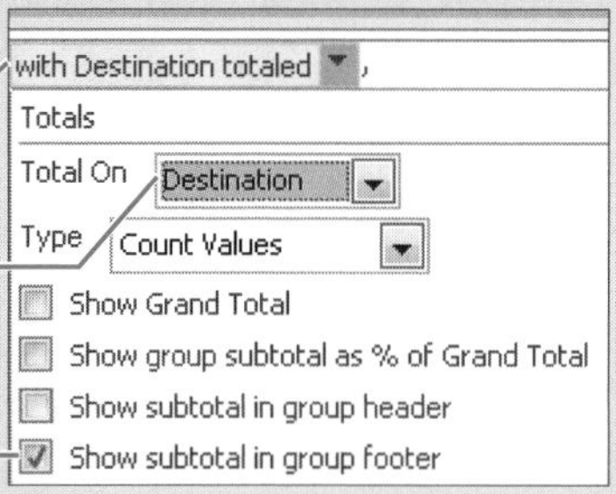

Access creates the count function in the Destination Footer section of the report.

4. Drag the **Page Footer** section bar down to make the Destination Footer section larger; then click the **Count** control and choose **Format→Font→Align Text Right** on the Ribbon.

5. Display the report in **Report View** and compare the listings for Australia/New Zealand on your report to the one shown here:

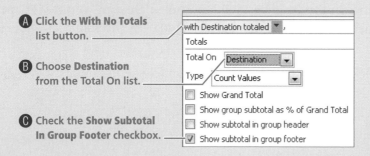

Total cruises to the first listed destination is 2.

6. **Save** the report, **print** a copy, and then **close** it.

REINFORCE YOUR SKILLS 8.6

Create Labels

Mailing labels is only one type of label you can create using the Label Wizard. You can also create file folder labels and many other types. In this exercise, you will create a simple file folder label to use for creating labels for Lagniappe Cruise destinations.

1. Select the **Cruises** table and choose **Create→Reports→Labels** to launch the Label Wizard.
2. Take the following actions on the Wizard screen indicated, clicking **Next** to advance to the next screen:

Screen	Action
1	Choose Label #8257
2	Choose Font Size 10
3	Move Destination to the Prototype Label
4	No changes
5	Type `Destination File Labels` as the report title.

3. **Print** a copy of the report and then **close** the report, **close** the database, and **exit** Access.

Apply Your Skills

APPLY YOUR SKILLS 8.1
Create a Report in Design View

Raritan Clinic East continues to work on their database. They have finalized forms and have moved on to creating reports. In this excercise, you will create a report using data from the Resources table.

1. **Open** the as-Raritan Clinic database in your Lesson 08 folder and **save** the database as a new file named **`as-Raritan Clinic Reports`**.
2. Create a new report in **Design View** that is based on the Resources table.
3. **Drag** controls for the following fields to the Detail section and place them side by side in the order shown: ResourceTypeID, ResourceFirstName, ResourceLastName.
4. **Delete** the label control for the **ResourceTypeID** field and move the labels for the name controls to the **Page Header** section.
5. **Save** the report using the report name **`Resources`** and **print** a copy of the report. Leave the report **open**.

APPLY YOUR SKILLS 8.2
Group Data in the Report

Grouping the resources by type helps locate resources when substitutes are needed. In this exercise, you will create a grouping level for the report you started in Apply Your Skills 8.1 and add a date control to the Report Footer section.

1. Display the Resources report in **Design View**.
2. Choose the **ResourceTypeID** control in the Detail section and set it as the **Group On** field.
3. Move the **ResourceTypeID** control to the **ResourceTypeID Header** section of the report.
4. Add the **Date** control without the Time control to the report and move it to the **Page Footer** section.
5. Adjust the size of the **Detail** Section.
6. **Save** changes to the report and leave it **open**.

APPLY YOUR SKILLS 8.3

Format the Report

The plain report you have created so far is a nice basic structure of a report. Formatting the report so that text appears more vivid and sections are more appropriately sized to report the data will improve the appearance of the report. In this exercise, you will apply a Theme to the report, format report controls, and size the report sections.

1. Display the Resources report in **Design View** and size the **Detail** section so that it is just tall enough to accommodate the controls.
2. Format the report by applying the **Opulent Theme** to the report.
3. Set **control properties** for the controls to improve their appearance.
4. **Align** the controls in the Detail section at the top.
5. Size the **Detail** and **ResourceTypeID Header** sections so that they are large enough for the controls they contain.
6. Switch to **Layout View** and adjust the sizes of the controls to display data appropriately on the report.
7. **Save** changes to the report, **print** a copy, and then **close** the report.

APPLY YOUR SKILLS 8.4

Add a Logo and Title to the Report

The Raritan Clinic East report now contains the data and format you want to display. In this exercise, you will add a title and logo to the report.

1. Display the Resources report in **Design View** and make the **Report Header** section active.
2. Add the as-Raritan Clinic Logo.jpg graphic to the **Report Header** section of the report and position it on the right side of the section.
3. Add a **title** to the report and position it on the left side of the **Report Header** section.
4. Type **`Resources by Type`** in the new title box and format the title by setting the font size to **40**.
5. **Size** and **position** the logo and title appropriately.
6. **Save** changes to the report and leave it **open** for the next exercise.

APPLY YOUR SKILLS 8.5

Add a Control and Edit the Control Source

The group header identifies the coded resource type ID. Unless those who view the report know what each type of resource represents, they will have no idea how many nurses, staff, etc., are listed. In this exercise, you will add a new control to the report and edit the control source property to select the appropriate table.

1. Display the Resources report in **Design View** and display the **Field List** panel.
2. Expand the field list for the **Resource Types** table and drag the **ResourceType** field to the **ResourceTypeID Header** section, positioning it beside the existing control in the section.
3. Copy the format from the **ResourcesID** control to the **ResourceTypeID** control in the group header section, align the controls appropriately, and delete unnecessary control labels.
4. Display the report in **Layout View** and size the controls in the group header section appropriately to display all data.
5. **Save** the report and leave it **open** for the next exercise.

APPLY YOUR SKILLS 8.6

Add Totals to Count the Entries in Report Groups

The report for the clinic database is almost complete. In this exercise, you will add totals that count the number of records for each group.

1. Display the Resources report in **Design View** and display the **Group, Sort, and Total** panel.
2. Create a total that counts the **resource records** for each resource type and displays the **total** in the group footer section.
3. Display the report in **Report View** and compare your report to the one shown here:

Each group total appears before the next group heading.

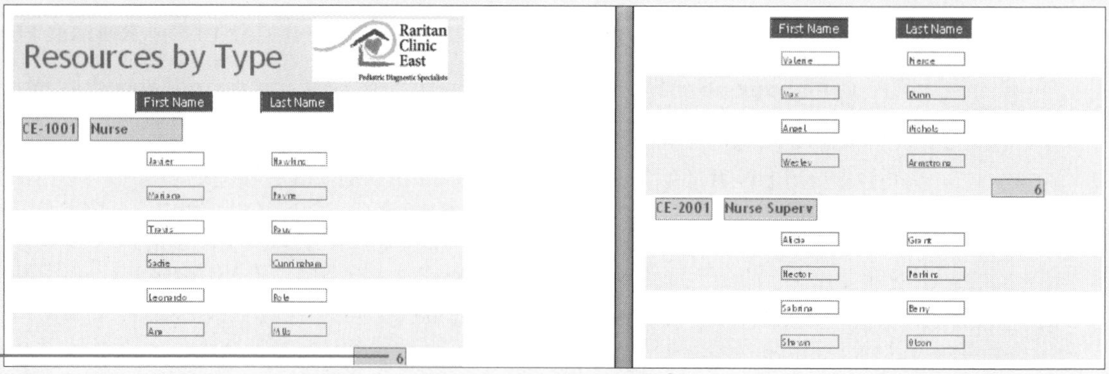

4. **Save** the report, **print** a copy, and then **close** the report, **close** the database, and **exit** Access.

Critical Thinking & Work-Readiness Skills

In the course of working through the following Microsoft Office-based Critical Thinking exercises, you will also be utilizing various work-readiness skills, some of which are listed next to each exercise. Go to labyrinthelab.com/workreadiness *to learn more about the work-readiness skills.*

8.1 Create a Report that Prints Labels

Green Clean is preparing to set up files for all customers in the database. They would like you to prepare a report for the database that they can use to create file folder labels. Follow these guidelines to prepare the report:

- Use the ct-Green Clean Reports (Lesson 08 folder).
- Format the labels so they print file folder label format from the Green Clean Customers table.
- Sort the labels on the Last Name field.
- Print a copy of the labels on plain paper.

WORK-READINESS SKILLS APPLIED

- Applying technology to a task
- Improving or designing systems
- Thinking creatively

8.2 Create, Format, and Total a Custom Report

Green Clean's corporate offices have just contracted with First Perk, an onsite coffee shop, to provide beverage service. First Perk has its own database for which they want to add custom reports. The manager explains that they would like a report that groups orders by sales person, totals each order, and totals all orders for each sales person.

Create a report that meets the manager's criteria using a query as a record source. Format the report using appropriate design elements, and save the report with the title **`Sales Summary`**. The logo for First Perk can be found in the Lesson 08 folder. Print the report.

WORK-READINESS SKILLS APPLIED

- Thinking creatively
- Making decisions
- Organizing and maintaining information

8.3 Use Teamwork to Design a Custom Report Layout

Green Clean's management team, none of them database experts, challenges your team of consultants to produce reports from their database that provide "higher value" information, though they are not specific in their requests. Collaborate with your team to identify the types of reports you believe Green Clean could effectively add to the database. Then, design a report layout that can be applied to the reports and create at least two new reports for Green Clean. Add the reports to the Green Clean Reports database you have used throughout this lesson. Customize the reports using your collaborative creative imaginations.

WORK-READINESS SKILLS APPLIED

- Seeing things in the mind's eye
- Thinking creatively
- Solving problems

Index

Numerics

A

B

C

D

E

F

S

T

U

V

Notes

Notes

Notes

Notes